MODERN FAMILIES

MODERN FAMILIES

STORIES OF EXTRAORDINARY JOURNEYS TO KINSHIP

JOSHUA GAMSON

Foreword by Melissa Harris-Perry

NEW YORK UNIVERSITY PRESS

New York

NEW YORK UNIVERSITY PRESS
New York
www.nyupress.org

First published in paperback in 2014

Frontispiece: William Haefeli / The New Yorker Collection / The Cartoon Bank.

References to Internet websites (URLs) were accurate at the time of writing. Neither the author nor New York University Press is responsible for URLs that may have expired or changed since the manuscript was prepared.

Library of Congress Cataloging-in-Publication Data
Gamson, Joshua, 1962-
Modern families : stories of extraordinary journeys to kinship /
Joshua Gamson ; foreword by Melissa Harris-Perry.
pages cm   Includes bibliographical references and index.
ISBN 978-1-4798-4246-9 (cl : alk. paper)
ISBN 978-1-4798-6973-2 (pb : alk. paper)
1. Families—History—21st century. 2. Racially mixed families.
3. Gay parents. 4. Human reproductive technology. 5. Kinship. I. Title.
HQ519.G36   2015
306.85097309'05—dc23   2015009609

New York University Press books are printed on acid-free paper, and their binding materials are chosen for strength and durability. We strive to use environmentally responsible suppliers and materials to the greatest extent possible in publishing our books.

Manufactured in the United States of America

10 9 8 7 6 5 4 3 2 1

Also available as an ebook

For Reba Sadie and Madeleine Blanche

CONTENTS

FOREWORD

That the personal is political has been a central tenet of feminist theory and practice for fifty years. It is the guiding philosophy on which I was raised. My own mother was a divorced white woman with a young daughter when she chose to love, but not marry, my African American father; to have a child with him; and to rear me in the American South less than a decade after the statutory end of Jim Crow. Throughout my childhood, the politics of personal choices sat at our kitchen table, awaited us on the doorstep, and stalked us through public spaces.

Mom was a staunch supporter of reproductive rights and served as part of an "underground railroad" that allowed women to access abortion services before *Roe v. Wade*. Along with her graduate school colleagues, she penned a slim volume about treating and avoiding sexually transmitted diseases titled *How to Have Intercourse without Getting Screwed*. She worked as a juvenile parole counselor and wrote a master's thesis on prostitution. Still, she firmly rejected multiple suggestions that she terminate her pregnancy to avoid having a biracial child who would be confused and rejected. I still remember my mother belting out the lyrics to Diana Ross and the Supremes' "Love Child" while she bustled around the house on Saturday mornings.

All of which made it surprising that I was such a conventional kid. Despite my public reputation—among some—as a fierce advocate for racial, gender, and LGBT equality, my private life progressed like a 1980s after-school special. I finished graduate school, had a big white wedding where I married my college sweetheart, moved to the big city, bought a place, swiftly and easily got pregnant, accomplished unmedicated childbirth, nursed my baby girl for nearly a year, and then started thinking about a second child. I had been raised on a lean diet of political investment in personal choices but was enjoying the feast of the normative—until it unraveled.

By the time my daughter started first grade, my marriage was over, the ugly custody dispute raged on, and after years of wrestling with the agony of fibroids, I had finally relinquished my uterus to hysterectomy. Being a black single mother facing the inequities of the family court system while learning to experience myself as a whole woman despite my inability to reproduce allowed me to wrestle in deeply personal ways with my feminist political commitments. But those experiences were nothing in comparison to the ideological complications I encountered when I entered the world of third-party, assisted, reproductive technology.

Third-party, assisted, reproductive technology must be the most obfuscating euphemism in contemporary discourse. What really happened is I met and married an astonishing human. This man had no children but became a doting and beloved parent to my daughter. And this man—whose very affection for my girl belied the irrelevance of genetic ties in family making—nonetheless wanted to have a child that was biologically tied to both of us. And while I had given up my broken uterus, I had kept my aging but active ovaries. So his dream of a "little us" was technically possible but ethically troubling, because this new life would require the involvement of a working uterus. And that uterus would reside within an actual person. And that person would be a woman. And that woman would receive financial compensation for carrying and giving birth to our baby. And I had absolutely no idea how to reconcile this personal choice with my own political commitments.

Research did little to help. Most texts fell into two dissatisfying genres: one of intellectual but bloodless academic texts that warn against the commercialization of reproduction without a full accounting for the genuine humanity in this process; and the second of triumphant personal narratives that pretend personal desire and positive outcomes are sufficient to transform troubling transactional aspects of unconventional family making into uncontroversial stories of love and destiny.

I needed to know if it was possible to reproduce ourselves without reproducing racism and misogyny. Could we expand our family without deepening imperialism and class inequality? I was searching for hope but not a free pass. This was a deeply personal choice with far-reaching political implications. I needed a clear-eyed guide through both. In short, I needed the book you are now holding.

In the stories that follow, you will encounter authentic, imperfect, thoughtful individuals making unconventional families by accessing a broad range of technological, medical, and legal choices that expand our definitions of parenting and kinship. As you read these stories, you will discover many satisfying new beginnings but no happy endings, because child rearing is process, not destination. These family-making journeys raise hard questions but offer no formulaic answers. These are stories of choices made consciously and sometimes uncomfortably to create and combine lives amid the messy human realities of desire, commerce, science, faith, community, and family. This collection is not a roadmap; it is a companion for all those who choose to navigate the world of modern kinship.

And for my second daughter, who was made of the genetic material of her parents and born of a beloved gestational surrogate on Valentine's Day, this book may someday help her understand all the questions that accompanied her extraordinary journey into our lives.

Melissa Harris-Perry
Presidential Endowed Chair in Politics and International Affairs
Executive Director, Pro Humanitate Institute
Director, Anna Julia Cooper Center
Wake Forest University
Host, MSNBC's *Melissa Harris-Perry*

ACKNOWLEDGMENTS

If it takes a village to raise a child, it takes a midsized town to nurture a book. I'm very grateful to the townspeople who helped me. For comments, support, and companionship, thanks to Amy Aronson, Sarah Cowan, William Gamson, Zelda Gamson, Ellen Levine, Stephen Levine, Sarah Anne Minkin, Rachel Neumann, Hagar Scher, France Winddance Twine, and Rhea Wilson. At the beginning of this project, I was supported by a fellowship from the John Simon Guggenheim Memorial Foundation, and the research was supported along the way by the University of San Francisco's Faculty Development Fund. The anonymous reviewers for NYU Press offered me a much-needed, friendly intellectual push. I'm deeply obliged to Ilene Kalish, my editor at NYU Press, whose unflagging belief in the project, along with critical commentary, motivated and invigorated me at crucial times. Richard Knight, my partner in life and in family making, encouraged me to keep writing in the midst of the rigors of child rearing and day jobs; he was a gracious, generous participant in the storytelling process, a fair critic, and an indulgent sounding board, and he remains, fifteen years in, an excellent playmate and ally. Most of all, I am grateful to the families, who are also my friends, who shared with me their time and stories: to be trusted with such cherished, delicate, and intimate tales was an honor that I can only hope this book returns.

"Tell me my origin story."

INTRODUCTION

Impertinent Questions

These kids I know were sitting at a Chinese restaurant in Berkeley a few years ago, on the evening of their preschool's Winter Gathering, the centerpiece of which is performances by the preschoolers of little shows they mostly wrote themselves. My daughter Reba, then five, was in the older group, and her show was to be about the adventures of a brown paper package: it gets picked up by two dogs, which are chased by two cats, which drop it in front of two mailmen, who deliver it to a Superboy, who takes it to two astronauts, who send it on a rocket into outer space, from which it floats down to earth and lands on two sleeping girls, Reba and her friend Donatella. Reba was practicing her line while munching a pot sticker: "A brown paper package tied up with strings, this is one of my favorite things!" Next to her, her friends Diego and Flora were playing with chopsticks, while several parents and grandparents chattered across her.

"If she doesn't have a mom," Diego asked me out of the blue, pointing to Reba, "how did she get born?" Diego was blond, almost five, obsessed with sports, missing a front tooth, and wore glasses. His father, Owen, looked at me with amusement and awaited my answer. It was noisy, but I saw Ronda, Flora's grandmother, lean toward us from two chairs down. One of Ronda's other grandchildren, Flora's cousin Milo, has two mothers.

"That's a great question," I said, buying a little time. For a second I wanted to ask what made him think of this question right now, then thought better of it. The five-year-old mind presents questions—why trees are called trees, what is the purpose of the rib cage, where water goes when you flush the toilet, whether *American Idol* is real—whose origins are mysterious and the tracing of which is often futile. Other paths of questioning reveal more.

"Do you want to try guessing?" I asked. Diego liked to puzzle things out. The week before, he'd thrown up on his way down the school staircase and had to be taken home, and I'd agreed to pop over to babysit so his parents could go to various work-related meetings. We'd played checkers. When his tears began to well up, I'd made some very bad moves, but I could see that he was as interested in pathways as in winning: if he made a move here, I might capture his guy, but if he moved there, I would get crowned.

He was in. "Did her grandma have her?" Diego asked. Owen's amusement grew, as did mine. The image of my mother or my mother-in-law pregnant with our child was charmingly repulsive.

"No, but that's a really good guess," I said, smiling at Owen.

"Maybe one of you guys had her," Diego suggested. Reba quieted a little bit beside me. She knew I usually told people with questions about her to just ask her directly.

"No, men's bodies can't get pregnant," I said, reminding him of the fact that sat behind his original question. "But we really wanted to have a baby, and since we couldn't get pregnant, we needed help." I could feel Diego's attention start to flag and ready itself for the next topic or activity, so I quickly cut to the chase. "So an old friend of ours helped us, and she got pregnant with Reba and carried her in her belly for nine months and then gave birth to her."

"Oh," said Diego, grabbing a pot sticker. "My chopstick holder is orange!"

"So's mine," said Reba.

"Mine, too," said Flora.

■　■　■

Almost five years earlier, a few months into Reba's life, on a work trip to Santa Fe we'd turned into a family vacation, my husband Richard and I were in a jewelry store looking for southwestern stuff to give as gifts. We'd plopped baby Reba on the floor to entertain herself and others.

"Where did you get her?" the proprietress asked, leaning over the counter to coo at Reba. In the beginning of Reba Sadie's life, we regularly encountered such impertinent questions from strangers—on the street, at the airport, in the park. "Where did you get her?" was a common one and also "How long have you had her?" Usually, these questions were preceded by compliments on our baby's cuteness—round face, bald head, observant eyes, quick smile—and asked in a kind tone, though one I found somewhat patronizing, the way you might ask a friend about a new puppy. The questioners clearly meant well. They seemed to be indicating that they really *got* us, that they understood our unusual family. They had no idea that they were communicating quite the opposite, triggering an urge to shoot down their presumptions, bam-bam-bam, until they were flustered, squashed, and ashamed.

Instead, I usually smiled. I tend not to rage in public. If they had a child with them, I'd sometimes say, "Long story. Where did you get yours?" Or I'd answer with a polite smile, "Oh, we've had her since way before she was born." Or I'd just repeat the question, all innocent-like: "Where did we get her? I don't understand what you mean." Richard is in many ways my mirror. Whereas my anger leaks out through the cracks in a cold wall, he sometimes rages hotly and openly, which quickly frees him to laugh and smile. So he let the Santa Fe jewelry store lady have it.

"What is it with you people?" he blasted. "Why do you always ask that?" Et cetera, until he was fully unloaded, by which time the saleswoman was sobbing.

The next thing I knew, I was outside corking the baby with a bottle, and Richard and the woman were deep in intimate conversation. It turned out she wanted kids but had been told that she was too old; she'd recently married a man with grown children who had no interest in adopting. She was grieving the life she'd thought she would have and saw in us some kind of possibility or familiar dream. She was identifying, not objectifying. And so, standing outside the store, Richard gave her a gift: he told her the whole story of Reba's willful and complicated creation, which we kept rather close: of this black Jewish baby, conceived by in vitro fertilization with one dad's sperm and the egg of a woman close to us, who almost wasn't but then became an embryo on the anniversary of the death of her namesake, my grandmother, then was implanted inside the ex-girlfriend of one of her fathers, who carried her in Virginia and birthed her in Massachusetts, from whose winter the family returned to her home in California to get on with it. While I was impatiently waiting, they were laughing a lot and crying some, and they parted with a hug.

It was she who suggested an answer to the question she'd asked. "The next time," she said, "just say, 'We conceived her.'" And that's what we took to saying. *We conceived her.* We imagined her, dreamed her up, and, with lots of help, brought her into being.

It wasn't long before the questioning subsided—as Reba Sadie's proximity to creation faded, so apparently did the issue of her beginnings— but that experience shifted and pushed me. I started to reinterpret, with more generosity, the constant questioning we'd received. The assumptions and presumptuousness were there, but behind them, I saw, was often not so much ignorance as curiosity and not so much the misrecognition of us as some kind of self-recognition. People really just wanted to know about origins: how a life and a family started when not everything was easy and scripted; how biology, social roles, choice, circumstance, and intention conspired to create and locate this little person; whether and how this child's entry into a family was the same as that of the kids they knew or had. The questions, in retrospect, weren't that different from a child's: *If she doesn't have a mom, how did she get born?*

And so I decided to answer them.

▪ ▪ ▪

As I started to compile the story of making my own family, it seemed that everywhere I turned I bumped into another child whose family was deliberately unconventional and whose entry into that family was somehow extraordinary. This one was the child of two mothers and was made with one mother's egg and the sperm of a man none of them has ever met; that one the child of two mothers and was made with the sperm of one mother's old friend, who remained prominent in her life as something between an uncle and a father. This one was born to a man and a woman in Ethiopia and was delivered by his natural grandmother to an orphanage when both his parents died in close succession and then to the arms of his mother, whom I've known for thirty-five years and who was raising him solo. These twins were made when their parents chose an egg donor from an online description, fertilized her eggs with some sperm from each of them, and implanted their embryonic selves into the uterus of another woman who had agreed to carry them for a fee. Those twins were made when their mother, who after much trying discovered she could not become pregnant and whose husband was sterile, used both donor eggs and donor sperm and gave birth to them months after being told that they would have to be removed to protect her body from a lethal infection. That one was made when his mothers, a couple, made an arrangement with his fathers, also a couple, to become parents together; these two were adopted from Nepal and India by Richard's best friend, who was raising them with her girlfriend and a gay couple in another four-parent family. Those are just a few of the kids I saw most days. Plus, there were these kids right here, my own two daughters.

When as a child in Ann Arbor I imagined being a father, I knew no such elaborate stories. Like almost everyone else I knew, my own creation story hardly seemed worth discussing. The reproductive biology, once learned, was assumed, as was some parental dating backstory that was none of anybody's business. We trotted my story out on birthdays, and even then it was entirely focused on the few hours surrounding birth. It goes like this: Two weeks after my due date, I showed no interest in emerging; this perhaps suggested an inherent tendency toward caution, laziness, or both. My parents, already annoyed at how much of their lives had been on hold since my sister's birth a couple of years earlier, went ahead with a party for a visiting scholar. Just as the party was getting going, my mother's contractions began, as if the sounds of small talk and clinking glasses were enough to summon me from the womb; this indicated an inherent taste for dramatic entrances, parties, or both. Anyway, the festivities continued while my parents were at the hospital and erupted into a cheer when my father called our house after midnight to announce to the partygoers that the baby boy had arrived. More glasses were clinked. The end.

I figured my future kids would each have a story like mine but with its own unique twist. Maybe it'd be about rushing to the hospital in a speeding car with a police escort and almost being born in a beaten-up Ford Escort. Maybe it'd be about arriving a little early, when we were on vacation at the beach or something, taking a taxi to a nearby hospital, and about entering the world to the smells of saltwater and taffy. The stories would be sweet, exciting, and brief.

That's not really how it worked out.

■　■　■

This book tells the tales of how several different families, including my own, were created against the grain of conventions and also often of institutions. The stories involve different types of unconventional family creation: adoption and assisted reproduction, gay and straight and transgendered parents, coupled and single- and multiparent families. They often began many years before any actual birth and involved constellations of characters far beyond mother, father, and doctors. Family creation was painstaking and often difficult, requiring inventiveness, persistence, and capital of various kinds. Often, parts of biological reproduction took place in a different body than that of the parents raising the child; sometimes, the model of kinship was made up virtually from scratch, often in tension with legally and socially sanctioned versions of family.

The stories here may satisfy curiosities, which is great, though not my main objective. I mean to offer an exceptional spot from which to view the norms, conventions, and institutions that regulate contemporary family making. You might do best to think of this not as a systematic study of unconventional family creation—it certainly is not that—but as a series of stories of that process told from inside a particular linked set of social networks. Or you might think of it as an oral history of how some people made their families in the early years of the twenty-first century. More broadly, you might read it as an intimate view of the much-remarked-on transformation of family structures, as seen through the experiences of people who have been, out of necessity as much as anything else, making their families up.

This book is forward looking, but it's also about capturing a period in a much-longer history of family creation and family discourse. As the historian Stephanie Coontz has put it, much family discourse is based on nostalgia for the "way we never were," a mythical *Leave It to Beaver* time when families were made up of a heterosexual man and a heterosexual woman, married and living together behind a white picket fence, raising together their biological offspring, with a clear division between male breadwinner and female child-rearing roles.[1] To the degree that such a "nuclear" family form ever existed, the psychologist Ross D. Parke points out in *Future Families*, it was dominant only for a brief period and only for some people.[2] Consult history for a minute. The form slave families took was hardly the nuclear one, the legal scholar Stephen Sugarman has noted, as slave couples weren't allowed to marry, male slaves couldn't possibly be breadwinners, and female slaves couldn't be stay-at-home mothers.[3] In the nineteenth century, moreover, poor immigrant women typically worked outside the home, and "multigenerational living arrangements were common."[4] Across the twentieth century, too, people raised kids who were not their own biological progeny—a sister's child born out of wedlock, the children of a second husband, and so on. Many children were born to parents who later came out as homosexual, too. Family arrangements have been far more complex and diverse than a single, normative family form could contain.

Still, even if the nuclear family is a historical myth, it's been very powerful as ideology. As Parke says, it "is the template against which other family forms are judged."[5] It has encouraged people whose families departed from the norm to treat those departures as family secrets, and that secrecy has in turn helped protect the notion that the One True Family is a husband, a wife, and their biological children. It has encouraged people to see variations—say, the broad kinship networks that have often characterized poor African American communities[6]—as deviant and pathological. Just a few years ago, in a major national survey conducted by the sociologist Brian Powell and his colleagues, 100 percent of respondents agreed that "husband, wife, children" counted as a family, and a single man or a single woman with children counted for around 94 percent; the percentage saying that two women or two men with children counted as a family hovered around 55 percent. "Husband, wife, no children" counted for 93 percent of the respondents, but "two men, no children" and "two women, no children" counted for just 26 percent.[7] The One True Family ideal is still so strong, that is, that a lot of people's arrangements just don't seem to count.

At the same time, there's no doubt that the heteronormative, biological family ideal has been losing its pride of place over the past few decades; that more than half the people surveyed by Powell and his colleagues saw same-sex parents as a family is actually quite remarkable, given that those very parents were born into a world where homosexuality was still criminalized. The cultural visibility of stepfamilies, adoptive families, mixed-race families, and same-sex families has expanded dramatically in recent years. This is perhaps best illustrated by the long-running television show *Modern Family*, which began airing in 2009: it features Jay, a white guy in his sixties who has remarried a much younger Colombian woman with whom he has a child, and the relationships between them and Jay's grown daughter, her husband, and their three kids and also Jay's grown son, his husband, and the girl they adopted from

Vietnam. It's television, so they all have lovely houses and none of their troubles is too troubling, but the show does present a telling contrast to the 1950s *Ozzie and Harriet* world that the show implicitly references. *Modern Family* was nominated for over a hundred major awards, including fifty-seven Emmy Awards, and won "Best Comedy" Emmys five years in a row. Family diversity is not just visible; it gets awards.

Even children's books, which have long reinforced the One True Family ideology—with adoptive, blended families, same-sex families, and even mixed-race families treated mainly as special topics—have begun to make family diversity more visible. As Todd Parr, an award-winning and best-selling children's book author and illustrator, summed it up it in *The Family Book*, a staple in many a home and preschool,

> Some families are big. Some families are small. Some families are the same color. Some families are different colors. All families like to hug each other! Some families live near each other. Some families live far from each other. Some families look alike. Some families look like their pets. All families are sad when they lose someone they love. Some families have a stepmom or stepdad and stepsisters or stepbrothers. Some families adopt children. Some families have two moms or two dads. Some families have one parent instead of two. All families like to celebrate special days together! There are lots of different ways to be a family.[8]

Years after becoming a best-seller, *The Family Book* was banned by a small Illinois school district after some parents complained about the page acknowledging two-mom and two-dad families, arguing that it raised "issues that shouldn't be taught at the elementary school level."[9] The ban appeared to be a sad and lonely one, though, indicating perhaps that even many defenders of the mythical "traditional family" now recognize that, when it comes to families, nontraditional is well on its way to becoming the new normal.

Much of this promotion of family diversity—and the cultural demotion of the One True Family ideology—reflects the simple fact that new family forms have become more common in recent decades and their existence thus harder to deny.[10] And that phenomenon is due in large part to the expansion of pathways to parenthood. A large cluster of social forces has converged over the past several decades to make it possible for people to pursue parenthood in nontraditional ways: the actions of social movements pushing for women's reproductive freedom and lesbian and gay family rights; the development of reproductive technologies that make it possible for sperm and ovum to meet without heterosexual intercourse and for women to carry babies that they did not conceive; the spread and normalization of divorce; the rise of women's labor-force participation and, for some women, delayed childbearing; the wars and worldwide economic inequalities that orphaned some children and left some parents without the means to provide for their children; the globalization of communication, commerce, and travel; the rise of reproduction-related entrepreneurship and social service professions, whose members have created organizations and programs devoted to easing alternative forms of family creation.

That's a lot. Each of these developments has been controversial, and each entails its own complex power struggles. The result, though, has been a gradual, forceful shattering of the ideology that the only real, natural, legitimate way for people to become a family is for a married man and woman to conceive a child through sexual intercourse and then raise it together in their home. It probably shouldn't be surprising to find people picking through the shards of that myth, not really meaning to be rude, trying to piece together the details of how, if not in the old-fashioned way, these new families came to be. The old origin stories no longer hold.

■　■　■

The view of unconventional family creation you get from this book is necessarily incomplete. As a collection, the stories in this book have quirks and limitations that reflect the boundaries of my own social networks. As a review of the sociological research on social networks put it simply, "contact between similar people occurs at a higher rate than among dissimilar people."[11] The social worlds I inhabit, like most, tend to be made up of people whose social class, educational background, political sensibilities, and work positions are not that distant from my own. Even as atypical family-making stories go, then, the stories here are neither exhaustive nor fully representative.

On a deeper level, though, the very fact that unconventional family creation is not all that uncommon among the people to whom I'm most connected is itself a revealing and important starting point. The kinds of paths to having children described in the pages that follow are—at least for now, at least in this country—taking place disproportionately within relatively privileged sectors of society, for whom family making has become increasingly a matter of choice, mostly for the obvious reason that neither private adoption nor assisted reproduction is cheap. They are also more commonly found in communities that embrace or at least tolerate "alternative" families, which tends to mean liberal enclaves, especially liberal enclaves with a critical mass of lesbian, gay, bisexual, transgender, and queer people. Where I live, for instance, geographically and culturally, unusual families are not all that unusual. Toss a stick around here, and it's pretty likely to land on a lesbian mother, a woman who chose to conceive or adopt on her own, or a middle-aged couple whose babies were created with some medical assistance; you might have to toss a handful, but you'd hit gay men raising kids after not too long.

This is not to stay that nontraditional families are found only among the relatively liberal fractions of the middle and upper-middle classes; single mothers, multigenerational families, foster families, and stepfamilies have long been widespread and cut across ethnic, racial, socioeconomic, and political boundaries, if unevenly so.[12] But the people who are setting out to have children solo or who lack one or another element they'd need to reproduce biologically (a uterus, sperm, or eggs, for instance) on the whole have more money and education than others do. For instance, according to the U.S. Department of Health and

Human Services, adopted children—especially internationally adopted children—are "less likely than are children in the general population to live in households with incomes below the poverty threshold."[13] Demographic information about the incomes of families made via assisted reproduction is harder to come by, but the costs of making a family via in vitro fertilization and surrogacy are not, and they run between $40,000 and $120,000, according to the Council for Responsible Genetics.[14] The rates of unmarried women giving birth remain much higher among African American and Hispanic women than white and Asian women, among younger than older women, and among low-income than high-income women,[15] but the active *pursuit* of single motherhood as a lifestyle choice has emerged almost exclusively among older, professional, middle-class, mostly white women.[16] As new ways of making families have become available, not everyone has been equally positioned—or equally motivated—to make use of them.

The social and geographic locations of unusual family-making forms can and will expand and change over time, I expect. The spread of new practices, ideas, and technologies often begins among "innovators" and "early adopters"—who are positioned by their social, educational, and financial resources to take risks and absorb failures—and becomes more widespread only later.[17] Many policies and social changes could shape the future possibilities for family-making choices—surrogacy laws, reduced costs and increased insurance coverage of assisted reproduction, tighter or looser adoption regulations, legal recognition of same-sex marriages, poverty-reduction policies, child-care and family-leave policies, support for poor families and single parents all shape choices about having and raising children. We shall see.

For now, the reminder is here again at the very start: there is no separation between the ways we make our families and the various social hierarchies in which we all find ourselves. There never has been, and there isn't now.

■ ■ ■

When I started thinking about this book, I figured I was well positioned to tell some unconventional family creation stories, plopped as I am somewhere near the epicenter of the phenomenon. My friends were upbeat about it, but they also seemed apprehensive, as if uncertain how to tell the stories and sometimes also whether to tell them at all. A few close friends declined, citing the need to keep a hard-won peace inside their family or concerns about the impact on the child later in life. When they did agree to talk, they were generous with their time and honesty, yet almost all of the participants outside my family (and even a couple within our own story) opted to have me use pseudonyms rather than to identify them or their family members by name. Later, I sent chapter drafts to all the central participants for both practical and ethical reasons—to make sure things were accurate and that people could consent anew to what was being disclosed about their lives—and this often generated new anxieties and new things-left-unsaid.

I get that. It's one of the things these family origin stories share with more typical ones: every family story has silences and secrets. More to the point, the farther away you get from the conventional, the less you can fit your story into a familiar script of family creation and the more you're likely to face disapproval. For those of us who grew up in a culture of disclosure—in which, for instance, coming out is an act of empowerment and Facebook is a verb—becoming parents has posed the jarring challenge of figuring out what not to tell. It's difficult to figure out how to be both honest and not damaging, how to narrate one's kids' atypical beginnings in a way that both celebrates and protects them, and how to do so in a way that cannot be easily hijacked by haters or pitiers. Knowing that creation stories become passed along as family legend can make it that much harder to decide how much of the less pretty detail to tell. Maybe some of us also harbor a teeny bit of shame or fear of being looked down on or are more committed to emphasizing the things that make us blend in than the things that mark our kids and family as different. These stories are hard to tell for the same reasons they are compelling: they are part of relatively new, not fully apprehended social changes; they are politically and ethically charged; they involve stigma, power, longing, defiance, fear, and the will to love; they involve complex relationships to normalcy; they feature children.

Looking at how others have told such stories can throw you off kilter, too. On the one hand, you can fill a large bookshelf with the memoirs of people who, like the folks in this book, really wanted to become parents and had to fight to get there. Your shelf would include books like Carey Goldberg, Beth Jones, and Pamela Ferdinand's single-women-and-sperm-donor memoir *Three Wishes* ("worried that somewhere between hot leads and hot dates they missed their chance for children," three journalists "decide to take matters into their own hands—with a little help from a local sperm bank")[18] and gay adoption memoirs like Dan Savage's snarky-sweet *The Kid*, in which on one page Savage is holding a new baby, looking "down at his tiny face, his head tucked into his little knit cap," watching "his eyes open and close," and on the next is "back at the Eagle, watching porn and playing pinball."[19] You'd have Scott Simon's adoption memoir *Baby, We Were Meant for Each Other* (about how Simon and his wife "found true love with two tiny strangers from the other side of the world" and about the "anxieties and tears along with hugs and smiles and the unparalleled joy of this blessed and special way of making a family")[20] and Rachel Lehman-Haupt's *In Her Own Sweet Time*, a single-career-woman-exploring-fertility-technology memoir ("the story of a young woman who wants it all" and who travels the world "to explore the many new choices available to women—egg freezing, single motherhood, and instant families—while grappling with her own ambitions, anxieties, and values").[21] And that's before you even get to the books about parenting itself.

The writer Anne Glusker, reviewing Peggy Orenstein's *Waiting for Daisy*,[22] a smart, unflinching account of Orenstein's road to motherhood—infertility, miscarriages, marital stress, almost-adoptions, almost-surrogacy—dubbed this genre Repro Lit.[23] Repro Lit narratives, which also often do double duty as how-to resources, are personal, moving, and celebratory. To the degree that institutional structures figure into these narratives, they tend to be either as obstacles to be overcome or as mechanisms for overcoming obstacles on the individuals' heroic journeys to parenthood.

On the other hand, reading academic writing on similar topics—assisted reproduction, adoption, surrogacy—you would be hard-pressed to find heroic-yet-anxious parents-to-be, true love, or tiny faces under little knit caps. Many scholars have described the emergence of what the sociologist Judith Stacey called "brave new families" as the cutting-edge of progressive social change,[24] or at least as potentially providing, in the words of the sociologist Suzanna Walters, "a template for imagining kinship in the future tense."[25] But when it comes to how those families are made, scholars tend to be much less enthusiastic. Feminists have long debated, for instance, whether surrogacy extends women's control over their bodies or takes the exploitation of women's bodies to horrific new lengths.[26] Back in the mid-1980s, the writer Gena Corea decried the "industrialization of reproduction" and the "reproductive supermarket,"[27] and the critical analysis of "reproductive labor," "reproductive tourism," and "commercial pregnancy" continues, for instance, in the sociologist France Winddance Twine's recent *Outsourcing the Womb*.[28] Drawing on the anthropologist Shellee Colen's framework of "stratified reproduction,"[29] Twine notes that surrogacy is "embedded in a transnational capitalist market that is structured by racial, ethnic, and class inequalities and by competing nation-state regulatory regimes," in which poorer women become "reproductive service workers" for wealthier people.[30] Others, like the anthropologist Diana Marre and the women's studies professor Laura Briggs, caution against the outsourcing of "pregnancy, childbirth, and sometimes the first years of babies' lives to less expensive places and/or mothers—literally, laborers,"[31] an aspect of what Arlie Hochschild has called, not admiringly, the larger-scale "outsourcing of intimacy."[32]

Adoption doesn't fare well either. Marre and Briggs, among many others, emphasize how international adoption is rooted in "inequalities between rich and poor nations, the history of race and racialization since the end of slavery in Europe's colonies and the United States, and relationships between indigenous and non-indigenous groups in the Americas and Australia"; emerged out of war; and remains "marked by the geographies of unequal power, as children move from poorer countries and families to wealthier ones."[33] E. J. Graff, from Brandeis University's Schuster Institute for Investigative Journalism, has convincingly demonstrated that the worldwide adoption industry—an extremely lucrative international business—is poorly regulated, often corrupt, and based on "the myth of a world orphan crisis."[34] Considering the long-standing debates over transracial adoption in the United States—basically, whether it's okay for African American children to be adopted into white families—the feminist law-and-society scholar Dorothy Roberts argues that adoption isn't just a means to providing children a loving home and parents an opportunity to parent but is also "a political institution reflecting social inequities, including race, class, and gender hierarchies, and serving powerful ideologies and interests. Most children awaiting adoption in the nation's foster care system are African American or Latino. Black children's 'need' for adoption results from biased decision-making and policies, including adoption policies, that systematically disadvantage Black families."[35] These are hardly the triumphant, poignant narratives of parenthood against the odds.

You might call the academic genre Repro Crit. Repro Crit narratives are intellectually challenging, politically charged, and quite discouraging. They focus mainly on institutional structures and the circulation of power in and through them; to the degree that individual parents-to-be figure into the analysis, they take their place mainly as illustrations of subordinate, dominant, or contradictory positions in an unequal social structure, which is, in these accounts, the more important story.

Such critical perspectives might be a buzz kill, placed against the happy endings of their Repro Lit counterparts, but they are also not wrong. The stories of the families in this book cannot be understood apart from the structural context that has made family creation a choice for people who would earlier have been excluded, the institutions that regulate reproduction and family creation, and the social inequalities of race, class, gender, sexuality, body, and nation that shape them. Yet neither are the personal memoirs of hard, rewarding journeys to parenthood just naive Pollyannaism. The stories of the families in this book cannot be understood apart from the ferocious, stubborn, creative drive that some people have to give and get this particular kind of intense love, which is also the insistence on leaving something behind. There are righteous battles fought here, real happy endings, actual children, and deep love. We have done beautiful things.

These two sorts of narratives—of rough, rewarding individual parenthood quests and of the troubling structural inequalities that shape family making—rarely even talk to each other. This book, though, is their love child. Together, they force us to take account of fortunes intertwined with misfortunes, of the inequalities that haunt the most intensely loving acts, of institutional obstinacies that spawn ferocious creativity, of family equality in a radically unequal world, of miracles linked to horrors, profits tied to love, bureaucracy and intimacy combined, the hard silences, contradictions, and raging beauties of it all. So here I am, with my bastard stories to deliver and impertinent questions and dazzling children to celebrate.

REBA, LIVE!

Just after New Year's in 2004, I had a dream that my college girlfriend Tamar was having a baby. It was a dream without much originality, just a string of clips from those birth scenes you see on TV medical shows: woman being wheeled, screaming, down the green halls of a hospital; calm, concerned face of doctor, saying things like "Just breathe" and "Blah-blah, stat!"; hospital room, sounds of baby cries, close-up of euphoric face of a woman, now mother, cooing and gazing into the face of a swaddled infant, now gurgling. The only difference was that the woman was Tamar, her freckled cheeks ruddy, her red hair matted with sweat.

A bloodless, simple birth in which bliss erases pain: it was as if even my dreams were required to acknowledge how far the reality of childbirth was from my reach. After all, it takes an awful lot of work to have a baby when, if you're a male couple like me and Richard, you're missing two of the three crucial elements. An extra penis is nice but not exactly needed.

After my coffee, I gave Tamar a call. We hadn't spoken in about a year, but I told her about the dream and asked her if something was going on, if she and her husband were maybe on the way to a baby.

"Nah," she said. "Andy and I decided we don't want kids. We have so many kids around us, godchildren and friends' kids. We like it this way, where they go home afterwards." I suggested that maybe the dream was metaphorical, probably about work or something, and we talked about various projects she was doing that could reasonably be likened to giving birth. Tamar was always something of a go-getter, and by now she was a pricey consultant to various conservation and sustainable-development nonprofits. Between trips to the Amazon, she was writing her first screenplay, the story of a big-city venture capitalist who loses her mother, inherits a farm and its family secrets, and then has to fight against everyone she thought she loved to save it. Tamar was giving birth to a lot of things.

Curious, I returned later to the question of actual kids. "I only have one regret," Tamar said. "I kind of wanted to experience pregnancy and childbirth. I was born into this body, you know, and I feel like I'm missing the chance to experience one of the most amazing things you can do in this kind of body." It is in Tamar's character to see the amazing side of what others suggest culminates in something a lot like shitting a watermelon. She has also been a feminist since childhood; she once organized a speculum party in her dorm room, in which she and her friends earnestly examined and appreciated their vaginas. Plus, she has a taste for emotional intensity.

"So you're saying you'd like to be pregnant and give birth to a child but not raise it," I summarized.

"Exactly," she said.

"Have I got a deal for you," I said.

I was four-fifths joking. Richard and I had just recently settled an argument about kid having that had lasted about four years and followed us from Manhattan to Oakland. We were both pretty sure we wanted kids. I'd grown up assuming I'd be a father, aged into the assumption that being gay meant I would not, and made the best of my freedom and semioutsider status. Years of other people's activism,[1] along with the rapid mainstreaming and heightened visibility of much gay life,[2] had undercut that assumption, and fatherhood had become imaginable again.

Richard had come around a similar circle, but that was where our similarities ended. He was the child of a postal-worker father and a mother who had worked as a secretary and a Walmart cashier; I was the child of two academics. He'd majored in biology at Stanford, a subject for which, as a critical-thinking political science major at Swarthmore, I'd required a tutor. When he'd finally taken off enough time to have a hobby, Richard had chosen genealogy. Now he wanted some genetic tie to a family lineage and thought that adoption, nice as it was, left too much unpredictable. He had done plenty of life saving in his time as an ER doctor and did not feel compelled to do more of it in order to have a family. I had nothing against breeding and felt as deserving of biological offspring as any straight person but was creeped out by the catalog-shopping and rent-a-womb aspects of surrogacy, which seemed to combine crass commercialism and a male sense of entitlement to female bodies. We'd concluded that our jointly held fantasy would be an intimate version of procreation—called "collaborative reproduction" in the assisted reproduction world, I later learned—with eggs from a relative and a friend or acquaintance to carry and give birth to a child. One of us would make deposits to a sperm bank, and then if we later decided to have another child, the other one would take his turn. We knew it was ludicrous, but it was clarifying nonetheless to have a vision. I told some of this to Tamar.

"I'll mull it over," she said. I figured she was kidding.

■　■　■

Tamar was turning forty that summer, and her husband, Andy, sent me a request to put together a page for a book he'd be giving her at the party in rural Virginia. Hoping for a few old photos, I prevailed on my mother to dig through a box of memorabilia I'd stowed at my parents' house on Martha's Vineyard. I had in mind perhaps a photo from our graduation, when my Grandpa Sam had taken one look at Tamar—a fair-skinned, ginger Jew born in Israel—and declared in full voice, to no one in particular, "She's not Jewish. She's Irish." Or maybe a snapshot from that same summer, when she and some friends and I had done mushrooms on the Vineyard and swooned at the awesome motion of individual grains of sand. My mother could find no photos but sent instead a package that included a long letter from Tamar, written over the winter break at the height of our romance, and a pile of stuff from her late mother, Nancy, also known as Duke.

Duke was a twice-married accomplished developmental psychologist, a brilliant academic, a powerhouse, and a total kook. She talked to people of all ages, including toddlers, as if they were peers. She was tiny, loyal, and willful. Her boundaries were unusual. Once, as boyfriend and girlfriend on a college-break visit to Green Bay, where Duke taught, Tamar and I took separate showers; Duke expressed concern about our relationship. She shared with her children the details of her sex life and expected nothing less in return. I'd come to love her, warily, and to admire her. In April 1986, she was diagnosed with late-stage breast cancer, and she died just a few months later, of cerebrospinal fluid cancer, at forty-six. The last time I spoke with Duke, she was on a heavy morphine drip. I was on my bed in the teensy apartment in the North End of Boston I shared with two roommates. "Joshie," she said, interrupting her own stream-of-consciousness good-bye, "remember this: you will have a guardian angel." As guardian angels go, you could do a lot worse.

In the package my mother forwarded were several articles Duke had sent me, one on "the psychological paradoxes of intimacy over the life cycle," another on being a Jewish militant atheist, another called "Beyond Oil of Olay: Bag Balm and Other Forms of Feminine Protection," and one called "Still Life with Dogs," about a two-week bout with the flu, which begins, "I might be dying." Also inside was an invited address on Judaism and feminism to the American Psychological Association in August 1985. In it, Duke quotes the *midrashim* on Genesis that Tamar and her sister wrote for a college class they'd taken together. Tamar, then nineteen, had written of the separation of male and female in the creation story and their reconciliation through the improbable pregnancies of Sarah (pregnant at ninety with Isaac) and Rebecca (barren for twenty years, only to give birth to twins Jacob and Esau). The logic of the interpretation wasn't easy to follow, but Tamar, Duke reported, "caused pregnancy to represent in symbol that which it is in biological fact, a unification of independent beings who require each other for the creation of new life." Tamar had also deemed the least likely births the most spiritually significant.

Tucked between two of Duke's articles was a letter she'd sent me, dated "The Sixth Night of Chanukah, 5746; 12 December 1986," printed on dot matrix. She wrote at length about her writing life, her complex relationship to Jews even as she toiled "isolated among the goyim," and the weather. "Now, briefly and gently, to family feelings," she then continued. Tamar and I had broken up a few months earlier—an event that boiled down, though no one including myself knew it yet, to gayness tugging at my pants leg. "Yes, Joshie, you found a place of your own in my heart a long time ago," Duke said. "That doesn't mean I don't miss seeing you and Tamar together. She's right, you know, to think of separation as a sort of death; the French say, *partir, c'est mourir un peu*, and I agree. But I also believe there can be a new life after such deaths. But here's a question for you, Joshie: What are you going to do now?" From across the distance of years and dimensions, the question was spooky, but spookier still was a sentence I found hovering a paragraph before. "When I think about what 'might have been' between Tamar and you," Duke wrote, "it is more often in terms of the large collection of baby items we have squirreled away in our minds for the first grandchild, for which you and Tamar looked like the most likely and most welcome candidates."

I made a copy of the letter and pasted the original onto a page for Tamar's birthday book.

■ ■ ■

When I'd begun to accept a gay identity in my early twenties, I hadn't entirely let go of my childhood assumption that one day I'd be a parent, but I'd certainly back-burnered it. When people put on sympathetic faces and told me how sad it was that I wouldn't have kids, I became snidely assertive. "As far as I know, my sperm are the same as before

I was gay," I'd sniff. "But then, I'm not very good with science." Really, though, back then I had no idea whether or how it was going to happen, now that I was probably not going to be romantically involved with women. Somewhere in the back of my head I knew technology was making things easier, but I didn't think that applied to me. I had some good lesbian friends with a baby, but as far as I knew they'd used a sperm-filled turkey baster. Not an option. I'd heard about "test tube babies" since the late 1970s, but that sounded too science-fictiony—the name "Baby M" didn't help—like a soft-core version of cloning. Anyway, I had a gay adolescence to progress through, a degree to finish, a body and heart to discover, a movement to join, an outsider identity to inhabit, and wild oats to sow.

By the time I'd met Richard in the late 1990s, when I was a professor with sown oats and an integrated gay identity, the technology for creating biological offspring without hetero sex had become more advanced and familiar. Over the course of a couple of decades, in fact, assisted reproduction had gone, in the journalist Liza Mundy's words, from "an oddball, fringe technology to being perhaps the most socially influential reproductive technology of the twenty-first century."[3] That technology seemed intended for others but available to me, which in itself held appeal: the tools of heterosexual pronatalism would be adapted for subversive queer family making.

Subverting heteronormativity might be one possibility, but assisted reproduction also came with dynamics that could hardly be called subversive. What brought assisted reproduction out of the oddball fringe was primarily a commercial industry that, once the technology was in place, successfully cashed in on the desires, and often desperation, of people who would prefer to have children through heterosexual intercourse but were having trouble doing so. Given the costs of assisted reproduction, the fertility industry was built largely on selling services to relatively well-off people, accentuating what some scholars call "reproductive stratification," in which, as the science studies researcher Charis Thompson puts it, the "haves and have-nots of [assisted reproduction technologies] are increasingly the socioeconomic haves and have-nots of society in general."[4] If Duke's what-might-have-been was going to become my what-might-be, it was most likely going to be in relation to commercialized reproduction, which joins "profound parental love" with "cold-blooded business truths," in which children are "desired, loved, celebrated, wanted, and obtained in a relentlessly commercialized process,"[5] and which facilitates the creation of some queer families even as it reinforces the distance between haves and have-nots.

I grew up enjoying the pleasures of commerce but suspicious of its amorality and wary of its manipulations. We were not allowed any toys that were advertised on television, and in my alternative high school and socialist-Zionist summer camp, it was assumed that commercials were capitalist propaganda; I'd kept my excitement about occasional McDonald's visits and trips to the shopping mall mostly quiet. But here I was, thirty years later, banging at the gates of a commercial industry. If we did want to make a family through biological procreation, we'd just have to enter the fertility marketplace. We'd have to treat a baby at least something like a commodity. We'd have to outsource to others the parts of the process we weren't equipped to provide, and probably pay for them.

At a personal level, that seemed manageable, but the bigger picture—the building of something so intimate as family through commercial exchanges—was disquieting. Egg donation, in vitro fertilization, and surrogacy might reasonably be seen as quintessential examples of the encroachment of a market mentality into aspects of intimate life that had previously been insulated from commercial forces. For instance, in *The Outsourced Self*, the sociologist Arlie Russell Hochschild details what she calls the "outsourcing" of intimacy, a "strange new emotional capitalism" in which the market has become present "in our bedrooms, at our breakfast tables, in our love lives, entangled in our deepest joys and sorrows."[6] Chief among her examples is surrogacy, in which "a person can now legally purchase an egg from one continent, sperm from another, and implant it in a 'womb for rent' in yet another."[7] She describes a couple who, turning to a surrogacy clinic in India, "saw their relationship with the surrogate as a mutually beneficial transaction" and "imagined themselves as outsourcers paying a stranger to provide a professionally supervised service," establishing with the gestational carrier "the sort of relationship one might establish with an obstetrician or dentist."[8] She describes an Indian surrogate who, "instructed to remain emotionally detached from her clients, her babies, and even from her womb" while doing "an extraordinarily personal thing," entered transactions that were "cursory, businesslike, and spanned differences in language, culture, ethnicity, nation, and, most of all, social class."[9]

Was that what we were choosing to do? I wondered. I was choosing, it seemed, to turn conception and childbirth into commercial exchanges, alienating myself, my partner, and the women involved from our bodies and our babies, replacing the personal and the attached with the impersonal and detached. This would be true even as I was setting out, with willing collaborators, to do something beautiful. This would be true even as I was participating in the radical transformation of kinship.

■   ■   ■

In my discussions with Tamar, it became quickly clear that she was not interested in getting pregnant with her own eggs. A genetic connection, she reasoned, would muddy the family waters and make it emotionally harder for her, and anyway she was getting old enough that a pregnancy via insemination wasn't very likely to take. We asked several people to consider donating eggs and somehow managed to get a yes from a person close to us. I'll call her Jane. Like Tamar, Jane was an intimate and a peer, from the same social class as the rest of us; at her request, her part of the story stays her own.

I took on a role a bit like that of a general contractor. Tamar, for her part, came to our ongoing conversations with lists of discussion topics. She wanted to know how we would feel about paying her, so that she could treat the experience at least partially as a job. Payment would help mark the boundary between a parental and nonparental relationship to the baby, which all of us involved wanted and needed; the terms of commerce, it turned out, were not just intrusions to be resisted. This arrangement sat well with Richard, who does not enjoy being indebted. My parents had already offered some financial help, which I'd rationalized to myself as gay reparations but knew was simply class advantage, and would be happy to see it go to Tamar, for whom my mother had served as a kind of surrogate mom after Tamar's own mother died.

Tamar also wanted to know how we would feel about our child making annual visits, without us, to her and Andy in Virginia, which even then I saw as a much-needed annual adult vacation for me and Richard. She wanted to know how we would feel about her breast-feeding, at least for the first week or two.

"I don't see why not," I said. "I guess what we're supposed to consider is the attachment you'll form to one another, which could make separating really hard." I'd been reading a lot of surrogacy websites.

Tamar paused. "I'm not worried about getting attached to this baby," she said. She had clearly already thought this one through. "I want to feel attached to this baby. I hope you want that, too." It was exactly what I wanted, in fact, the opposite of the conventional surrogacy-industry wisdom, which saw a carrier's emotional attachment to the child she was carrying as the first step toward her decision to screw over the intended parents and keep the kid. Given the supposed health benefits of breast milk,[10] Tamar added, her proposed plan after we took the baby home would be to pump her breasts for the first six weeks and FedEx the milk to California.

"You drive a hard bargain," I told her. I had the sense that she had already investigated the best place to purchase dry ice and packing foam. I knew she was in.

■　■　■

I would have been fine with a bastard child, but Richard had already proposed, on Thanksgiving of 2003, about two weeks after the Massachusetts Supreme Court ruled that denying marriage rights to gay couples was unconstitutional. Richard is a boisterous fellow at a party, known for his unbridled laugh, a bunch of chortles followed by a deep, full-throated set of heaving guffaws, but he detests public speaking. That night, he had stood in front of fifteen drunken friends and a turkey carcass, sweat beads forming on his brow, wine glass in hand. He'd explained that before the Massachusetts decision, he had thought civil unions would do just fine—they could keep the word "marriage" if they wanted—but that he'd now decided he wouldn't put up with second-class citizenship, that he'd had more than enough of that in his life. He'd talked about how his own parents' marriage—white mother, black father—had been illegal in many places. Then his face had started to break and leak tears onto the golden tablecloth, and as soon as it did, several other people at the table started to cry. He wanted to know if I would marry him, in Massachusetts.

I took a swig of wine and said yes to Richard and good-bye to the last shreds of my frayed self-image as a nonconformist. So maybe this is what it turned out I wanted my life to be: married, with a child who was not even considered illegitimate, in a house with a picket fence, like a poster for the mainstreaming of gayness.[11] Status elevation and the blanket of normalcy weren't the main conscious motivations for marrying and having a kid, but they were hard to disentangle from the more selfless motivation of steadfast love. Entering the institutions of marriage and family was for me a healing victory, yet I could not help but notice that it was also a victory for those institutions and their enforcement of normalcy. Richard, who despised hypocrisy but harbored little animosity toward social norms, had no such concerns. I shrugged, focused on the love part, and enjoyed myself.

Richard and I were married the next August in a tearjerker of a black-Jewish gay ceremony (cantor, gospel singer, "Somewhere over the Rainbow") in my parents' yard on Martha's Vineyard, with a hundred-plus witnesses, during a brief patch of sunshine between Tropical Storm Bonnie and Hurricane Charley. Our friend Rebecca, whose gift was to plan and execute a "wedding so pretty it'll make your teeth hurt," had purchased every sunflower available on the island and adorned the deck railings with tulle. From my spot under the chuppah, I could see the table where I'd sat with my parents, just before leaving for graduate school in California, and told them I was maybe gay, to which my father, who is usually mild mannered and who taught courses on social movements and social justice, replied that it made him sick to his stomach. The wedding tent was set up on the field to which my mother had quickly fled that day, where she had violently pulled up weeds and screamed, in a madwoman voice I heard neither before nor since, that I always did whatever the fuck I wanted anyway. They had more than come around in the seventeen years since. They'd arranged a column item about the wedding in the *Vineyard Gazette* and would soon be carried on chairs with their son's husband's mother, waving handkerchiefs and bouncing above a crowd of sweaty hora dancers.

One photo from the wedding shows Andy, Tamar, Richard, and me, raising our champagne glasses to the camera. We had decided to make a baby together, but only our immediate families knew; we didn't want to jinx it or subject ourselves to questions we didn't want to answer or go public. What we were toasting was our little secret.

■ ■ ■

Eight months later, in April 2005, Team Baby descended on northern Virginia, near the Genetics and IVF Institute, which we had chosen because it was near Tamar and Andy and got good reviews online. We stayed in a plantation-style Marriott near Dulles that had an extravagant floral centerpiece and Tara-ish columns in the rotunda, with wide staircases leading up to meeting rooms named after early presidents.

The fertility institute was located in a small, bland office park in Fairfax, and it looked right at home. The waiting room reminded me just how little medical institutions were set up for people like us. Checking in at the front desk, we could fit our roles into none of their forms. Mom-kid combos beamed from the shiny covers of parenting magazines. The few waiting women and the receptionist watched us with curiosity and caution, as if our laughter might be mocking them. It had become clear months earlier that we asked more questions of the institute's staff than they were used to answering, and it occurred to me now that perhaps they were accustomed to clients for whom asking questions meant dwelling on things they didn't want to think about—a sense of a betraying or failed or aging body, maybe, or an unbecoming desperation to reproduce. Tamar had once scanned and sent me the response of the fertility doctor to her probing about time lines, drugs, and the like, a careless hieroglyphic of scribbles, dots, and numbers that clearly assumed the reader was uninterested in deciphering it. We'd arranged for her to switch doctors. In the waiting room, we were incongruous, a bunch of fertile people loosed in the land of infertility.

While Jane's eggs were being "harvested"—an odd word, I thought, meant to make the grueling procedure sound like picking vegetables from a garden—I browsed the agency's brochures, one of which advertised the availability, for an additional fee, of eggs from women who "hold or are pursuing advanced degrees in medicine or another academic specialty," known at the institute as "doctoral donors."

"Daddy," I said, in my best spoiled voice, "I want a doctoral donor." No one was amused.

Dr. Hearns-Stokes, to whose care we had switched after Tamar's experience with the patronizing scribbler, emerged from the wings. Everything went just fine, she reported, and the donor just needs to rest.

"We have nine viable eggs," she said. Not a great number—twelve to fifteen would be great—but good enough. She looked at Richard and did a double take. "You look familiar."

"Rhonda?" Richard asked.

They had overlapped in medical school, where the black students knew each other by sight, if not by name. While they were catching up, I imagined the sperm we'd frozen waking up and wagging their tails slowly, like groggy runners at an early-morning road race, ready to fertilize Jane's eggs.

The next day after breakfast, the doctor called. "I don't have good news," she told me. "None of the eggs fertilized." I handed the phone to

Richard and put my head down on the pillow. The doctor explained that our only option now was intracytoplasmic sperm injection, or ICSI, in which a single sperm is manually placed into an egg. She described ICSI at this stage as an "emergency rescue" procedure, which did not sound hopeful to me, and said she was very sorry, which sounded even less so.

I cried into my pillow for the next hour and a half, with Richard draped over me now and then. The strength, drama, and duration of the cry took both of us by surprise. It was childlike, with those lengthy, open-mouthed silent breaths that toddlers take before they let out a wail, followed by retching sobs. I heard moans. It was a deep, loss-of-faith sort of grief: I'd been acting as a sort of project manager, a practical role that had apparently hidden from me my own irrational belief in the power of focused, loving, bountiful good intention. My aunt Mimi, a good Wiccan, had even cast a spell. In a lull between sobs, I considered the possibility that I'd been in California too long. Then I took a nap.

When I called my parents with the news, my mother was on her way to Shabbat services to say kaddish for her mother, Reba Ladin, whose *yahrtzeit* was that day. Grandma Reba had been like a playmate to me as a kid. On visits to north Philadelphia, my sister and I had accompanied her to Cow Town, a nearby flea market where she sold reject clothing. She'd taught us the Russian word for "snot" and let us wear aprons filled with coins. When she moved to Atlantic City, Reba would go play nickel slots with one of her boyfriends while I tried to win stuffed animals at the skeeball arcade. Reba grew up in a Ukrainian shtetl whose name translates to Oniontown, and before coming to her new American life as a teenager, she had witnessed pogroms; but she laughed easily. Born on a date unrecorded and later given the opportunity to make up her birthday, she'd chosen Valentine's Day. When Richard and I were fantasizing girl-baby names—we wanted names with a family connection and ones that could be plausibly both black and Jewish—Reba had made the short list.

■　■　■

The evening of the failed fertilization, Richard and I drove out to Andy and Tamar's house, a log cabin at the end of a dirt road, on a hill below a horse pasture and above an algae-covered pond. While we had been wallowing in our hotel rooms, they had prepared a Shabbat dinner. Tamar lit the candles. Andy, who is not Jewish, produced his signature hummus and said the *bracha* over the challah in a thick West Virginia accent. It's the anniversary of my grandmother's death, I announced after the kiddush, while we were still holding our wine glasses. Tamar observed that the day before had been the anniversary of her mother's cancer diagnosis. We toasted them, and since there seemed to be a convergence of dead women, we added our other departed mothers and grandmothers. To my Grandma Reba, also known as Rivka, and to my Grandma Blanche, who had once been a glamorous actress; to Tamar's mother, the guardian angel, and to Andy's; to Richard's grandmother Georgia, also known as Sugar, who had been able to silence children in church with one glance; and to his grandmother Olive and to his great-grandmother Sadie and his great-great-grandmother Talitha, whose steely-eyed portrait has always hung in our homes beside that of her husband, Volney: we clinked our glasses, thanked them, kindly asked them to see that an egg fertilized, and drank our wine. *Lchaim*, we said.

After dinner, Andy put on some music. He chose Sister Sledge's "We Are Family." We pushed back the table a bit, and we danced and sang along, drunk enough to remember the words. *We are family. I got all my sisters with me. We are family. Get up everybody and sing.*

The next morning, Dr. Hearns-Stokes called. When the technicians had gone to do the ICSI procedure, they'd found that one of the eggs had fertilized late. In addition, one of the ICSI eggs had fertilized. We could go ahead and transfer the embryos into Tamar, she said, though the odds of a pregnancy weren't good. Tamar, who for months had been physically and mentally preparing for her role, wanted to follow it all the way through. Otherwise, she said, it would be like she'd trained for a relay race and never been handed the baton. I asked Richard whether he thought it was worth my changing my plane ticket, which had me returning to Oakland that night. "The doctor said the odds of a pregnancy are 'slim to none,'" he told me. "That's doctor talk for 'It's not going to happen.'" I went home.

That Monday morning, Richard, Andy, and Tamar went back to the clinic for the embryo transfer, a simple procedure in which the minuscule embryos are sent through a catheter into the uterus. Tamar lay on the table, legs raised, with Andy and Richard on each side. Andy suggested that they hold hands. The room was a bit cramped, and on one side was a small sliding window much like you'd find at a Burger King drive-thru. The window slid open, and a voice called out, in a manner that reminded Richard of a short-order cook, "Embryos for Gamson." They all watched on the ultrasound screen as a tiny dot gently traveled, like a slow-motion spitball, to its destination. Richard requested pictures of the embryos, which he later scanned into our computers. One was two cells, the other four. I could show you their pictures.

Tamar was told to lie low for the day, not to move around too much. Andy was at work, so she and Richard decided to get some French fries and watch a couple of DVDs at her house. The first movie Tamar selected was *Finding Neverland*, about *Peter Pan* writer J. M. Barrie and the family that inspired him. As the opening credits rolled, Tamar started to weep. Richard, concerned, asked her what was the matter.

"It's so sad," Tamar said.

"But it hasn't started yet," Richard pointed out.

"I know," she said, "but it's going to be so sad."

■   ■   ■

Two Thursdays later, I was packing my bags in the back of our blue Mini, getting ready to head to the airport for a trip to Los Angeles, when I looked up at the front steps and saw Richard motioning to me from our little front porch. He looked stricken. He was leaning over, one hand on his leg, breathing heavily, waving me toward him with his other hand, which also held the phone. His face, usually caramel, was yellowish. My first thought was that his uncle, who had been sick, had died. I ran up and grabbed the phone and heard, to my surprise, Tamar's voice.

"Guess what?" she said, while Richard lit a cigarette. "I'm pregnant."

"What?"

"I'm pregnant."

"What?" I said again. I laughed and headed down to Los Angeles in a daze.

That afternoon, Richard pulled the mail from our mailbox. This in itself was an unusual event. I am the mail getter, sorter, and distributor. Typically, if I'm not around, the mail simply accumulates in the mailbox until there's no more room. That day, Richard, apparently thrown off his routines by the news, absent-mindedly opened the mailbox. Inside was one of our weekly promotional cards from a nearby casino, sent to us to encourage our gambling addiction with offers of free hotel rooms, meals, shows, and "bonus cash." We went there more than we could afford, no doubt, though once, after Richard had won a $1,200 slot jackpot, we'd splurged and wound up sitting in folding chairs about ten feet from a wobbling, spitting, sweaty Liza Minnelli, who uncomplainingly performed in the bingo room, converted for the night into a theater.

The card on this particular day had a simple declaration on one side: "Reba Live!" The other side provided more specific information about Reba McIntyre's upcoming performance. Richard, a bit freaked out, put the card on the fridge.

"I guess we'd better name her Reba," I said when he told me the story that night. When even casinos are sending messages from the great beyond, we agreed, you'd better not mess around.

■　■　■

Kinship is always a set of social relationships mapped onto nature, but it's pretty well established for most people: the person who carried and gave birth to you is your mother, the person who "got her pregnant" is your father, their parents are your grandparents, and so on. Assisted reproduction arrangements mess that all up. To put it back together again involves an elaborate dance—"ontological choreography," the sociologist Charis Thompson calls it—aimed at "producing parents, children, and everything that is needed for their recognition as such."[12] Body parts, medical instruments, treatment protocols, laws, ideas about kinship, bureaucratic forms, social norms, and money have to be brought together in particular ways. The choreography is complex, and the dance can easily collapse, either failing to produce a child or failing to produce agreement on who that child's parents are.

The legal choreography is particularly tricky, especially for same-sex couples working with surrogates. On the one hand, legal conflicts over parenthood in the United States have gradually moved the legal conception of parenthood away from "socially fixed and biologically natural and toward something that is more voluntaristic and enforceable through contracts expressing procreational intent."[13] This makes it possible to make a family in which the biological contributors are not necessarily the parents and in which kinship is established by contract. On the other hand, the definitions of family at the state level—where laws governing family are written and enacted—have tended, not surprisingly, to rely on the model of two-heterosexual-parent families. Since laws and policies regarding assisted reproduction have been developed in relation to marriage, the legal scholar Richard Storrow argues, "the effect has been to restrict the use of assisted reproduction to those in socially sanctioned intimate relationships and to erect barriers to those who are not in such relationships."[14] For instance, the "legal definition of infertility in insurance legislation is informed by the medical definition of infertility, the inability of an opposite-sex couple to achieve a pregnancy after a year of engaging in regular and unprotected sexual intercourse"; access to insurance coverage is thus blocked for those whose infertility is social rather than medical, namely, single people and same-sex couples, who must either have, or have access to, other resources.[15]

On top of all that mess, definitions of family are "widely variable, contingent, and prone to an excess of idiosyncratic judicial discretion," as the sociologist Maureen Sullivan puts it.[16] That contingency can be a setback or an opportunity, depending on which judge, and in which court, a case is being considered. The same is true of surrogacy law. Some states have statutes, administrative processes, or common law that explicitly allow surrogacy, and some of the states that do allow it prohibit arrangements in which gestational carriers are paid, which they see as baby selling. Some restrict surrogacy to married couples—and restrict marriage to a man and a woman—or only to those with a demonstrated "medical need."[17] Right now, at least, no state surrogacy laws have any explicit consideration of gay fathers. In some states, like California, gay couples can get prebirth orders designating them the parents, but that is up to individual judges. If the surrogate is in a different state than the intended parents, things get even messier. As one legal scholar, Tiffany Palmer, put it years after my experience, gay men pursuing surrogacy "find themselves caught between the wildly variant patchwork of laws that govern both surrogacy and the nation's equally non-uniform re- lationship recognition laws, creating a jurisdictional roulette for estab- lishing parental rights."[18] They also find themselves facing thousands of dollars of legal fees.

The very things that, at least for now, make it possible to rework kin- ship through assisted reproduction also require considerable money and cultural capital. You need the money, and the sense that the law is yours to use, just to enter the legal dance. Even then, you'd better be careful where your foot lands.

■　■　■

At Tamar's six-week sonogram, she called from the doctor's table and put her cell phone on speaker. She described what she was looking at as a tiny little ball with a beating heart. She put the phone up to the ultrasound, and we all listened to the heartbeat for the first time. Tamar gave us weekly reports, mostly about how much the fetus liked to swim. In one sonogram, Tamar swore the fetus was waving as it moved across the screen. Tamar was hardly sick, and the fetus got consistently high scores on her medical testing, which Tamar communicated with a tone that indicated pride not just in a budding overachiever but also in a job well done.

She came by that pride honestly. Tamar approached pregnancy with the conscientiousness and grit that I recognized from our college years, when I could usually track her down at her reserved library carrel. She learned everything there was to learn about fetal development and posed the question of amniocentesis versus nuchal translucency testing before I even knew that fetuses had nuchals, translucent or otherwise. She researched, she charted. She kept her receipts and tracked her expenses on Excel. A few months into her pregnancy, we drove down to Monterey, where Tamar had a business meeting. At lunch, she whipped out a card summarizing which fish were and were not recommended during pregnancy; she'd made an extra copy for us. When she was diagnosed later with gestational diabetes, her detailed tracking of her blood-sugar numbers elicited dumbfounded looks from doctors. She dealt with curiosity seekers with finesse and smiling bite, disarming them with the isn't-it-wonderful news that she was carrying a baby for dear friends, two guys who could not have one on their own. I imagined she left little space for disapproval; naysayers no doubt left the conversation sorry they'd opened their mouths. She saw her mission as personal and political.

Still, we had to sue her. We had already decided against having the birth in Virginia, where laws were hostile to surrogacy, let alone same-sex parenting. If labor started earlier than expected, Tamar and Andy would dart over the nearby bridge to a hospital in Maryland, but barring such an emergency, our plan was to head up to Massachusetts, hang out at my parents' house, and have the baby there, in the only state where Richard and I were then legally married. Left alone, though, the baby's presumptive legal parents would be Tamar and Andy—egg donors do not have parental rights, and neither did we—in which case we'd have to adopt our own kid. At best, Tamar would be considered the legal mother and the one-of-us-who-provided-sperm the legal father, in which case we'd still have a legal mess on our hands. Tamar and Andy wanted no legal responsibility for the baby, and we wanted all of it, so we decided to try to get a court order so that, as our complaint to the Probate and Family Court of Dukes County, Commonwealth of Massachusetts, put it, "the child's birth record may be established in accordance with those true and accurate facts regarding the child's parentage." Richard was disturbed by the suit—he did not like the idea of a document in which we and our friends were legal adversaries, which might be misread by future genealogists—but I couldn't help but admire the big balls of a system that so casually insisted our collaboration be recorded as a dispute. What a perfect perversion: generosity reflected back to us as animosity. At least, I thought, we get the pleasure of being a difficult meal for the legal system to digest.

The twenty-week ultrasound fell around the time of a conference in Philadelphia, so I arranged to pop down to Virginia for the event. "Do you want to know the sex?" the technician asked Tamar, after the usual assurances that the fetus had ten fingers, ten toes, the appropriate bones, and a reasonably sized head. Tamar turned to me, ignoring the technician's assumptions about parentage. Neither Richard nor I wanted to be surprised, he because he doesn't like surprises of any kind and me because I wanted to start collecting hand-me-down clothes, which don't tend to come gender neutral. We had entertained boy names, but what with the casino flyer and all the dead foremothers, we figured we were having a girl.

"Yes, please," I said.

"A girl," the tech said.

"Are you sure?" I asked. I searched the screen for the spot where one might find genitalia, distracted by a facial profile that seemed to indicate an oversized schnozz.

"I never say 100 percent," she replied flatly, "but I can tell you for certain that this child has no penis." That seemed a pretty good indicator, so we called Richard to tell him he was probably having a little Reba Sadie.

"Yeah, our kids had that nose when they were newborns," one of our relatives told us when we sent her the ultrasound photo. "She'll grow into it." I was not reassured, but she promised to start digging around in the basement for baby clothes.

▪ ▪ ▪

In mid-December 2005, Richard and I took a trip to New York City, staying in a dank, cramped Days Inn on Ninety-Fourth Street whose only real virtue was that it was near where we used to live, two blocks from the Equinox gym where we first met and just up the street from the park bench where I'd made my first attempts to get him to notice me. We knew this trip to New York was likely to be our last as free adults for quite some time, so we went to see *Sweeney Todd* and stayed out late. Then we made our way down to Virginia to start the rest of our lives.

Tamar picked us up at Dulles—Andy was to join us a few days later—and we road-tripped it together in her Subaru up to Martha's Vineyard, she in the back seat with her ridiculous belly, now filled with more than eight pounds of baby, and a body pillow. We ventured onto the deck of the ferry as we left Woods Hole for Vineyard Haven. The mist was salty and cold and familiar. *How strange to be here like this, with these two*, I thought, as we scooted back inside to the snack bar. I'd made the trip several times with each of them before, and here they were, these two who had walked in from different lifetimes, laughing it up in the hard green seats with our swimming baby-in-waiting and the ghosts of our earlier selves. Tamar took a drink of cold water, which she said sometimes woke up Reba, and lifted up the bottom of her sweatshirt. Richard touched her stomach to feel the kicks, and even his big hand just looked like a small Michigan resting on her pale, unmarked globe. Maybe I had lived just one lifetime after all.

My father, Bill, picked us up at the ferry landing, and the familiar sight of him putting down his *Newsweek* to scan the passenger ramp for us, older but always with the same routine—the *Newsweek*, the scan, the nod and smile—comforted me like soup. My mother, Zelda, greeted us at home with a leg of lamb, packages of baby clothes and carriers that had arrived from various corners of the island, and local gossip. Martha's

Vineyard is basically a small town in the off-season, and my mother takes pride in knowing the central island stories in circulation at any one time: the two runaway goats that occupied the Levines' house while they were gone, opening drawers, sleeping in beds, and generally having a party; the battle between Laurie David, the environmentalist and then-wife to Larry David, and her neighbors, one of whom she had served with a restraining order. This time, however, we were at the center of a Vineyard story, which seemed both delicious and vaguely uncomfortable to my mother, as though reveling in her *naches* would somehow cheapen the experience. Still, what a juicy story were we, especially in the dullish winter: the gay son and his husband (he's a doctor, I hear), married just the year before (Wendy catered it, you know), walking around town with the college girlfriend (I think the bearded guy is her husband), who is going to deliver a baby for them (I wonder which one is the father). My mother took us to the Town Clerk's office, where people greeted us with knowing good cheer and attempts to extract fresh information, and a few days later to the Hebrew Center's annual Chanukah party, where our reputations had clearly preceded us. When we walked down the streets of Oak Bluffs and Vineyard Haven, I knew we were the subjects of sightings. In July, you might spot Michael J. Fox, Jamie Lee Curtis, Spike Lee, a Gyllenhaal or two. The pickings were slimmer in December, though, and aside from the occasional weekend appearance of Alan Dershowitz or Mary Steenburgen, we were pretty much it.

My mother was certainly not averse to talking in general terms about our arrival to friends, acquaintances, and people who looked vaguely familiar, but she brought to bear on the situation a seriousness of intent and an efficient management style that bore more than passing resemblance to those of Tamar, who had once worked at the research center my mother founded and ran in Boston. My mother knows how to get things done, in part because she spent her professional life studying organizations and serving on their boards and in part because she enjoys making lists and then crossing things off. She arranged massages for all of us, a facial and hair trim for Tamar, and places to stay for the various family members who were due to arrive around the same time as Reba Sadie. Like Richard, she had turned herself into a genealogist and keeper of family lore and was finely attuned to the problem of forgetting. So she arranged for two people to interview Tamar, Andy, Richard, and me and delegated to my father the task of tracking down a decent tape recorder. She herself began keeping a sort of journal record of our stay, with brief summaries of each day's events, that she entitled "It Takes Two Fathers, a Surrogate, Her Husband, Three Grandparents, a Dog, Three Cousins, an Egg Donor, Two Aunts, an Uncle, Four Houses, and an Island to Birth a Baby: Notes from a Modern Confinement." At Richard's behest, she stuck closely to the facts, which suited her social scientific sensibilities, if not her grandmaternal ones, in entries like this one, from December 19: "At the guesthouse, Josh washes loads of beautiful hand-me-downs that are probably already clean. As things accumulate, he piles them up in the kids' room at the guesthouse and on the bed of the front guest room at our house. J and R deal with the legal procedures that will allow them to be recognized as the legal parents of the baby." And this, from a few days later: "J, R, T and A go to the MV Hospital. Non-stress tests on the baby show that she is perfect on all. Nurse notes this."

We hunkered down in the guesthouse to await the baby, like roosting birds on Valium. We played and replayed the cluster of CDs I'd gifted to my parents over the years—Shawn Colvin, Angie Stone, Robbie Robertson, Meshell Ndegeocello—that had been sent to entertain guests. Richard strung small lights along the living room's perimeter and set up a small Christmas tree next to a green Tibetan chest, decorating it with ornaments he'd bought on the island. The fireplace was lit each morning as the coffee was brewing and burned itself out after that evening's movie. We read fiction punctuated by meals. We stared spacily out at the bare trees, their trunks and crooked branches mottled with light-green moss, and the occasional snowflake. My mother's dog, Rosie, a kissy and deeply feeling mutt, took to spending most of her time over there, since our crew promised not only extra attention but also looser rules regarding furniture and human food. She often took naps with

Andy and Tamar, or Tamar and the body pillow, and when she did, she rested her body against the baby. We entered a sort of group marriage, annoying one another with dishwasher-loading styles and inappropriate whistling; occasionally one dyad would peel off for a walk, an argument, or both. Mostly we ate. On Christmas Day, Richard cooked an elaborate meal that included mac-and-cheese, collard greens, and sweet potato pie; it was also the first night of Chanukah, so we lit several menorahs, read and sang from a Chanukah booklet my mom had photocopied, and heard her position on whether contemporary political significance could be imposed on the story of the Maccabees. When now and again we ventured out—to see the doctor and nurse-midwife, to get groceries—we returned with chocolate fondants from an Oak Bluffs café. We became bored, impatient, and a little chubby.

It was clear that the baby, weighing in at around nine pounds a week before her due date, was chubby and patient. No one doubted she was fully cooked. Our mentions of inducing labor, however, had already been met by the nurse-midwife, a calm and clear woman named Cathy with long hair and kind eyes, with firm recommendations of patience. We tried every trick we'd heard, thought we'd heard, or uncovered on the Internet: a long hike in the Menemsha hills, lobster and eggplant parmesan and spicy food, raspberry-leaf tea and primrose oil, and, Tamar reported to our tittering discomfort, stimulation of nipples and other body parts. We called to Reba Sadie, sang to her through Tamar's protuberance, cooed and commanded. She stayed put, paddling about contentedly in her dark sea of amniotic fluid. My sister and her family came from Newton, ate latkes and exchanged gifts with us, and when there was no action after a couple of days, returned home.

A couple of days after Christmas, my mother reported, "Third trip to the hospital. All is well. They all discuss the possibility of inducing labor, perhaps later in the week. They go to lunch at Art Cliff Diner and decide they definitely want to go ahead with it at that time. By the time they call back, another patient has been scheduled for inducing on Thursday. This is James Taylor's niece and Hugh and Jeanne Taylor's daughter, who is having twins and whose blood pressure is high. They all seem a bit disappointed but regroup."

"Goddam Taylors," I said, back at the house, putting on an old James Taylor album.

By the time James Taylor's niece's twins were born, a few days later, we had already set new goals. We had gotten it into our heads that Reba Sadie would be the first baby born on the island in the new year, grabbing a coveted spot on the pages of the local papers that would look terrific in the baby scrapbook Richard was already starting to imagine.

▪ ▪ ▪

"Big national and international news of the day," my mom wrote on Reba's due date, January 4, 2006. "The lobbyist Jack Abramoff has pleaded guilty to bribing public officials and cheating Indian tribes and may implicate powerful politicians, including Bush and Tom ('The Hammer') DeLay, the already disgraced former Speaker of the House. And later we learn that Ariel Sharon has had a massive stroke that will probably finish him—throwing the political scene in Israel into uncertainty."

From Oakland came the news that our friends Eric and Loren had welcomed a son, a black–white Jewish mix named Matteo, whom they were coparenting with a lesbian couple; the week before, our friends Gretchen and Ilana had welcomed a daughter, a black–white Jewish mix named Noa. Reba would be the third in the string of biracial Jews born to queer parents in our immediate circles within a month of each other.

In local news, still no Reba, though the labor and delivery team was throwing drugs her way. Tamar had entered the hospital the day before and taken Cervidil to soften her cervix and stimulate labor. She'd started having contractions, but the labor didn't really take off. "I'm at the early stage," Tamar, who took it as part of her job to narrate the experience for us and a grown-up Reba, told our video camera, "where I still have my sense of humor." In the interim, Richard's mother, Betty, had arrived from San Diego, along with his sister Amy, a labor-and-delivery nurse, and both had come directly to the hospital. A nice young heterosexual couple had slipped in after New Year's, snagged the first-Vineyard-baby-of-the-year slot, and left; we told ourselves it was probably for the best, since our Massachusetts marriage was based on the shaky assertion that we were part-time residents there, a claim that, despite the fact that our names were in the phone book, might not withstand the attention brought by local coverage of our baby's arrival.

We had moved into the labor and delivery area, where Tamar had started a Pitocin drip, to induce and strengthen her contractions. Outside, sleet was falling. "Today is Reba's birthday," I'd told everyone, as if confident assertion would make it so.

We'd had a choice of two rooms and chose the darker, cozier one with a big bathtub. We'd done our best to entertain and distract Tamar. Carrie, a short-haired, good-humored nurse, had told a story of chasing James Taylor down the hall on his recent hospital visit and not knowing what to say once she got his attention, though he did say her name five times and thrice shook her hand. We'd put some country music on the CD player, and Andy and Richard had danced a goofy jig. I'd massaged Tamar's back and played the music mix I'd made for the occasion. Andy had quietly sung to Tamar, a cappella, a Kate Wolf song in which a lilac and an apple converse about "life in another time." Andy sings simply, with a West Virginia twang that sounds like bygone days. *Oh, no, said the Apple, there are so few, who come here on the mountain this way, and when they do, they don't often see why we're growing here, so far away.* When it seemed that no amount of drugs, songs, stories, baths, and jigs would get this baby moving—the contractions were regular and painful but didn't increase in intensity, and Tamar's cervix was barely dilated—we had ordered a pizza, wheeled Tamar out to the waiting area, and agreed to try again the next day.

Later that evening, Richard quietly told me that he had just had his last cigarette. He had always been a bit taciturn about smoking; hands were washed, breath was minty, alibis were available. He had said little to me about quitting, beyond the promise that he'd do so before the baby was born, but I'd seen the patch and smelled the nicotine gum on his breath. He had propelled himself out of Williamsport, Pennsylvania, through Stanford and into doctordom; in the end, though cigarettes put up a good fight, they were no match for Richard's will. Even if it's minutes before the deadline, Richard always delivers on a promise.

■ ■ ■

The afternoon of Reba's due date, Cathy, the nurse-midwife, broke Tamar's water. "It's odorless," Tamar reported for the video record. "Copious and clear. It was like a flood. Three towels soaked through." My parents were called in. "Today is Reba's birthday," I announced, for the second day in a row. By eight-thirty, Tamar agreed to an epidural, both for pain reduction and because Cathy suggested it might increase the chances of a vaginal delivery. Everyone except Tamar was predicting a Caesarean, but out of respect for Tamar's wishes, Cathy was holding off calling the doctor, who would no doubt want to come in right away and cut her open.[19] Several hours later, Tamar, now into the early hours of day three of her labor, looked wearily at Cathy. "Do you think it's safe to say we've tried everything?" she asked. "Do you think I've done everything I can to get this baby out?" Cathy nodded and picked up the phone to call the doctor.

"Today is Reba's birthday," I chirped at seven in the morning, as Richard and Andy and I were getting into our scrubs, masks, and caps. The three of us stood inside the delivery room, and Amy watched from a windowed room just above us. Richard's mother and mine, who had slept overnight on matching couches in the maternity visiting area, were waiting outside the door; my father was on his way. "Suction," one doctor said. "Blah-blah, stat!" another may have said. From where I stood, Tamar reminded me of a woman in a magic show being sawed in half, divided as she was by a waist-level screen. The top half was placid, her eyes blinking slowly, her head turned a bit to look at her husband; it seemed to have no connection to the bottom half, where three men poked away frantically with gloved hands dripping blood.

Out of the wreckage of Tamar's lower body our baby was pulled.

Cries of "Oh, my God!" came from various quarters, probably due to her size—over nine pounds and long—but the first thing I noticed were her lips, both facial and vulval, all of which were bright red and engorged.

"Well, she's a girl," Richard said, laughing at the sight. Andy cut the baby's umbilical cord.

"Feisty one," said a nurse, suctioning and cleaning the baby, who was crying and grabbing at the various cords around her. The nurses swaddled her like a burrito, and Amy, a sweet, young, blond nurse who had spent big chunks of the ordeal with us, asked who was going to get her first. Richard and I looked at each other.

"Take her to Tamar," I said. Tamar, cheeks ruddy, hair matted, crying, gazed dopily at the swaddled infant, who was already starting to look around a bit. A few seconds of cooing at the baby exhausted Tamar, and Nurse Amy brought her back over to me and Richard.

"Hi, Reba Sadie," I said. I didn't wipe my tears away; there are times when it's only right to overflow. I thought, *This is the first time I am seeing your face, Reba Sadie.* I thought, *You found us.* Richard held her up toward the fluorescent-lit ceiling, Kunta Kinte style, crying and chuckling. We took her out to the hallway to meet her grandparents. My mother turned to Richard's. "Look at those lips," she whispered.

Later, a nurse asked us whether we wanted to keep the placenta. "Sure," Richard said. When Reba Sadie and Tamar were released a few days later, the placenta went with us. We had heard of traditions (Navajo, Maori, Igbo) in which the placenta is ritually planted to root and protect the child and of a Chinese tradition of drying and eating the placenta; we thought we might want to bury it. I put it in the guesthouse freezer, wrapped in thick blue plastic and marked, perhaps redundantly, "Placenta—do not eat!" We would bury it in the summer, when the ground was soft again, laughing and holding our noses, under the oak tree where we were married.

■　■　■

The day before we were all to leave, my parents made us dinner at their house and left us there to eat it while they babysat at the guesthouse. The centerpiece was an orchid my sister and niece had bought for my mother at the flea market that summer. Earlier in the day, I'd been readying things with my mother, Reba Sadie perched in a red car-seat carrier, just next to the orchid. "There were six flowers on it when we got it, and they all fell off," my mother had told the baby, who almost appeared to be listening. "Now here's a new one that just came on. You know when it opened? The night that you were born. We're calling it our Reba orchid. It's yellow with fuchsia, and it has all kinds of little parts that look like a vagina." Over fettuccine and pesto that night, we talked on video to future versions of Reba. The combination of sleep deprivation, hormones, wine, and intimacy proved irresistible, and pretty much anything anyone said made someone else cry. When Tamar reported on our success with feedings ("every two to three hours, we're keeping meticulous records, and one of your daddies is always there"), I filmed the tears coming to Richard's eyes.

"What do you want Reba to know about who you are and who you are to her?" I asked, recording. Just the question made me cry a little.

"I'm not sure who I am to her yet," Tamar answered, drying her tears without interrupting the drama of the moment. "She'll have to figure that out as she grows up. But who she is to me: she's this wonderful little person I helped bring into the world, and I'm really glad she's here. Her dads needed a little help birthing her, since neither one of them has a uterus, and I do, so she got put inside of me when she was two cells big, and she grew inside of me for nine months." She covered her mouth, crying hard now but readying a punch line nonetheless. "I tried to take really good care of her, and I think I did a pretty good job, 'cause she came out really, really big."

"Why are you crying?" I asked.

"I'm crying because there's a lot of hormones right now," Tamar said, blowing her nose. "And I'm also crying because I'm going to miss her. I was very glad to help her grow and bring her into this world. It's really hard to let her go now that she's no longer inside me. I want to be part of her life. I will be part of her life." Looking back, it sounds like something you'd hear on *Oprah*, but at the time it was just like listening to the inside of a heart.

When a camera is around, Andy tends to ham it up, southern style. For his part, he said when Reba came to visit Virginia, he was "lookin' forward to gittin' her out in the woods and takin' her to catch some fish." It was clear that he meant it, too. Then he cleared his throat and pushed his long, straight, enviable hair back behind his ears. He sang for Reba the song that he'd made up earlier in the week and that had been stuck in my head through what had been passing for sleep that week. The tune was from the spiritual "Children, Go Where I Send Thee," which I'd grown up hearing Peter, Paul, and Mary sing, never thinking too much about the baby born, born, born in Bethlehem. Andy had inserted lyrics that were equal parts love and cheese. *Children, go where I send thee. How shall I send thee?* Andy sang. *I'm gonna send you one by one. One for the little bitty Reba, wrapped in swaddling clothing, lying in her daddies' arms, born, born, born on the Vineyard.* Everyone but Andy got a shout-out in his song—Richard and me (two), the grandparents (three), Richard's siblings (four), my sister's family (five), the hospital stay itself (six), even the "luck of the embryos" (seven), Cathy and the nurses (eight), and the Apgar score (nine). He ended not with the apostles but with Tamar: *Ten for the belly mommy.* We did our best to join in. The last time, I closed my eyes. *One for the little bitty Reba, wrapped in swaddling clothing, lying in her daddies' arms, born, born, born on the Vineyard.* I would not have been surprised to hear the orchid singing along.

When it came my turn to talk to the camera, I chose to tell a story that by then had become famous, not just among our crew—which included my sister, brother-in-law, and their three kids, who had returned for a first look at the baby—but also across the entire Martha's Vineyard Hospital and presumably outward from there. On the first day of Reba's life,

I'd laid down with her skin to skin, which sounded nice, until she unfurled a massive, tarry, dark-green pile of meconium, and I'd panicked while trying to put on her diaper, leading to a tussle in which both of us became covered in baby crap, so much that the night nurse, Rachel, later reported that in twelve years of nursing she had never seen such a sight.

You could hear Richard harrumphing off camera as I told the story. "Those Gamsons," he was saying. "They just *love* to talk about poop."

The next morning, the four of us took a walk on the beach with my mother, her dog Rosie, and a bundled-up baby, to say our good-byes. We didn't talk much. When Tamar and Andy drove off, my mom held the baby while Richard and I chased after their car, waving and crying, like the movie wives of soldiers chasing the train carrying away their husbands.

■ ■ ■

Nine days after Reba Sadie was born, she, Richard, and I took an early-morning JetBlue flight back to California. Richard covered her carrier with a long blanket, lest she catch some airborne illness. I kept uncovering her, to show her off to others and myself, but Richard informed me that the emergency-room workup for a child under four weeks with a high fever includes a spinal tap. I covered her back up. We fed Reba on the breast milk Tamar had pumped and packed for us in ice; another shipment would arrive in Oakland the next day. A flight attendant brought us a certificate for first-time flyers, and we filled in Reba's name.

I peeked at Reba under her protective blanket. "Oh, my God, it's a baby!" I said to Richard, who smiled obligingly. *You worked awfully hard to be here*, I thought to the baby. *There are easier ways in, you know.* In my more mystical moments, I imagine souls, like teensy fairies, hovering around and twittering to one another about finding a body and a family in which to become a living person. Some choose the safe and well-trod route, while others lazily jump at the first accidental pregnancy they stumble on; they risk wondering whether the opening they'd come through resulted from yearning, thoughtless conformity, or one beer too many. *Reba Sadie, I'll tell you what,* I thought. *You will not wonder how you got here.*

When the mystical moment passed, I thought also of the strange mix of creativity, convention, marginalization, commercialization, intimacy, and privilege that had made us into Reba's parents. We'd found openings in the law, accessed it because we had the will and wherewithal to do so, used it to mark our kinship intentions, and recorded our intentions in part by suing people we loved. Without consciously meaning to, we'd created a team that undercut some of the more overtly exploitative and intimacy-eroding aspects of much assisted reproduction. The "strange new emotional capitalism"[20] and "reproductive stratification"[21] were there, for sure—there in the fact that we could afford this at all, there in the interactions with fertility clinics, there in the surrogacy-industry warnings against emotionally attached surrogates—but also kept at bay. We'd deepened our connections to each other and to Tamar and Andy in a burst of intensified closeness, sometimes evading and sometimes embracing market transactions, even as Tamar and Jane also served as bodily outsourcers and we as paying customers. We'd built a family that most of our lives had been denied us through a commercial fertility industry built for others. We'd worked hard against the alienation of people from bodies fostered by both the science and commerce of assisted reproduction. We'd broken down old cultural categories, reshuffling the relationship between bodies and parental status, at least in part facilitated by a class system that we at best left unchallenged. We fought against the norms of what constitutes a family and in doing so reinforced the norm-proffering power of the institution of family. Like every other baby, ours was a creature of a particular political moment, within particular social institutions, of a class structure, legal system, and technological order, of ideas about nature, gender, kinship, and sexuality. *How extraordinary you are,* I thought. *And how ordinary, too.*

In my carry-on bag that morning was Reba's birth record, handed to us the day before by Sandy, a rosy-cheeked hospital records clerk with braces on her teeth. When we'd first arrived at her department, Sandy had not known what to make of the group of us, but over the weeks she had made many phone calls regarding the issue of how the Commonwealth might allow her to provide a birth record that didn't say "mother" and "father." Over the weeks, she had become a confederate. The birth certificate she produced listed us as Parent A and Parent B. It doesn't matter which is which.

STRANGER THINGS HAVE HAPPENED

A few years ago, my old friend Rahel and I took our kids to a New York City playground on the banks of the Hudson. The playground was filled with fountains, all linked by a long, shallow channel. Reba and Rahel's son, Yisak, both four, ran through the spray, catching water in their mouths to gargle while spinning in circles. Later, we walked along the High Line, which had recently been transformed from deteriorating elevated train route to lush and groovy pedestrian walkway. We stopped at an amphitheater that ends with a big Plexiglas wall overlooking Tenth Avenue. Yisak and Reba danced in front of the glass, giggling and shaking their behinds, unwilling to stop until we suggested popsicles.

"Reba Sadie, Reba Sadie," Yisak shouted during dessert that night at an Argentine joint on upper Broadway. He is a wiry cocoa-brown boy with a voice that sounds as if he has mild nasal congestion. He doesn't sit still for long. "Reba Sadie! We are going to get married. I can stand up on my hands! I am coming to California, and we are getting married." This was not Reba's first marriage proposal; she'd promised her hand to a girl named Sada at preschool, and both she and Yisak had by then held many mock weddings with boys, girls, and several of their favorite foods. But I looked at Rahel, and she looked at me.

"Such *naches*," I said, throwing up my hands, calling up one of the few bits of Yiddish I learned from my mother. Such pleasure.

Rahel laughed. "We should only be so lucky," she said. Then: "Inside voice, Yissy."

And maybe they will wind up together, I thought. *Stranger things have happened.* There was, for instance, the fact that we were here, through some combination of great will and luck, some thirty years after Rahel and I came into each other's lives as midwestern adolescents, me now married to the man sitting next to me, she eyeing the son who floated into her arms in an Addis Ababa orphanage along a river of broken plans and others' misfortunes, that son now jumping on a banquette in an Argentine restaurant in New York, me eyeing the two girls I'd thought for so long would be refused me, one covered in dulce de leche and the other keeled over in laughter. *Stranger things have already happened.*

Of course, though that moment may have been meant to be, it was not just kismet. Behind this sweet, unexpected moment is pain and bitterness, ferocity and resolve. And behind those stand a bunch of social forces and institutions that cause pain, facilitate joy, and demand ferocity. Poverty, AIDS, and international adoption politics brought Yisak from his first parents into an orphanage and then to Rahel. Rahel's relative advantages, along with her persistence and scrappiness, made it possible for her to consider solo motherhood in the first place and to navigate the complex path to him. The story is what the story is, I thought, unusual and ordinary, with distant voices whispering beneath the chattering of our children as they ran out onto 125th Street.

■ ■ ■

I first met Rahel at a socialist Zionist summer camp in Michigan between seventh and eighth grades, when she was still Rachel. We were shy misfits who found comfort and community in a place where Israeli folk dancing was cool and competitive games were frowned on; there was no private property other than clothing, toiletries, and sleeping bags. Campers could be heard discussing Marx or doing values-clarification exercises, and goofiness was held in high regard. We were the last ones picked for anything that required hand-eye coordination, but goofy we could do. I was known for my "underwear mobile," a carefully displayed collection of colored briefs with vinyl decals—a rooster, a car, a baby—that I'd gotten from my grandmother Reba's reject-clothing store. Rachel, round cheeked and farsighted, worked a klutzy charm and a snorty giggle that became her trademark. She and I bonded as costars in one of the camp plays, Edward Albee's absurdist *The American Dream*, a satirical take on the American family that we did not understand. She played Mommy, and I played Daddy.

The play, which Albee said was an attack on artificial values, on "complacency, cruelty, emasculation and vacuity" and on "the fiction that everything in this slipping land of ours is peachy-keen,"[1] is set in the living room of Mommy and Daddy, also occupied by Grandma. They receive two guests, one of whom, Mrs. Barker, turns out to be an adoption agent Mommy and Daddy had encountered twenty years before, and the other, the Young Man, turns out to be the twin of the baby they'd adopted and then eventually killed. Rahel in a dowdy frock and I in Bermuda shorts, we tried to mimic middle-aged people, listening to Grandma's speech as delivered by a redhead named Shira. We had sprinkled talcum powder in our hair, and as Shira walked along the makeshift stage, her feet roused a light white dust.

"Once upon a time," Grandma says, "there was a man very much like Daddy, and a woman very much like Mommy." One afternoon, they went to a place "very much like the Bye-Bye Adoption Service" to talk to a lady who did Good Works there. "They were very sad and very hopeful," Grandma says, "and they cried and smiled and bit their fingers, and they said all the most intimate things. The woman, who was very much like Mommy, said that she and the man who was very much like Daddy had never been blessed with anything like a bumble of joy."

"A what?" asks Mrs. Barker, played by a dark-haired girl named Ilana.

"A bumble; a bumble of joy," Grandma responds.

"Oh, like bundle," says Mrs. Barker.

"Well, yes; very much like it," says Grandma. "Bundle, bumble; who cares?"[2]

■　■　■

When Rahel and I were older teenagers, we were camp counselors together for a group of thirteen-year-olds. Rahel, by then using the Hebrew version of her name—the "Ray" now "Rah," the *ch* now the guttural Hebrew *h*, the emphasis now on the second syllable—had lost much of the insecurity and awkwardness, as had I. She still seemed to have a hard time believing in her own authority, but she was already proving to be an effective organizer and programmer, coming up with smart activities and using her laugh and a façade of ditziness to her own advantage.

We lost touch a bit in college, but I got occasional news of Rahel from my sister, Jenny, who overlapped with her first at the University of Michigan and then in Israel, where both had immigrated in the mid-1980s. Rahel had taken a job as a part-time secretary and translator for a group that did trainings for Israeli social justice organizations, and she had worked her way up to a director position. She was single and surrounded by good friends. The few times I visited Israel in those intervening years, I always stayed for a few nights in Rahel's Jerusalem apartment. While she worked, I tootled around the town I'd known well as a kid, and at night we ate chopped salad and drank red wine. She had come into her own in Israel, as though starting fresh in a new place had allowed her to finally shake off the parts of herself she had outgrown but had been unable to shed.

At thirty-four, Rahel had hit a turning point. For years, her life had been centered on her career, and she struggled to figure out how she could ever make room within it for anything else. She was exhausted and satisfied by work and acutely aware that she was a long way from being the mother she always imagined she'd be. She had a tendency to fall for men who were in love with other women. So she took a break. She took her sick mother to Europe. She spent a few months in New York City, reconnecting with old friends. She helped a friend start a nonprofit. She explored Malaysia, Indonesia, and India, where she meditated and did yoga. She unexpectedly met a man, a curly-haired, green-eyed wanderer seven years her junior, and began a torrid affair. It was like a Jewish *Eat, Pray, Love.*

When Rahel returned to Israel, refreshed and full of optimism about love and motherhood, her old life took right back over. Two of her bosses were leaving, and her new boss quickly promoted her. She threw herself into the job—heading up an eighteen-month strategic planning process—and decided to let her biological clock tick for the next two years. She organized a funding summit in a lavish Tuscan villa, and it ticked. She met with a former Israeli prime minister, and it tocked. She met with the leaders of international organizations, and it ticked. Still no man and no baby. And then suddenly, stunning everyone including herself, Rahel walked into the office of the executive director and resigned. *If I don't figure out the rest of my life*, she thought, *I won't have a life.*

I had been wavering about whether to move into Richard's apartment a few blocks away from mine when Rahel called to say she had quit her job and was moving to New York City. I offered her my apartment, my telephone number with its coveted 212 area code, and some of the furniture that wouldn't fit in Richard's place. Rahel has since moved twice, but she still has the digits and the furniture. There are very few things more tangibly familial than sharing a phone number and coffee table across a lifetime.

I was not surprised to discover that Rahel had arrived in New York with a three-point plan. She is a planner by nature and profession, known within her myriad circles as a legendary networker, and she networked her way to a job shortly after her arrival. But as her sojourns to Southeast Asia had reminded me, she is also something of a mystic. She's a longtime meditator and took up yoga long before it became hip. On her previous stint in New York, she had referred me to a friend nearby who had weekly phone sessions with a psychic rabbi in Jerusalem whose method was to swing an amulet over a set of letters representing multiple-choice answers to questions you never told him; needless to say, I gave him a call. These, and do-gooders the world over, were the sorts of people Rahel knew.

Rahel intended to work, accumulating money and seniority so that she could take maternity leave, go on as many dates as she needed to, and have a baby within two years. If she didn't meet someone within that time frame, she would have a baby on her own. The plan had Rahel's practicality, optimism, and self-reliance. It also exhibited her tendency to process things for a long time. She was thirty-eight.

Then, that September, the first jet hit the Twin Towers while Rahel was at the Equinox gym on Ninety-Second Street. She watched the news on the gym televisions and called friends. The second jet hit while she was on the downtown subway. For New Yorkers, among the many effects of the trauma of September 11 was a kind of hollowness and a magnification of what was missing from one's life, brought on by witnessing such sudden and horrific endings. Rahel walked with a colleague the hundred blocks uptown to her neighborhood. The sky was dark with soot, and the smell of smoke diminished a little with each block. Rahel felt as though she might float off with the ashes. The only thing that could keep her tethered, she thought, was having a family of her own. Two years suddenly seemed like too long to wait.

Not long afterward, the nonprofit organization she was working for shut its doors, and Rahel decided that the time had finally arrived for her to do the two things she'd been wanting to do for many years: start a business and make a baby. She would just have to do it all herself. She had a checkup and blood work done and set about searching for the right sperm. She joined Single Mothers by Choice—a national organization founded in 1981 that has grown into a network of over thirteen thousand women with multiple chapters[3]—went to a couple of meetings, and spent time on its website. The home page showed three women: a "thinker" (smiling, looking off into the distance), a "tryer" (eyes closed, fingers crossed), and a "mother" (smiling, holding smiling infant). She began a first round of consultations with trusted friends, most of whom were supportive but, having had many conversations about babies with her before, dubious. Rahel intended to show her friends, who saw her as a perpetual thinker, that she was now, at long last, a real tryer.

∎ ∎ ∎

Anyone who has spent more than a few hours with kids knows that raising a child while also trying to make enough money to survive and have a semblance of a personal life is a struggle even for two parents; five parents seems like about the right number. Still, single parenthood has been on the rise in the United States for decades now. About a quarter of children under eighteen lived with a single parent in 2010, about three times more than in the 1960s; most of these (87 percent) were in mother-headed families.[4] A bunch of major social changes fostered the rise of one-mom families: higher divorce rates and the increased social acceptability of divorce;[5] women's increased financial independence; legal decisions that "shook husbands' unchallenged authority within marriage over their wives and the children they bore";[6] the legalization of birth control, which allowed women more control over the timing of pregnancy; the rise of medical technologies that have made it possible to conceive a child with the sperm of a man without the need for the rest of him; the decreasing stigma placed on children born "out of wedlock," a term that now sounds almost quaint. These changes, as the sociologist Rosanna Hertz puts it, have begun "rendering sexual intimacy between husbands and wives obsolete as *the* critical familial bond."[7] About half the women who become single mothers get there through divorce, but that route has actually been declining as the percentage of women who become mothers without ever marrying has been increasing.[8]

The decision making around single motherhood is clearly very different for people of different races and classes. This is clear not just in the statistics—around half of African American children and around a quarter of Latino kids live only with their mothers[9]—but also in the conditions shaping women's choices. As the sociologists Kathryn Edin and Maria Kefalas, who spent years conversing with low-income single mothers in Philadelphia and Camden, describe it, most young, poor women revere marriage, seeing it as "something they aspired to but feared they might never achieve."[10] Not so with having kids. Without "the chance to go to college and embark on careers—attractive possibilities that provide strong motivation to put off having children—poor young women grab eagerly at the source of accomplishment within their reach: becoming a mother."[11] They know full well that being a poor single mother is less than ideal, but it is not nearly as tragic to them as missing the chance to have children; and the path out of poverty, let alone into a "career," tends to be blocked at every turn. They mostly don't plan on being pregnant at a young age, but when it happens, they often embrace motherhood.

Middle-class single mothers have usually approached from the opposite direction, pursuing the educational and career paths open to them and delaying parenthood. Often, as Hertz describes it in *Single by Chance, Mothers by Choice*, they've kept busy at work, clinging "to the belief that marriage was an essential credential for motherhood"[12] and "hoping the right partner would materialize and start the sequence."[13] At a certain point, when no partner materializes, they start to rethink the sequence, reading up on single motherhood, testing the waters with friends, family, and online strangers, and building a new identity and support structure in anticipation. They go back and forth, considering the pros and the cons, sometimes for years, until, often suddenly, a catalytic event occurs—a breakup, a death, a medical intervention—that, Hertz writes, "disrupts the ping-pong-like contemplation" and "crystallizes their desires, focusing a decision: a future without a child is simply unbearable."[14]

This was Rahel, unique in her details and yet also typical of women of her class and generation: living her independent life, fulfilled at work, busy while hoping to meet the man who would be father to her children; gradually undoing the assumption that coupledom was a requirement of parenthood; thinking, talking, thinking; stable enough financially to imagine bearing the costs of having and raising a child alone; walking amid the ashes of lives suddenly cut short, trying on the new identity of single mother.

■ ■ ■

Rahel had plenty of models around her, including Richard and me, of people who'd made families in nontraditional ways, building them on voluntary relationships and contracts and such. Her gay friends, who had long since seen the holes and coercions in the traditional model of family, seemed like a good starting point. Rahel went first to her best friend, Jacob. She loved so much about him, including his thick, curly, black hair, his fierce intellect, and his loyalty. His head sometimes superseded his heart, true, but perhaps that was not genetic.

"There is no one I trust more than you," she said. "Will you be the father of my child?" He declined, firmly and immediately. He had married his boyfriend, Paul, just months before Paul had died from cancer. Before Paul's diagnosis, he and Jacob had begun to talk about having children. Now, Jacob wasn't sure he wanted children, but he was sure that if he created any, it would be within a committed love relationship. Rahel was wounded, but she understood. And Jacob assured her that, should she have a child, he would become a favorite uncle.

Next she came to Richard and me. "You are two of my dearest friends," she said over the phone. "Will you be the fathers of my child?" The previous summer, Rahel had been one of the chuppah holders at our wedding. We'd assigned her the job of explaining the Jewish symbols of the ceremony to the attendees. She'd described the wedding canopy, the chuppah, as symbolizing the home that we would share. "But as you can see," she'd said, "this symbolic home is open on all four sides. The open sides are symbolic of the openness and welcome which are required to create a new life together. The chuppah invites all of us to be an ongoing part of their lives." The idea of the three of us making a kid together—she as legal mother, we as long-distance godfathers—was intriguing and sort of gorgeous.

When Richard requested that the future child be raised in both Jewish tradition and the black church, though, Rahel was uneasy. She knew Richard had left religion behind long ago and wanted to support her prospective child's black identity, but she could not imagine taking her child to church. Plus, there were probably hints in that conversation of future battles over how she should raise her child. The advantages of going it alone were becoming clearer.

■   ■   ■

For weeks, Rahel perused sperm donors on the Internet. She was drawn finally to a young guy with dark hair and green eyes. His profile said he was an artist living in California. She developed a crush on him. He sounded a little bit like Sam, the man she had met on her *Eat, Pray, Love* sojourns six years earlier.

"I don't know you well, but I think you are talented, and I, too, like Joni Mitchell," she said, in her head, to her computer screen one night, sipping red wine in her apartment. "Will you be the father of my child?"

And so she had her plan.

Just after she placed her sperm order, Rahel got an unexpected phone call from Sam. He was in New York on business and asked her to dinner. It felt like he had fallen from the sky, though more precisely he had come from Nebraska. They talked at dinner and talked some more back at her apartment, but as had been the case during their affair, talking seemed to get in the way of what their bodies wanted to do. Rahel was briefly tempted to simply keep her mouth shut, consider his sudden appearance a gift from the universe, and hope to get a baby out of the deal. That kind of deception, however, was not in her personality structure, so in a break during the make-out session, she told him of her plans to try to get pregnant. He was unsurprised, and it seemed to turn him on.

"Well, how about me?" Sam said, his breathing slowly ramping down.

"What about you?" Rahel said.

"Well, you want a baby, and you're looking for a donor, and I've got sperm," he said, holding her hand. "What if I'm your donor and a kind of occasionally involved father? I want to be in your life anyway, no matter what, so why not like this?"

Rahel laughed. *Is this happening?* she wondered.

And so she had a revised plan. It was a more pleasurable one than those that had come before. She told herself she could handle the fact that Sam wasn't interested in monogamy; he was a friend with benefits, and now he had a specific contribution to make to her life. The fertility specialists, having poked and assessed Rahel several times, tested Sam's sperm count, which was shockingly high. Sam and Rahel had sex whenever and wherever they could: on his visits to New York and hers to Nebraska, inside and out—in the woods, on a mountaintop—daytime and night.

After a couple of months, Rahel was still not pregnant. Concerned that timing might be an issue, she asked Sam to leave some sperm with her in New York on his next visit. One Sunday morning, they stopped at the clinic. Rahel, dressed in a suit, was on her way to a board meeting; Sam was on his way to Penn Station to catch a train to Washington, DC. They had little time to spare. Inside the small "donation room," the porn was not working for Sam, so he asked Rahel to help. The lab technician politely waited outside the door, and when Rahel and Sam emerged a few minutes later, flushed and amused, Sam handed over six vials for freezing. The clinic later reported that this was the largest sample they had ever received in a single donation.

Not long after breaking this record, Sam left for Costa Rica for four months. Rahel found the frozen version of him not nearly as exciting as the fresh one, yet neither was managing to knock her up. When he returned from his trip, Sam announced that he was no longer so comfortable with the pregnancy project and withdrew. Rahel was sad but a bit relieved. If Sam was one of those people who got going when the going got rough, it was probably better he should go.

She returned to the green-eyed California sperm, but beneath her determined-yet-Zen surface, the suspicion that the problem was her own body, not the sperm, was growing stronger. This was, of course, what many fertility doctors had suggested would be her biggest obstacle—eggs too old and so forth—but Rahel had resisted the treatments she now suddenly chased. Over the next months, she took Clomid, injected hormones, had ultrasounds, and switched doctors twice. She tried two cycles of in vitro fertilization, and when that didn't work, tried one last cycle, this one with fresh sperm from a generous, cute, gay friend dispensed while John Kerry debated George W. Bush. She spent several thousand of the dollars she had been saving.

Rahel went for the results of her last IVF treatment not long after Bush was reelected. A kind, Indian-born doctor on rotation gave her the news that she was, once again, not pregnant. He seemed baffled by her grief.

"It's over, it's over, it's over," Rahel chanted between sobs.

Of course, like in many stories, what looks like an ending is really a beginning. While Rahel was sobbing, her son was getting ready to be born to another mother.

■　■　■

That winter, Rahel went into hibernation in her apartment on 103rd Street, which was small enough that the refrigerator was in the hallway. She worked, ate takeout, and slept. Friends called, and she sometimes took weeks to get back to them. Her hormones were still out of whack. Surprising things made her cry—a subway ad, an offer of a bite of pizza—and she was prone to sudden fits of total bitchiness. She emerged from her cave to walk the freezing city in a melancholic daze. *I thought I was living a self-directed, self-determined life*, she told herself, aware even as she was thinking it of the working-woman clichés her head was feeding her, *when what I was really doing was making a series of horrible mistakes that are going to leave me a miserable human being.*

In January, Rahel was wandering the halls at a conference, pretending that she was still the together professional she was known to be, when she ran into a colleague named Jonathan. She did not know him well, but she admired him.

"You look awful," he said, kindly.

"Thanks," Rahel said. She wasn't surprised by the comment. She'd had a crying jag in the conference-center bathroom and could barely manage to run a brush through her hair. Something in Jonathan's tone, plus her knowledge of his family—he and his wife, a Reconstructionist rabbi named Karen, had three biological kids and two kids adopted from Ethiopia—allowed Rahel to drop her façade. She told Jonathan that she was indeed a basket case, unable to accept that she would never have a baby, and he put his hands on her shoulders, turned her body slightly to the right, and pointed.

"See that woman?" he said. "Go talk to her right now." It was his wife, Karen. Rahel had met her once in passing and had heard she was writing a book about the spiritual aspects of adoption. She walked over and introduced herself. Karen took one look at her and invited her to sit down. Stuff spilled out of Rahel the way it sometimes does with friendly strangers: how one plan after another had ended in disappointment, how angry at herself she was for taking so long to get going on her family, how she was mourning her lost motherhood even as her own mother declined into dementia. Karen listened rabbinically, with deep attention and empathy, while two of her kids played under the table.

"Okay, look," said the rabbi, after a while. She was no longer in empathy mode; she was now directive and definitive. "It's sad, yes. Be sad. But here's the thing. You will be a mother. You should be a mother." Rahel sensed a change in tone, as though Rabbi Karen was suddenly speaking as a prophet rather than a colleague's wise spouse. The rabbi looked at Rahel.

"I think your child is in Ethiopia," she said.

"My child?" Rahel asked.

"Your child is in Ethiopia," Rabbi Karen repeated. It felt to Rahel like a moment of conception. Then suddenly, as if snapping out of a brief trance, Karen turned practical. She recommended an agency called Broad Vistas and wrote down a few phone numbers. It was like a visit from an angel who is also a receptionist.

The very idea that a baby half a world away could be "yours" is complicated. After all, that imagined child has a life already of some kind and had, may still have, people who consider the child theirs. On what grounds can you claim that child as your own? What conditions—global ones, economic ones—have made it reasonable to think such thoughts? What do you do with the inequities that make it seem to make sense? What do you do with the fact that this child may be yours because others have abandoned her, presumably in a situation of shattering pain? Why is it so hard to imagine someone in Ethiopia being told that "their" baby awaits them in New York City?

Often, in the storytelling about adoption, parents speak of the fate that brought them and their child together. This is not self-delusion: the joining of *this* child to *this* parent really is, in a practical sense, a matter of chance, and depending on your belief system, chance might reasonably be understood as destiny. But fate can also be a way of not dealing with big, uncomfortable parts of the story, by suggesting, falsely, that the child was always already yours. As the sociologist Sara Dorow puts it, "Abandonment and adoption are two sides of the same coin; it is separation and rupture that make adoption possible."[15] That is a hard coin to hold softly in your hand. It is difficult to reconcile the first parents' hardship and the second parents' joy, to ignore the "the ghosts of unsettled pasts, foreclosed relationships, and excluded others that haunt the present and push for recognition."[16] The notion of fated family keeps these complications at bay, suggesting that there were never choices, that the injustice, pain, and complications of kinship are generated not by people and institutions but by the stars. It is no wonder that we want, if only for a moment, to turn things over to angels who prophesize our destiny.

■ ■ ■

When Rahel's brother came out as gay, her father took to reading anything he could find related to the topic: homosexuality, definitions and history of; sexual orientation, science of; gay child, how to love your.

In that way, though not in many others that she cares to acknowledge, Rahel is like her dad. When an emotional challenge arises, a full intellectual investigation is launched. Anxiety is met with study.

Rahel had thought plenty about adoption and had often imagined herself with four kids, a mix of adopted and biological. Somehow, though, it was too much to give up the whole fantasy—pregnancy, a partner—all at once. So she researched. She subscribed to the magazine *Adoptive Families*. She interviewed adoptive mothers on walks through Central Park. She went to adoption fairs and workshops. She went to hear a speech by Dr. Jane Aronson, sometimes called the Orphan Doctor, who later served as pediatrician to Angelina Jolie's Ethiopia-born child. By the time spring arrived, Rahel had amassed a small library of books about adoption—transracial adoption, single-mom adoption, first-person narratives of adopted children—ordering six books at a time from Amazon and scouring the shelves of Barnes & Noble, systematically freaking herself out. She researched fetal alcohol syndrome, malnutrition, and learning disabilities among adoptive kids.[17] She read books about the attachment disorders that sometimes accompany adoption—kids whose early trauma makes bonding very difficult.[18] She sought out horror stories of "disrupted" and "dissolved" adoptions, in which adoptive parents who, after the child is in their home, decide that the child is more than they can handle.

Her decision to adopt was finalized at a retreat in Connecticut for progressive social change. Part of the training was a sort of chipping away at the ego in an attempt to get to the essence of your purpose, through an exercise called a vision stand: you stand up in front of the room and describe your vision, which you have been working on for months in preparation. When Rahel was called up, she quickly began bawling. She knew she was supposed to be talking about her social-change vision, but she couldn't get to that right now; her purpose, she said, was to be a mom. The trainees were also required to come up with three "promises" to their vision. Rahel promised: *Surrender. Let other people in. Keep it real.*

The decision itself was personal, but to implement it Rahel would have to negotiate the complicated dictates of adoption structures. She quickly ruled out domestic adoption. Agency after agency told her that, in a system in which most birth mothers are single women—and in which birth mothers choose their child's family on the basis of prospective parents' profiles—the least appealing placements were with other single women, unless they were rich and famous. She was, she realized, the lowest person on the adoption totem pole. The rest of the world wasn't that much more welcoming. The former Soviet Union had too much fetal alcohol syndrome.[19] Vietnam, Guatemala, and Nepal had been opening and closing their adoption programs due to political conflict and corruption scandals.[20] Single parents had long waits for Chinese adoptions and then were only allowed to adopt special-needs kids, and all prospective parents were required to have a body mass index below 40, a rule that would not disqualify Rahel but that she found hideous.[21]

Rahel made a list of things that she could deal with and things she could not. Nutritional deficits and possible subsequent learning disabilities: okay. Harsh orphanage conditions and possible subsequent attachment difficulties: not okay. Kid whose skin is a different color from hers: fine. Long wait and problems for single women: not okay. Restrictions on meeting the birth family: not okay. The map got smaller and smaller until her finger landed on Ethiopia. Her child, she realized months after her encounter with the rabbi, was in Ethiopia. It was not fate that led Rahel there but laws, bureaucratic rules, politics, and social conditions.

That June, Rahel submitted her paperwork to Broad Vistas. The requirements were extensive: an autobiographical essay addressing sixteen questions, a copy of her birth certificate and her most recent tax forms, photographs of herself and her apartment building, several signed agreement forms. And that was just the first round. Soon she would need to provide fingerprints, letters of reference, a therapist's release of information, statements from her accountant, notarized powers of attorney. She would take basic adoption courses, where she would always be the only single woman in the room and, through a weird combination of assumptions, presumed to be lesbian. There would be a home visit and, after that, another round of forms.

Rahel found the bureaucratic process comforting, delightful even. She began to think of it as gestation, with paperwork in place of weight gain and nausea. Each piece of paper lifted her spirits a bit more. You filled out a form and then another and then the next. You signed here and then again here and also here. At the end of all of these forms was a child. Sometimes, flipping through the monotonous pages, she almost thought she could see a baby's face peeking back at her.

As Rahel was preparing to submit her paperwork, her parents and brother came to town to witness her receiving a leadership award from a Jewish service organization, and she told them of her plans to adopt. Her father, with mild excitement, peppered her with logistical questions. Her mother was showing signs of dementia; she'd packed a random assortment of clothes and only half the fancy outfit she'd selected for the event. Although she struggled to understand Rahel's plans, she knew that she, like Rahel, felt hopeful and happy.

■　■　■

Rahel's essay for the adoption agency ran fifteen single-spaced pages. How odd it is, she thought, to present yourself to strangers, in a manner bland enough not to offend yet with enough honest personal detail to distinguish you, for the purpose of convincing them to allow you to spend the rest of your life taking care of someone. Though it was technically accurate—she is indeed a "positive person who enjoys friends, work, and the rather unpredictable journey of life," with "a good sense of humor and appreciation of the absurd" and "a strong capacity for connection and forging deep, lasting friendships"—it didn't sound much like her. While she was writing it, she thought a lot about the things she dared not write: that her childhood had been complicated; that she had a terrible temper; that her father struggled with mental illness and her mother, who had always been eccentric, thrifty, an activist and arts lover, and fiercely loving, now barely recognized Rahel.

She knew that race would be on the minds of her readers, as it was on hers. "I have thought a lot about the issue of raising a child who will be from a different culture and race," she wrote. This I knew to be true. When Rahel was in high school, a friend of her brother had moved in with her family when his own home life became too difficult. Over the next few years, Rahel watched him struggle to get things she took for granted—education, stable employment, an everyday life devoid of suspicion and stares—as he, a black teenager, became a member of her family. This was not a qualification for raising a black child, of course. Rahel acknowledged how much she still had to learn and wrote of her hope: that "over time my awareness will increase and I will find strategies to help my child feel secure and proud in all of his or her identities." She'd read about the public debates in the 1970s over transracial adoption, triggered by the National Association of Black Social Workers' opposition to the adoption of black children by white parents, "citing concerns about racial identity and survival skills as the basis of their objections,"[22] and though the controversy had long since receded, she took seriously those concerns and the weight she would carry as the white mother of a black child. Rahel simply didn't doubt her ability to help her child navigate through a racist world or to love a child who neither looked much like her nor moved through the world with the privileges her own light skin provides.

"You're going to be very confusing to people on the Upper West Side," I suggested to Rahel on my next visit to the Upper West Side. We were walking down Broadway on our way to a Vietnamese restaurant, and it seemed that everywhere I looked I saw brown-skinned women—Caribbean, mostly—pushing Maclaren strollers containing white children. Although Rahel knew that her race and class positioned her to create her little family, she was happy that her family did not sit too easily within the culture of liberal, white entitlement in which she had landed. In a weird way, I felt, it connected her budding family to mine, both of us outside conventions in more ways than one. We imagined that the families we were making, and the children we were shepherding, might be flexible enough to hold many identities beyond the black-white categories that others would constantly apply.

In any case, Rahel now met most apparent challenges with a sort of surrender. She had concluded that all of her careful planning, all of her attempts to control her fate through studying, medicine, and denial, had failed *in order* to make room for the child she was going to have. In her autographical essay to the agency, Rahel wrote that she believed that "there is something spiritual to this process" and of what she would teach her child: that "a power greater than ourselves brought us together." She could not say, of course, that distinctly unspiritual powers were at work, including those of the people who were reading her essay; she referred instead to the familiar discourse of fate. Still, even knowing that her own constrained choices as a single woman combined with a fucked-up world to provide the conditions for her family, even knowing that most people cannot pull together the $30,000 the whole endeavor would wind up costing, she thought the real power might be found in dropping the reins and seeing where the horses would take her. Or where the bureaucracy would take her: whatever child was ready for adoption when her forms arrived at the top of the pile would be her child. I imagined Rahel at the edge of a cliff, arms spread like a bird or a diver, calmly dropping in a soft, slow fall into a pile of forms. "In the end," said a poster she bought at the time, "what matters most is how well you live—how well did you live, how well did you love, how well did you learn to let go."

"I do not have any pets," Rahel's autobiographical essay concluded. "My building does not allow them. I have never owned a gun and never would own a gun. There are no safety hazards in my home that I can think of. The building is required to test for lead paint and to put window guards in the windows. I have certifications that can be provided on demand."

■　■　■

My birthday and Rahel's are twelve days apart. I called her that November of 2005, when we were turning forty-three. I was expecting a baby in January, and so, in a way, was she. She had turned in the last of her documents, a thick dossier for the Ethiopian authorities, just before her birthday. Now all she could do was wait.

Rahel had not anticipated how difficult the waiting would be. Compared to the tedious paperwork, it was excruciating. She jumped whenever the phone rang. She distracted herself with work. Each bit of the waiting was a reminder of that fact that, despite all of her supportive and excited friends, only she had her heart and soul on hold, waiting for the heart and soul that she believed were waiting for her. She was at peace with becoming a mother on her own, but *oh*, she thought, *the loneliness of waiting*.

One afternoon in mid-February of 2006, she was meeting with a colleague named Staci at the café in Bloomingdale's—not her kind of place, really—when she noticed a phone message from Ellen, the social worker at Broad Vistas. Rahel had first met Ellen when she'd taken the Long Island Railroad to the Broad Vistas office, which was located in a small town with cute little houses, their curtains fluttering in open windows. Ellen's tiny office was plastered with holiday cards of every permutation of family: adopted children with biological ones, parents and kids of all colors. Rahel had felt at home—the smiling white baby "success story" photos she'd seen on fertility-clinic walls had always rubbed her the wrong way—and when she saw that Ellen had a bluebird tattoo on her forearm, she was certain she'd been sent in the right direction. Sometimes since then, Ellen had called just to check in on Rahel. Rahel excused herself to return the call.

"Well, you got a match," said Ellen, who tended not to waste time or words. Rahel was silent. "Where are you? Can I fax you some pictures of the child and a medical profile? And then you have forty-eight hours to tell me if we're moving ahead."

When Rahel returned to the table, she was hyperventilating. It felt like the birth of her child.

"Can I get you something?" Staci said after Rahel quickly filled her in on the call.

"I'm so sorry," Rahel said. Staci was barely an acquaintance. "I'm not usually so dramatic."

"Don't be ridiculous," Staci said, unknowingly beginning a friendship. "I have a fax machine at my house."

Rahel laid eyes on Yisak for the first time at Staci's apartment. In both pictures she received, he was wearing a plaid jump suit. He had a bald head with a single tuft of hair on top, and he was crying.

Yisak had been born, the documents said, on April 3, 2005. His father had died two months later, at the age of twenty-eight, of tetanus, and his mother had died of bronchitis three months after that, at age twenty-three. He had two living grandparents and a living uncle. He had been transported by car from the Sidama region to the Vistas House in Addis Ababa. He had been in the orphanage for just three days. He was eating and sleeping well but not yet interacting with other children or staff. *Well, no wonder you are crying, sweetie*, Rahel said to the picture. *You must think you are alone in this world.*

There is really no way to know how alone he had been or felt, though, and not just because he was a little baby. Extreme poverty, a poor health care system, AIDS stigma, and an almost nonexistent communication infrastructure erased and perhaps distorted the details of Yisak's first family beyond the most basic. Like so many adoption stories, this one is nearly silent on the details; one might wonder how the biological parents met each other, what they said to each other in their quieter moments, where they were when they got the news of the pregnancy and how they met it, what music they liked, how they fought and worked and laughed, what they smelled like, what they sounded like, what they looked like. Many adoptive parents, especially in transnational adoption, have almost no information from which to paint a picture of the biological family. For some, this may come as a secret relief, since even tidbits of information can call into question the exclusivity of the child's adoptive relationship—not so for Rahel, though, who values knowledge above comfort.

One could certainly venture some guesses, given the situation in Ethiopia at the time. Ethiopia, as the writer Melissa Fay Greene has described it, has a "huge population, droughts and food crises, nonindustrial means of production, huge debt-service obligations, massive military spending, ongoing border disputes with Eritrea, and state ownership of land," which have all kept the people "rural, unemployed, and destitute" even as they have watched revolutionaries become dictators and government after government fail.[23] The vast majority of the population lives on less then two dollars a day. Health spending in 2002, a few years before Yisak was born, was around two dollars per person per year.[24] When HIV/AIDS hit the African continent, Ethiopia was unprepared in every way to cope: two million Ethiopians were infected with HIV by 2000; one of every eleven people living with HIV/AIDS was Ethiopian; information was slow to travel, due to widespread illiteracy, and urban myths were quick to develop (you could get HIV from drinking the milk of a cow that had eaten grass on which an HIV-positive man had discarded a used condom or from meat bought from an HIV-positive butcher), as was the belief that AIDS was a punishment for sin.[25] Shame, ostracism, and silence were as common as the disease. Anti-AIDS medicines, when they were developed, were slow to reach Ethiopia, in part because, as Greene puts it, "rich countries and their global organizations and multinational drug companies [were] reluctant to share the antiretrovirals."[26] By 2001, it was estimated that there were nearly a million Ethiopian children orphaned by AIDS.[27]

That was the larger story, but when it came to Yisak's particular one, Rahel could know very little. Once, in an Ethiopian village, there was a sick father, a sick mother, grandparents, an uncle, and a baby.

■ ■ ■

Rahel grabbed the medical record from Staci's fax machine and took a cab to the office of her medical consultant, a pediatrician who specialized in the health of adoptive kids. Their relationship was expensive and chilly. Once, during one of Rahel's visits, the doctor had taken a call from her art dealer and then attempted to get a table at Bouley in Tribeca. Still, Rahel would have been surprised to hear she'd ever made a medical error.

"He probably has rickets," the doctor said. "That probably means he hasn't been getting milk. A vitamin D deficiency can mean potential brain damage, too, though all I see right now is rickets. That'll clear when you start him on a vitamin-reinforced diet. But also, he has a large head circumference, which can mean swelling, which can mean brain damage."

Rahel's heart sank.

"Oh," she said. "I see."

"But sometimes," the doctor said, "it just means he's got a big head." Rahel smiled. She could handle a little boy with a big head.

The doctor did not smile back. "The thing that concerns me the most, though," she said, "is that his parents both died within months of each other in their early twenties. In Ethiopia, the cause of death on birth certificates is completely unreliable. They write whatever they want because the village person who's recording it is almost never a medical professional. I doubt this was tetanus and bronchitis. I think they were HIV-positive, and they both died of AIDS. And this baby hasn't had a proper AIDS test. You want to know, so you can decide if this is the child you want to raise."

Rahel took a breath. The doctor was explaining that, while the baby had tested negative on the ELISA test for HIV antibodies, because of the "window period"—the time between infection and the appearance of anti-HIV antibodies—a negative ELISA test did not rule out HIV infection.[28] She could only know his status definitively with something called a PCR test, which actually detects the genetic material of HIV.[29] Rahel did not think, *I can't parent a sick child* or *I don't want a child with HIV because he's going to die*. She knew quite a bit about retrovirals and the management of HIV and knew plenty of people who knew more. She thought, *I have to get this kid that test*. Her reasoning was mainly financial: if she adopted him and found out afterward that he was HIV-positive, insurance companies could refuse to cover treatments for a "preexisting condition," which she could never in a million years afford to pay for.

This was a challenge and a choice, of course, structured by privilege. The advice to, as the doctor put it, "decide if this is the child you want to raise" implies that one is in a position to pick and choose. For Rahel to make her family, moreover, she would need to confront the weakness of the global medical system, especially the unreliable reporting, testing, and treatment of HIV/AIDS in Ethiopia. She'd need the social, financial, and cultural capital to navigate a domestic insurance system and multiple medical systems across national boundaries.

This kind of challenge was well within Rahel's existing skill set, comfort zone, and social location. It gave her focus. Within hours, she had begun activating her networks, researching laboratories from New York City to Nairobi, familiarizing herself with terms like "polymerase chain reaction" and "reagents," and writing careful and pointed e-mails to the adoption agency. To Rahel's shock, the adoption agency seemed surprised that a PCR test might be necessary and was unequipped to arrange for one. The one laboratory in Addis Ababa that could conduct the test, they told her, was overwhelmed by demand and devoid of supply; the test kits are expensive and require a level of refrigeration beyond the Ethiopian lab's capacity. Her options, they said, were to sign a waiver saying the adoption was full and final no matter what or to be patient while they tried to get Yisak tested again. The adoption was on hold.

Six weeks passed. "Waiting stinks, but it is the way things are," the adoption doctor said when Rahel consulted her about the situation. "Part of adoption is waiting and having to grin and bear the time that the child has to stay in an orphanage. You are not alone here. This is the undercurrent of all adoptions." Rahel was not comforted. She imagined Yisak in the orphanage, alone, wondering where he was and where his parents were.

In her own mind, she was already his new mother. In her e-mails seeking advice and help, she took to referring to Yisak as "my son." After so many years of waiting for her child, this new round of waiting turned Rahel into something of a madwoman, if a highly effective one. The only thing standing between them was the test, and this knowledge sent Rahel into overdrive. She offered to locate test kits and have them FedExed to Ethiopia but was told they wouldn't survive the trip. She spoke with a friend of a friend from an Ethiopian HIV center, a vice president of the Gay Men's Health Crisis, a nurse practitioner at Montefiore Hospital, an epidemiologist at Johns Hopkins, an acquaintance at an international women-and-AIDS program, and a friend who worked for the United Nations. On a work trip to Israel, the head of HIV Infection and Infectious Diseases at Hadassah Hospital—a friend of a friend—put her in touch with an Ethiopian laboratory doctor, who told her of another clinic that had the test kits, and another Israeli friend connected her to a doctor working for the Joint Distribution Committee in Ethiopia, who told her about the Pasteur Institute in Addis Ababa, which turned out also to have the kits. She heard from another friend that the U.S. embassy required double HIV testing for Ethiopian babies before they'd issue a visa—a protection, the friend suggested, for American insurance companies. She presented this information to the adoption agency and waited.

It's hard to imagine what someone without Rahel's professional background, social class advantages, and social networks would have done. Perhaps they would have signed the waiver and taken the chance of adopting a child whose health problems they could not afford to address. Perhaps, seeking to avoid the risk, they would simply have waited for another child. One wonders, if Rahel had been less Rahel-ish, whether Yisak would ever have met her.

Finally, late in April, Rahel received notice that Yisak had received the PCR test at one of the clinics she'd uncovered. He was negative. She booked her flight to Ethiopia the next day.

A few weeks before, she had sent to Ethiopia a picture of herself, in the hopes that someone might put it near Yisak in the orphanage. She'd written a few lines on the back in Amharic, which she'd been studying.

She packed in her carry-on bag a picture of her new son. Her friend Shari had recently been in Ethiopia for a conference and had gone to the orphanage and taken pictures of Yisak, now finally smiling, to replace the sad-faced photo Rahel had posted on her fridge. In the photo she packed, he had a devilish gleam in his eye that Rahel thought she somehow recognized.

■ ■ ■

Boarding the plane on the Friday night before Memorial Day 2006, Rahel imagined she heard the trumpeting crescendo of her aloneness. Her siblings were deep in their own family lives, her mother was rapidly disappearing into dementia, and her father was supportive but exhausted. Her friend Jacob had been planning to accompany her, but the drawn-out saga of the HIV test had screwed up the timing for him. She had asked her friend Sarah, in Israel, but Sarah and her husband were trying to make their own baby, and the shots required to travel to Ethiopia could interfere with conception; they planned for the husband, Amir, to join Rahel later. *Oh, well*, Rahel told herself as the plane revved up. *Solo it is.* She reckoned she would soon enough be hankering for time to herself.

The cheapest flight took her through Amsterdam, with a full day layover. Getting to this point had been like stamping barefoot along a prickly trail, but now she felt like she was strolling a well-lit street littered with gifts from strangers. Her friend Maya had a Syrian friend who'd recently left Amsterdam after living there many years. The Syrian stranger had sent her mysterious instructions: "When you get to Amsterdam, go to the Jordaan district, to the Small World Café, and ask for the owner. He will have some things for you." At the tiny café, she found a fifty-dollar gift certificate from Maya for the café, and she bought herself a big meal. She walked along the canal and took herself into a nearby artsy-indie movie theater with a 1920s vibe and watched a film about the Russian ballet. Afterward, strolling back through Amsterdam on her way to an art museum, her last venture as a free woman, Rahel felt like someone was holding her hand.

Rahel fell asleep on the tarmac in Amsterdam, and when she woke up, she was in Ethiopia. The driver from the orphanage, whose name was Johannes, recognized her immediately.

"I know your son very well," Johannes told Rahel after he'd loaded her luggage into the van. He was married to a Dutch woman, and he spoke English well. "I drove him from his village to Addis. My wife held him the whole time. He cried all the way, and he ate all her sandwich and drank her water." He laughed. Rahel looked out the window at the city and smiled. *I know your son.*

As they drove through the dusty streets of Addis Ababa, Rahel watched as descriptions she had read of the place rolled by, real now, accompanied by the city's waking sounds: the prayer song from the Grand Mosque, chants from the Ethiopian Orthodox cathedral, soon to be joined, as the writer Greene had described it, by "animal bleats and taxi horns and shouts from market vendors, and the commotion of thousands of pedestrians";[30] high-rises, cathedrals, and open markets; motorcycles, camels, and nomads; and "beggars of every description," including "the blind and the lepers, and the mentally ill and the malnourished, and the orphans and the dying."[31]

The orphanage was in a gated compound. Johannes parked near the guesthouse for visiting families, which was next to the house for infants and a few hundred feet from another house for babies over a year old.

"You want to go see your baby?" Johannes asked, expectantly. Rahel's luggage was still in the van.

"Like this?" Rahel asked. "I haven't even brushed my teeth." She was not sure she wanted to meet her son for the first time with bad breath, unkempt hair, and smelly armpits. Johannes looked confused.

"You can go whenever you want," he said. "But if you want, I'll take you now."

Rahel took a breath. She could hear the babies inside the small building right in front of her.

"Yes, now," she said, shaking her head. "Of course, right now. Thank you. Please."

There were six babies in the house, each in its own crib. One woman was dressing a baby, and another was collecting laundry. Rahel saw Yisak immediately. He looked up, and she could see that he recognized her. Maybe it was the eight-by-ten photo of her tacked to the inside of his crib, or maybe it was the fact that she was the only white woman in the room. She walked toward him, and he reached his arms up, as if he'd been waiting only a morning instead of a lifetime. He was bony, light, and squirmy, but the tears in his eyes matched the tears in hers. The nanny and the laundress quietly watched. *This is the moment I became a mother*, Rahel's tired head thought. She felt the chilling layers of fear, doubt, and worry liquefy and evaporate. *This is all going to be fine*, she thought.

"It's really going to be fine," she said to Yisak.

At the orphanage, where Rahel stayed for a week waiting for Yisak's release to be finalized, two nannies alternated twenty-four-hour shifts, sleeping on a cot in the room with the babies. Other staff took care of laundry, food, and light medical care, so the nanny could direct all of her attention to the six babies. There were not many toys, but the babies seemed to enjoy the few that were there. Often, the nannies put two kids together in a crib for playtime. Most nights, Yisak slept with Rahel in her room.

Each morning, after bottles, the nanny removed each baby's pants and diapers and took them outside for an hour. Rahel loved this time the best: the airing of the babies. Each morning, after coffee, she went to watch Yisak and his colleagues crawl, sun shining on skinny tushies, in the dirt of the yard.

A few days into her stay, another gift arrived, this time from Israel: Amir, husband of Rahel's friend Sarah. He'd been a medic in the army and was good with kids. He arrived from Tel Aviv, just a few hours away by plane, with two duffel bags filled with toys, medicines, Pedialyte to hydrate Yisak, an Israeli baby formula bulked up with corn flour to fatten him up, enough of it all to share with the other kids, and a fifth of Scotch for Rahel. At night, when Yisak seemed overstimulated and crabby in Rahel's arms, Amir took the baby up to the roof in a sling and walked him into a deep sleep. *It's like having the perfect temporary husband*, Rahel thought one night as she and Amir sat wordlessly sipping Scotch: a practical helper with no emotional needs and a wife of his own.

Rahel took a trip, without the baby, to visit Yisak's birth family. Many adoptive parents, lacking anything beyond a sketch of their child's story and not wanting to threaten their own status as parents, wind up telling their kids about the place they came from but not their first family.[32] Rahel wanted more. She wanted to fill in as many pieces of his story as she could. A man named Abraham drove her, Amir, and another family seven hours along a long, bumpy road, to a small village near Sedek'a in Sidama; it was hot, and they were breathing dust. Along the way, they picked up a translator and a social worker. The closest parking area was a twenty-minute walk to the village. Fura was a collection of mud huts with thatched roofs and a couple of tin-roofed buildings. It had lush vegetation but no running water.

When Rahel and the others emerged out of the woods, children came running toward them. One of them went to find Amaresh Yohannes, Yisak's grandmother, who came quickly. She and Rahel locked eyes. Then Amaresh left, returning with four other grandchildren, Yisak's first cousins, all of whose parents had died, most likely of AIDS-related diseases. They sat, quite formally, on a small circle of hard benches. Rahel gave Amaresh Yohannes framed pictures of Yisak, and they looked at them together.

This is what Rahel learned about Yisak's family. The men are tenant farmers, making their living by farming *enset*, a plant in the banana family. They leave for weeks at a time, to work farm lands that are far from the village, while the women, children, and elders stay in Fura. When Yisak's mother had become pregnant with him, she and his father had been living in another village but returned to Fura when his father got very sick. When both parents died just months after Yisak's birth, Amaresh had tried to take care of the baby. She had no money for formula, so she'd mashed bread into water and fed it to him. The baby became very sick. He wasn't getting better, and he wasn't growing. He was very, very hungry. Amaresh had strapped him to her back and walked fifteen kilometers to the nearest clinic.

At the clinic, the staff had given her a case of formula. The social worker happened to be at the clinic that day, and the staff had suggested that she might want to consider placing Yisak in orphanage care. Amaresh met with the social worker, and two days later she delivered him to the orphanage in Addis Ababa.

"I can't take care of a baby," Yisak's grandmother said to Rahel through the translator that day on the bench. "I don't have food for a baby, and my roof leaks, and I don't have a proper home for a baby. I'm an old woman. I shouldn't be working, but I still work, and my husband still works." She gestured to the cousins. "And we have all these other children that we're taking care of," she said.

"What do you wish for Yisak?" Rahel asked her.

"I want him to get an education," Yisak's grandmother answered. "I want him to be a good person. I want him to be a kind person, a person who helps others." Rahel began crying, and soon everyone else in the circle was, too. Nobody said exactly what they were crying about. I can only imagine the waves of tears: a wave for the loss of a son and daughter-in-law; a wave for the education their son will have and another for what his cousins will not have; a wave for the hunger of a baby and for bread mashed in water; a wave for the leaky roof and one for the love underneath it; a wave for the joy that cannot be disconnected from grief; a wave for lives you might have lived and another for the stories that cannot be told; a wave for the world that is so unjust and another for the unimaginable connections between strangers; a wave for being a mother alone and another for being surrounded by family; waves for gratitude, anger, beauty, resentment, relief, and hope; a wave for the picture of the little boy with the soft tuft of hair.

On the long plane ride home from Ethiopia, Yisak cried inconsolably, taking only a few small breaks across the twenty-some hours of travel. During one of his brief periods of calm, Rahel looked over the photos she'd taken at the orphanage. Among them were pictures of another baby, younger then the one now fidgeting on her lap. Before she'd left New York, an intended mother had contacted her and asked her to take some pictures of the baby girl she was expecting to adopt. At the orphanage, both the girl and Yisak had battled the same bacterial infection. Two days after Rahel took her pictures, the girl died.

Yisak started up his wailing again. *Oh my God, I think I've made a terrible mistake*, Rahel thought, like most new parents do, five hours in. She was naive to the possibility, she later discovered, of a much greater horror than a baby who won't stop crying. Many Westerners adopting from Ethiopia over the coming years would face, or choose not to face, the evidence that, with high demand for healthy infants and big adoption fees, deceitful middlemen were taking some Ethiopian children away from their families, many of whom believed their children would later return to help support them.[33] Even at the time, adoption agencies allowed adoptive parents to financially sponsor members of their child's birth family, which meant that someone like Amaresh might see giving up one child as a means to garnering material support for the others under her care; this practice was later curtailed under criticism that it amounted to offering money in exchange for babies. Through the adoption agency, Rahel would support humanitarian programs in the region where Yisak's first family lived, including the building of a maternity clinic, in the hopes that other women would receive the health support that Yisak's first mother did not. She would place a framed photo of Amaresh on her Manhattan bookshelf—it sits there now—but she would never know for sure if Amaresh had been subject to misleading enticements or broken promises.

Sometimes, as an older child of seven or eight, when Yisak could sit still long enough, he would suddenly burst into tears.

"Mom," he would cry, collapsing in Rahel's arms, "I miss my first mother." No amount of planning, no hand of fate, no money or paperwork, no boyfriend or husband, could have made their story any different. There was nothing she could do but be sad with him, until the storm passed and he dashed off to throw a Frisbee in the air and chase it down. She knew he could not possibly remember his first mother, but she knew just what he meant.

BIRTH CONTROL

I see Aldo a couple of times a week at the schoolyard, when I drop off or pick up Reba. He's not really a mischief maker, but he reminds me of one of the Little Rascals from the 1930s *Our Gang* flicks. His light-brown hair sticks up a bit at the back, his sharp blue eyes darting quickly toward a ball in the air or on the ground, and though he always seems to be running to or from something, he sometimes humors me with a high five on his way.

I've known Aldo since before he was born. His mothers, Maureen and Julia, used to live down the street from me and Richard. We saw them at yard sales and walking on the street and had a vague gays-on-the-block understanding. When Reba was a newborn, Maureen was pregnant. Once, walking with the baby on my chest, I ran into her and her dog.

"How's it going?" she asked. It might have been just a casual how's-it-going, but since her belly had recently ballooned, I took it to be more of a request for a report from the front lines. I was sleepy.

"I won't lie to you," I said, then probably something along the lines of "It's beautiful, for sure. You know, the miracle of life and the tiny fingers and how much they need you and all. But really, it's kind of awful, too. I feel insane and hormonal. It's relentless and there's no end in sight. Nobody really wants to tell you that."

"Thanks for that," she said, drily.

"Oh, but you know, ask me again after my nap," I said.

The next week I saw Julia on the block. She commented on the diaper bag slung over my shoulder and asked me why I chose it. I offered what I suspect was an overly lengthy treatise on the bag's pros and cons. Julia was surprisingly attentive. It turned out she was on the verge of buying one, had done extensive research, and was closing in on a decision. Now that she saw mine, she was reconsidering. I could see that my attempt to be helpful had backfired.

I assumed at the time that I was talking to my local lesbian couple made pregnant through donor insemination, the most recent in a long line of such lesbian mothers I'd known since my college friend Becky and her girlfriend had their son in the late 1990s, and my friend Liz, Becky's ex-girlfriend, had given birth to a boy not long after. I knew my own fortune was good, but I also envied these lesbians and their turkey-baster pregnancies. Encountering Julia and Maureen, I imagined their path to parenthood was so much easier, and cheaper, than my own.

Of course, envy is often based on misperception. As I got to know Julia and Maureen a bit better, I came to find out that the fetus Maureen was carrying was indeed made with donor sperm from a sperm bank—no surprise there—but that the egg was not actually her own. The sperm were used to fertilize Julia's eggs in vitro, and then Maureen was impregnated with embryos to which she had no genetic link. As I got to know them better still, I came to find out the layers of complexity beneath that one. They seemed to be such forthright, secure women that I hadn't imagined that being gay had actually been for each a lonely, unthinkable thing, pushed down until it appeared in the unstable form of an identity crisis. Slowly, I came to discover what Maureen and Julia had pushed through to get to those moments of parental chitchat on the street: the struggles to imagine themselves as a couple in the first place, as they each moved against and toward social conformity; the need to protect themselves against doubting families and to occupy their space on their family trees; the fear of losing control and the fear of controlling too much; the ambivalent relationship to a system that equates biological parenthood with authentic parenthood.

▪ ▪ ▪

To get to Aldo, both Maureen and Julia would first have to stumble individually across the minefields of normalcy and shame. Julia, for her part, was an obedient only child. Her parents routinely told her what a perfect daughter she was, especially compared to her messy, noisy, dirty cousins, whose visits to the house they likened to tornadoes. In her house, life was set to a quiet soundtrack of classical music, and dinner was at six o'clock, don't be late. Julia's fear of disappointing her parents became such an integral part of her family dynamic that she did not even know it was there. Each decision had to be the right one, so she developed a habit of painstaking cost-benefit deliberation before taking any action. She worked hard and tried not to stand out. When it came to gender and sexuality, she made a safe space for herself in the middle. She loved horses, avoided dresses, did hair and makeup on her Barbie Styling Head, and played sports. She favored a plain appearance. As a teenager, she was into boys in a Fantasy Boyfriend kind of way. The thought of intimacy with girls was not even a tiny blip on her radar, but neither did she lust after boys. When in middle school she read an Ann Landers column discussing fellatio, she resolved with disgust that she would never do such a thing. Even through college, she maintained a safe trajectory of romantic heterosexual fantasy and asexual reality.

Maureen grew up in a much more chaotic environment, the second of four kids. In her house, the Tooth Fairy might arrive a few days late, and the legs of coffee tables were pockmarked where the dogs had chewed on them. Her father was a military chaplain, and the family moved around a lot. Maureen was shy and chubby—not the best characteristics for someone who was starting a new social life every couple of years—a bit of a misfit, and like Julia, she ducked under the radar. At home, she took on the role of caregiver for her baby brother, even insisting that his parents move his crib into her room; the role suited her, giving her both a sense of value and cover. When her family settled in a small town in rural Maryland, where her father became a local minister and she a high schooler, she felt the stirrings of rebellion. She didn't like to get in trouble, though, which meant her rebellion would have to remain invisible. In church she played the good minister's daughter, but in her head she thought maybe God didn't exist. In school she followed the rules, but in her head she announced that dating, homecoming, and prom were a big fat waste of time. She let people think she was a small-town Maryland girl, but in her head she was already on a bus for a big city and not looking back.

Julia and Maureen met during their first year at Washington College in the late 1980s. That summer, when they were both working and living on campus, Julia took to dropping by the library after her shift in the Admissions Office to hang out until Maureen's library shift ended. They became great friends. When they both transferred to different colleges the next year—Maureen moving to Philadelphia, Julia to Oakland—they wrote long, loving letters, but it seemed about as likely that one day they would be married to each other and having a baby as that they would lead expeditions to Saturn. In fact, so casual and unexamined was the heterosexism they carried with them that such a suggestion would have appeared at the time as an insult.

A year after they were both done with college, Julia invited Maureen to drive back from her parents' house in New Jersey to Oakland. Maureen, fed up with working in a prison library for a crazy boss, eventually agreed. Road-tripping it in the summer of 1994, they camped out under the stars and splurged on charming bed-and-breakfasts. They shared beds and the intimacy of sunsets. It was as romantic as it was chaste. Once, looking down on the New Mexico countryside from the peak of the Sandia Mountains, Julia put her arm around Maureen and rested her head sadly on her shoulder.

"What's the matter, sweetie?" Maureen asked.

"It's so gorgeous and so powerful here," Julia said. "If only I could share it with someone I'm in love with." Nothing, not even the spirit of Georgia O'Keefe, not even the fact that they were behaving like a young couple in love, could get them to see each other as that someone.

Maureen nodded. She understood: they were both waiting for the man they were destined to marry, which would make them normal. She'd had a boyfriend in college for a while and wasn't even a little bit in love with him, but when he broke up with her, she had fallen apart. She'd dropped out of school for a semester and started therapy, where she talked mostly about how being dumped proved that she would never be normal.

Still, when the trip was through, Maureen made plans to move to California, where she would move in with Julia. After college, while Maureen pulled herself together in Baltimore, she had befriended some gay people, and though she was determined not to be one of them, they weren't really buying it.

"You're in love with Julia," her friend Sherri announced to her one night over cocktails. By then, Maureen had allowed the possibility that she was bisexual to surface, then she shoved it back down whenever she could.

"No, I'm not," Maureen protested, thinking about how much she missed Julia. "We're best friends. We're soul mates."

"Yeah, exactly," Sherri said. "Well, you're going to be roommates soon. You at least need to tell her that you're gay."

"But I'm not," Maureen protested. A few hours later, at three a.m., Maureen called Julia from a pay phone, full of drink and drama. She might be bisexual, she said. If Julia didn't want her to come to California after all, she'd understand, she said. Julia, who understood herself to be straight, was comforting. Of course Maureen should come to California; this changed nothing.

Maureen left for California the next week. In a way, she was still running away from home, but she was also on the run from the nagging fear of being abnormal and also, without really knowing it, running toward something.

■　■　■

The goal of a life others recognize as "normal" seems at best a modest one. In fact, the pursuit of normalcy, which has a long history in lesbian and gay politics, has been roundly, and I think soundly, criticized. The idea that our worth is contingent on others' perception of us as normal is dangerous—for people who are deemed abnormal and absorb the conclusion that this makes them unworthy, it can be lethal. That idea needs to be challenged. Seeking to be assimilated into the-way-things-are does nothing to change the way things are, and the way things are is the very problem to begin with: powerful people define normalcy so that respect, status, rights, and resources flow to those who fit the definition and are denied to those who don't.

When normalcy becomes a movement platform, as it pretty much has for mainstream gay and lesbian organizations over the past two decades, it bolsters the status of the already privileged and further marginalizes those who can't or don't want to conform. As the writer and activist Mattilda Bernstein Sycamore puts it in *That's Revolting!*, when a "1950s model of white-picket-fence, 'we're just like you' normalcy" takes over and "the dominant signs of straight conformity . . . become the ultimate measures of gay success," the politics becomes more about "obtaining straight privilege than challenging power." Earlier queer struggles "to create new ways of loving, lusting for, and caring for one another" are swept aside and largely forgotten in favor of access to institutions like the military and marriage.[1] In this situation, the social theorist Michael Warner points out in *The Trouble with Normal*, a hierarchy emerges, in which "respectable" gays—those who don't "challenge the norms of straight culture, who [do] not flaunt sexuality, and who [do] not insist on living differently from ordinary folk"—stand above "shameful" ones.[2] Embracing the normal standard "merely throws shame on those farther down the ladder of respectability," while suggesting that "the taken-for-granted norms of common sense are the only criteria of value."[3]

If the celebration of normalcy is politically problematic, it has some logical weirdnesses, too. After all, Warner points out, if by normal we mean typical, there's no great argument to be made for it; no one is really normal in the statistical sense, and many of the things people seem to want—to be famous or a genius or exceptionally endowed—are statistically abnormal. And if by normal we mean nonpathological, there are other ways to respond to the charge that you're a freak besides trying to be as ordinary as possible. You can measure yourself by the norms you and yours have generated and not by someone else's "yardstick of normalcy."[4] You can refuse the stigma of pathology yet also refuse to be absorbable. You can reject the notion of pathology altogether. You can, as they say, let your freak flag fly.

Still, I'm not so sure you should have to. Gayness and other stigmatized differences are not in and of themselves a moral prescription to fight, and even if you do go that direction, you'll encounter strict norms among the rebellious, too. Perhaps freedom can also just mean making room for people to choose or reject normalcy or to cobble together a mix. This may not make full intellectual sense, but that may be in part because our relationship to normalcy is guided by more emotional logics. I suspect that what Warner calls "the lure of the normal" can only be understood if it is recognized as more than just a seduction.

In any case, I try not to be too judgy about people wanting normalcy, not least because my own life has turned out to be pretty conventional. Going up against social norms is really, really hard—an exhausting, David-versus-Goliath effort, since by definition you're going up against something most people take as just how things are and must be. For another, when the world tells you that your being is pathological, deviant, unlike everybody else, it makes good sense to try to object and resist—especially, as Warner asserts, in America, "where normal probably outranks all other social aspirations."[5] Plus, there are many pleasures to be had in a normal life. Some derive from respectability's privileges, but it seems unfair to assume that those are the only pleasures of a so-called normal life. Getting to normal can feel, for some folks, like coming home.

What is clear—the common ground between critics and defenders of normalcy pursuits—is that normal isn't just a set of ideas but an unavoidable structure. You don't set the terms of the hierarchy of normalcy; you figure out how to respond to them, how to make a life within and against them. To paraphrase Karl Marx, we make our own normal, but not under circumstances we have chosen, the traditions of the past weighing on the decisions of the present. Your individual choices, even if you protest that you don't intend them to do so, can further normalize you or do the opposite, since those choices are markers in a structure that exists independently of its particular occupants. In the structures of normalcy, as in the other inescapable hierarchies in which we operate (gender, class, race, nation, and so on), those choices are necessarily political ones, even when they don't feel like it. The personal, as feminists have reminded us since the 1970s, is political.

And so there you might be: trying to figure out if you are the kind of normal the world insists on, and if you're not, could you still be okay, and whether you have to give up the life you have imagined for yourself in order to fight the coercive normative structure or hold on to it because it is your life to live and no one else's.

■   ■   ■

Shortly after Maureen moved into Julia's apartment in Oakland in 1995, she found a Parents and Friends of Lesbians and Gays (PFLAG) pamphlet on her bed, left there by Julia. It was called "Be Yourself: Questions and Answers for Gay and Lesbian Youth." Maureen was pushing twenty-five and trying as hard as she could not to be lesbian, but she was touched nonetheless.

They each had their own bed, but almost every night Julia would slide into Maureen's bed to chat, against Maureen's halfhearted protests. One night around Thanksgiving, tipsy, they decided to try kissing—just out of curiosity, they told each other. The next morning, they agreed that it would never happen again. But then it did, and then again, and then another time. They would have sex at night and in the daylight pretend they were just best friends. They could barely talk about it. Instead, they wrote long notes to each other, and Julia did cost-benefit analyses of the situation in her head. When they did speak out loud about it, it was mainly to worry about what others would say if they found out.

"If only you were Calvin," Julia told Maureen.

"You can call me Calvin," Maureen said. She realized she was happy.

After a while, the secrecy became more burdensome than the thing itself. When they told their closest friends—another pair of female best friends—and all they got back was love, they started to tell other friends. A few months later, emboldened, they told Julia's parents, who reacted disdainfully and so activated her fears of making the wrong decision and of losing her perfect-child status, which led her to doubt herself some more, which Maureen then resented. It took many months to get back on track, but they stuck with it. Julia knew she had suddenly become to her parents a person they could not decipher, an alien creature. You might say that staying with Maureen was Julia's first act of rebellion.

Julia still had her moments. One night in 1996, Maureen found a toy ring on the floor of the bookstore where she worked. She brought it home to Julia.

"I want to marry you," she said.

"That's just silly," Julia replied. As in: this is great for now, but I have other plans.

Maureen no longer did. She's the type of loyal person who will only leave if you tell her to go away; Julia's ambivalence alone was not enough to get her to exit the relationship. Anyway, she now knew that she could still have the family she had always wanted. She was sure she wanted to marry Julia. She had been mothering people for as long as she could remember, and she loved the idea that her body, which had never done her any favors, could do something as beautiful as make a child. She was sure she wanted to have kids with Julia, too.

"No kids," Julia said. She was not unclear.

■ ■ ■

Life became routine over the next couple of years, almost what each of them had once imagined normal would be. They were a couple. They were out at their jobs. They had broken up and gotten back together again. Julia's parents had resumed talking to her; her mother, who had once offered to travel to California to help Julia break up with Maureen, now declared that love is love. They threw parties at their new apartment on Alcatraz Avenue. They almost forgot they were lesbians.

Maureen tried, for a while, to respect the fact that Julia didn't want to have kids, but her resentment started to leak out—in snide remarks at parties, in sad looks at passing strollers—and eventually Julia called her on it. They spent months in couples counseling trying on each other's perspective. Julia pretended that having children meant not intolerable chaos but, if she Maureened herself for a minute, unpredictable good fun. Maureen looked at their childless friends as Julia might, seeing not empty selfishness but freedom, adventure, travel, and early retirement.

"It would just seem a little lonely," Maureen said. Somehow, those words struck Julia. Over the months, Julia visualized having a kid so often that she began to be saddened when she imagined not having one. Over Thai dinner in Berkeley on her birthday, she told Maureen she was ready to have a kid.

"Great," Maureen said. "But we have to get married first."

"You're nuts," said Julia. It was 2003, and even Massachusetts hadn't yet legalized same-sex marriage.

"I want wedding photos," Maureen said. "My kid has to see wedding photos. That's what you do. Kids see wedding photos of their parents." She knew the story she wanted to be able to tell, and she wanted the pictures to go with it. She was like an immigrant working to get her kid the life that had been out of her reach; her kid would at least start from the conventional script of normalcy.

Around the time Richard and I were getting married, Maureen and Julia were, too. It wasn't legal, but since they'd already been planning a big party, they skipped the whole Gavin Newsom–led San Francisco wedding scene so as not to steal their own thunder. They got married in the boathouse at Lake Merritt in downtown Oakland. Lake Merritt, oddly, has gondolas. They rented them all for the night and hired an accordionist, and all night their friends and family were serenaded on gondolas.

Some family members had refused to come, and others came and stayed off to themselves, disapproving, or got ugly drunk. Julia's father refused their request to say a prayer at the wedding, but Maureen's younger brother gave a brief, booze-fueled speech that he admitted was based on a book on "winning toasts" he'd read on the plane. When her older brother stood up for his toast, though, he started tearing up before he could get any words out. Then, bawling, he recalled how hard it had been for his sister and Julia to tell anyone about their relationship and how Maureen had been shaking when she finally told him.

"And when they have their child," he said, catching Maureen's startled stare but not in time to stop himself, "that will be the luckiest kid in the world." There were murmurs in the crowd. Julia and Maureen had only told a few people they intended to have kids and hadn't even begun the process, and over the days that followed, friends and family members, thinking perhaps they had just heard a baby announcement, gently probed for more information. Maureen didn't care. She got the girl. She got the wedding. She got the photos of the wedding to show a future child. And now she'd just have to get the baby.

■ ■ ■

Julia agreed to take over the practical question of how to make a baby happen. On and off for months, Julia had been researching online, reading books, dragging Maureen to adoption seminars, going on message boards. Nothing seemed quite right.

Truth be told, she was a bit of a mess. Trying to have a kid is not easy for people who like control. Since you don't really know how your or somebody else's body is going to perform, pregnancy is a bit of a crap shoot, and unless you're cloning, you have no idea what child is going to emerge from the womb anyway. In most adoptions, you know very little about the child's medical history, genetic background, or even sometimes early childhood, so it seems like things could crop up at any time (unusual illnesses, behavioral problems) for which you're not prepared. The unpredictability of it all freaked Julia out.

Control was only one piece of her worries. Julia's worst fear was that she would have a child and be unable to feel a connection, that she would look at it as her parents looked at her during the aftermath of her coming out or like she looked at their dog, as a thing apart, a lovable but unfathomable being. Each available family-making option seemed only to increase her alienation. Raising a child born in another place, she'd want to expose the child to his or her heritage of origin, which would not be hers, which would then disconnect her from the child; it was hard to imagine adopting a baby from China and then insisting that his or her cultural heritage was Polish and Italian rather than Chinese. Every lesbian mother Julia and Maureen knew had used donor insemination, but the idea of Maureen and a sperm donor making a baby left Julia feeling sidelined. They thought maybe the trick would be to use a sperm donor who brought something of Julia's genetics into the mix; so they'd considered asking a cousin, but they didn't really want the kinds of familial complications that could bring. Julia wanted Maureen to have the pregnancy she so craved, but she also wanted to be connected to the child by something that felt more substantial than being the "other" mother. She just couldn't find a way in.

In her most honest moments, Julia knew she thought of a child that wasn't biologically connected to her as an alien—not as in immigrant but as in unfamiliar species—and she didn't want to bring home an extraterrestrial. Only a biological connection would convince her that the baby was hers. She wanted to look at Maureen's belly and know, the way most straight fathers-to-be do, that a part of her was growing there. The problem was, she didn't have the stuff to knock up her wife. So there they were. Julia really, really wanted to have a child that was genetically hers, but she didn't want to carry a baby. Maureen really, really wanted to have a baby but didn't care that much about her own genetic reproduction.

One night in bed, Julia rolled over and nudged Maureen.

"I wish I could get you pregnant," she said. "I wish you could have my baby."

"Yeah, right," said Maureen. "Hold on a sec. Let me go get my magic wand."

A lightbulb had already gone off for Julia, though. She'd heard of "test tube babies," but she'd associated that with infertile couples and surrogates, neither of which they were. But now there seemed no reason that Maureen couldn't take the surrogate role, carrying a child made with someone else's donated egg, and no reason Julia couldn't be that someone. The next day, Julia went online to do some more research. She typed various combinations of "lesbian," "mothers," "eggs," "sperm," "donor," clicking around, and eventually stumbled onto the website of a woman conducting dissertation research about lesbians using in vitro fertilization to become coparents. That was it: Julia's egg, donor sperm, Maureen's womb. It seemed outlandish but also exactly what they were looking for. Maureen could have her baby. Maybe they didn't need a magic wand.

A few days later, Julia called their local fertility clinic—the same one, it turned out, that helped Richard and me conceive Reba Sadie with Tamar and Jane—and made an appointment to see Dr. Szymanski. They could make this happen, he said. It would cost around $12,000. They would have to dig into their savings and take out a home equity loan, but that wasn't so far out of reach as to be a deal breaker; they had, like most people who can even consider assisted reproduction without insurance coverage, a bit of money in the bank and assets they could leverage to pay for family making.

Dr. Szymanski reminds some people a bit of Santa Claus: white beard below smooth noggin, twinkly blue eyes, working hard with his bustling staff to get you a big gift. He finishes many sentences with a friendly, eastern-European-accented "Oh-kaaaay?" He is all scientist, though. It took him a while to understand the problem for which IVF promised a solution for Julia and Maureen. The first time he saw Maureen's uterus, he was not enthused. He explained that because it was relatively small, her uterus brought some risks to both a baby and the woman carrying it.

"You could use Julia's uterus," he suggested, helpfully. "Oh-kaaaay?"

■　■　■

That the resolution Maureen and Julia chose involved elaborate medical procedures when simpler avenues to parenthood were available to them is telling. It might at first seem odd that people who are making up new kinds of families outside a heteronormative framework—which is so reliant on the argument that nature dictates heterosexuality—would be so attached to the notion that nature tells you what makes a real parent. One of the contributions of queer family making has been to push forward the claim that "families we choose" are just as authentic as those tied by "blood" and to demote biology and genetics from their privileged place as determinants of kinship.[6] Yet in this family, as in many others, biogenetic ties were seen as the ultimate arbiter of parenthood.

This is perhaps made less strange by the simple recognition that straight and queer people operate inside the same, or at least largely overlapping, cultural worlds. As the sociologist Laura Mamo puts it, "Assisted reproductive technologies and sperm banks provide the institutional and technical practices necessary to bypass social conventions of the heterosexual family, but they do not necessarily bypass cultural and social ideals of what and who makes a family."[7] In the cultural world we collectively occupy, the assumption that a genetic relationship to a child is what makes you his or her real parent is still nearly unassailable. The law can step in and establish parenthood, but that's no match for a DNA test. Adopted children are asked about, and sometimes search for, their "real" parents. And even if many of us have what anthropologists have called "fictive kin"—people we consider relatives but with whom we share neither biological nor legal ties—the very term is a reminder that these are not considered the truest of family. "The power of biogenetic determinism," as the sociologist Maureen Sullivan found in her study of lesbians who made families through donor insemination, is "resilient and protean" and never "loses its grip."[8]

That grip isn't direct and linear, though. It sets the key terms for decisions about and narratives of kinship but doesn't dictate them. Indeed, it's striking not just how strong biological and genetic assumptions are but also how malleable they turn out to be. Suzanne Pelka—the anthropologist Julia discovered on her web search, who studied lesbian couples using IVF—argues, for instance, that whether, how, and which biological and genetic links are "imagined to create 'real' kinship" varies by context. A pregnant woman with no genetic ties to the fetus she is carrying can be seen as a "benign vessel" but not a parent (if she is carrying the baby for other intended parents) or as a mother whose maternity is legitimated by pregnancy (if she is the intended mother carrying a fetus conceived with someone else's egg). A man who contributes genetic material to a baby might be considered a father or a "donor," depending on context. Intentionality, Pelka concludes, shapes how genetic and biological ties are built into perceived kinship.[9]

For people getting assistance with reproduction, biology and genetics often become not simple determinants of parenthood, then, but central symbols of kinship; rather than "a prerequisite for relatedness," Mamo suggests, "biology is transformed into a mere signpost of parenthood." Trying to conceive a child who physically resembles both parents, for example, may stem in part from a narcissistic desire to see oneself reflected, or one's genes continued onward, but more deeply is an attempt to create what Mamo calls "affinity ties," in which biogenetic connections are used to mark "likenesses" that fall somewhere between "blood" ties and "social" ones.[10] Finding a sperm donor who shares one parent's cultural heritage—which less charitably appears as ethnocentrism—does the same. In this kind of family creation process, the anthropologist Corinne Hayden concludes, parents-to-be "simultaneously affirm the importance of blood as a symbol and challenge the American cultural assumption that biology is a self-evident, singular fact and the natural baseline on which kinship is built."[11]

Because the relationship to "biogenetic determinism" is often deliberate but not necessarily examined, inventive but also at times ambivalent or even contradictory, the creation story can be hard to tell. Nature marks Julia as mother through her eggs and Maureen through her pregnancy; they become, to themselves and to those who know their story, comothers, each with her own biological link to their child. What, then, can be said, or must not be said, of the man whose genetic material the child will carry, who by this same biogenetic logic might reasonably be seen as the father of their child?

■ ■ ■

Straight people who have kids in the typical way don't usually give much thought to how to bring the two sides of the family together. It comes up in naming, for sure—a child might carry the first name of a grandfather or great-grandmother and share one or both parents' last names—but law, custom, and nature pretty much bury the question of how a child can emerge who is (and maybe even looks like) the combination of the two parents and their families' cultural heritages. With Maureen and Julia, as with many unconventional family makers, the melding came to the fore as a practical, hyperintentional project.

The deliberate melding of their families was only partly going to be achieved through the combination of Julia's eggs and Maureen's uterus. After all, there would be a set of genes in the mix—from the sperm side— that would be neither Julia's nor Maureen's. When they were considering sperm donors, Julia had lists of pros and cons; though it looks somewhat irrational to her now, this was a process she thought she could control. She wanted a brown-eyed donor with brown-eyed parents, thinking this would give them a brown-eyed child. She also wanted, like many prospective parents generating "affinity ties," a child that looked like some combination of them. Both she and Maureen were around five foot five, so she wouldn't consider donors taller than six two. She signed up for the sperm bank's "photo matching" service, geared to meet exactly this desire for genetic affinity, in which the agency searches its database for donors who look like the parents-to-be. The photos she received were, oddly and without explanation, of Nordic-looking men, so Julia went at it on her own. After much sorting and spreadsheeting, she presented a dozen or so sperm donors to Maureen: artsy French Canadian; Italian American psychologist; German American brunet; computer geek. They each considered them independently and then talked about them, like judges at a talent show, the photos and files laid out on the dining-room table. After they narrowed the pool to four, each disclosed her favorite. It was the same guy, happily. Thus did egg meet sperm.

Maureen would have been happy with any of the contenders, really. She just wanted to be able to get the sperm and then forget about the donor. This wasn't too hard, in a way, since there wasn't really a person here but his sperm. As long as his genetics weren't too distant from theirs, no stranger would be visible in the body of a child, and that was how they wanted it. Indeed, they chose their donor largely because they could see pieces of themselves in him, because he was someone around whom they could build their own story in order, paradoxically, to write him out of it.

They didn't know his name, of course, but their friend Meredith called him Rocco. Rocco had hints of each side of Maureen and Julia's family, carrying their story without intruding into it. Maureen's family is Irish American, and Julia's is Italian and Polish; Rocco was Italian Irish. Like Julia, he was from New Jersey. He was Italian like her father's family, the Barzinis, and an artist like many in her mother's family, the Molnars. Maureen had worked in libraries, bookstores, and then developing software for libraries; Rocco's mother was a librarian. He was like a superficial composite of bits of their cultures, features, and personalities.

The fact that the actual man was unknown to them gave them some useful latitude. The conventional creation script on which they were building their story centers around the dyad—a couple, albeit a lesbian one, making a baby—and there's not a lot of room for strangers. Perhaps his sperm had produced scores of children, like the "God of Sperm" in Michigan whose donations over the years had produced an estimated four-hundred-plus progeny;[12] they would never know and chose to believe that theirs would be the only one, and there was no evidence to the contrary. They wanted a donor who would be willing to be known and contacted if the child wanted that in adulthood—that's not a decision they wanted to foreclose for their kid—and one day he might become a different part of their creation story. For now, though, he was his sperm and a character in the story they were making up. Soon, after they fertilized the eggs, it would be easy to proceed as if this baby was just something they had made without third-party involvement. Sometimes, even now, they forget about Rocco or whatever his name might really be.

■   ■   ■

Maureen and Julia were relieved to have a project they could work on together. A baby became not a set of wrought and abstract decisions but Things You Have To Do. They had to synchronize their bodies through shots and pills, so that Julia's follicles were stimulated to produce eggs and Maureen's womb was prepared to receive and hold on to an embryo. Maureen made them a schedule, read the instructions, and administered the shots.

They planned for the Egg Harvest, as they called it, around Thanksgiving, but Julia's hormone levels weren't high enough. On the second try, a few months later, they harvested nearly a dozen eggs, which were fertilized in Dr. Szymanski's laboratory, and then transferred a single embryo into Maureen's uterus. Figuring that with no impediments and a fresh embryo they'd have a baby in a snap, they were demolished by the news that they were not pregnant.

Even so, Julia liked the sense of control the medical process provided. In place of mystery and chaos were a set of actions and checked boxes: get this dosage right, stick that needle in at the right time, check this and that level. The doctor, who said Maureen's uterine lining wasn't thickening enough, prescribed some new drugs, and Julia culled advice from any source claiming to increase their odds. She read that eating eggs would ready a body for pregnancy, so she made lots and lots of egg salad, which Maureen dutifully ate. She arranged for Maureen to get acupuncture, which Maureen despised but endured. She lugged over from a friend's house a heavy statue of a fertility goddess and set it up in their bedroom.

None of this seemed to work. Maureen was disappointed but not especially surprised. She knew this medical approach satisfied their different desires, but at the same time she was a little repulsed by the whole process of making a baby in a lab. It seemed like they were playing God, trying to control a process that did not want to be controlled. Every time they went to Dr. Szymanski's office, she cringed at the cutesy picture on his wall of a baby in a test tube. The poster was meant to make you feel comfortable, to destigmatize the "test tube baby," but it had the opposite effect on Maureen. It was all so clinical and sci-fi. It made the whole thing seem like a cheat.

"You like the illusion of control," she told Julia, finally fed up with the drugs, egg salad, and needles. "I get that. But there is only so much you can control. And I'm sorry, but this is actually my body." She quit acupuncture. The next time they made a transfer, she said, they would follow her own natural cycle, without all the drugs.

On the date of the next transfer—their fourth and final try—Dr. Szymanski announced with pleasure that Maureen's endometrial lining was the right thickness. Maureen flashed Julia an I-told-you-so glance. They went one last time into the tiny room adjacent to the laboratory, and Dr. Szymanski transferred two embryos through a long, skinny tube from their petri dishes into Maureen's womb.

They went home to pack. A few weeks earlier, exhausted by the ups and downs of the process, they'd decided to get off the roller coaster and take a vacation in Hawaii. That way, if once again they faced the disappointment of no pregnancy, at least they'd be on a beach in the sun.

Shortly after they landed in Kona, they went to a local clinic for a blood test, which would be sent back to Dr. Szymanski's office for processing. Their statistical odds of a pregnancy had gone way down, according to the doctor, but just in case, Maureen went easy on the Mai

Tais. That night, flipping through the channels, she landed on a National Geographic special called "In the Womb," which used special effects and ultrasound movies to show the fetal development of cats, dogs, and humans. They watched it in superstitious, reverent silence.

Two days into the trip, the nurse from the Oakland clinic called to tell them the blood tests indicated a pregnancy. They tried not to get too excited and more or less failed. They stopped at Barnes & Noble on the way back from the clinic to pick up a copy of *What to Expect When You're Expecting*, which Maureen had been wanting to read for ages but Julia had feared would bring bad juju to their pregnancy attempts.

While Maureen read her pregnancy book on the beach, bathing in the sun and in her own relief, Julia began to worry. They had met their goal, step by step. She had done her job—finding the donor, making the egg salad, pushing the acupuncture—but now that there was nothing for her to do, all she could think about was what could go wrong. They'd used medicine to make a child that would otherwise be impossible. They were like lesbian Dr. Frankensteins. They had monkeyed with something that should be left to nature or God or the universe or whatever. They would be punished. She brought out her old understanding of lesbianism as unnatural and wrong, dusted it off, and set it next to the other reasons that made her irrationally certain Maureen would lose the baby. Or worse, she thought: *What we did was sort of monstrous, so the likely result is a monster baby.*

"Why don't you have morning sickness?" Julia asked Maureen. "That's a bad sign." Maureen, seeing where this was headed, told her the book said that not all women get morning sickness and went back to reading.

"What if your uterus isn't big enough?" Julia said. Maureen sighed and told Julia she had great confidence in her uterus.

Over the next months of the pregnancy, Julia's anxiety about what could go wrong went from a full-blown panic attack to a persistent hum of nervousness. She queried Maureen regularly about her level of exhaustion ("I'm tired, okay?"), the tenderness of her boobs ("Yup, still tender"), and vaginal discharge ("Do you really want to know?"). Although Maureen assured her that there was a live baby in there, Julia needed scientific proof. She bought a fetal Doppler machine to listen for a heartbeat. After the week-twenty ultrasound, when she could see the living fetus, she finally relaxed a bit and began focusing on baby-product research. Inside Maureen was not a creature with two heads or a long, scaly tail but a tiny humanoid.

Julia still worried, but her anxieties became more reasonably focused on homophobia. The whole world was not Oakland, after all, and most of the world did not even think lesbian mothers could or should exist. She readied herself for the moments that people would confront them, insisting that they were doing damage, noting with disdain the absence of a father. Maureen added in related practical concerns. She worried that someone might try to take the baby away from one parent if, God forbid, the other one were to suddenly die. They tightened up the legal side as much as they could. They became domestic partners, since same-sex marriage wasn't yet legal in California. They signed an agreement drafted by a lawyer stating their intentions to both be the parents of the coming child and prepared second-parent-adoption papers so that Julia could adopt their baby, made from her own egg, after it was born.

Julia did not know what to say when friends congratulated her on the pregnancy. People seemed to be congratulating her for being a so-cial mother—they did not tell people the whole story, so that was all they could see—which Julia was not convinced was enough to qualify her. The very genetic connection that made her feel like a "real" mother worthy of congratulations, the whole point of the elaborate switcheroo they had spent so much effort and money orchestrating, was unknown to the congratulators. She said thanks, to be polite, but as she did she wondered, *Who do they think I am to this baby?*

Maureen wore pregnancy with a beatific smile. She walked around thinking, *I got this. This I can do.* She liked being big without feeling fat, the pregnancy wiping away some of her earlier distaste for and distrust of her own body now that it was finally serving rather than betraying her. She loved getting special pregnant-woman treatment, young men helping her get things down from the shelves at Safeway, women chatting her up about due dates and strollers, people who would otherwise not have glanced at her offering their seats on BART. She would tell people about the other mother if they asked, but mostly she just let people see her as a straight pregnant lady, blending into the normative woodwork as she had as a child. She felt powerful and in charge. She felt like a "normal" woman, and she was, her pregnancy like an escalator moving up the normalcy structure.

■ ■ ■

The baby was facing the wrong way, its feet rather than head facing the exit, and the obstetrician said it was too risky to try to turn it around. Julia arranged for Maureen to return to the acupuncturist, who had her lay upside down on a board while burning various herbs near her pinky toes. She took Maureen to a swimming pool to do head stands. Maureen knew this wasn't just her control habits kicking in but also love: a breech baby would mean a C-section, Maureen really wanted to deliver vaginally, and Julia was trying to help Maureen get exactly what she wanted.

Maureen's mother wanted to know what colors they were painting the nursery so she could coordinate the quilt she was making, which was a barely veiled attempt to extract hints about the baby's sex. Their parents all thought that Julia and Maureen knew the answer but were refusing to tell, but they had requested not to know. It's not so much that they wanted to be surprised. Given how tightly managed the process had been, they had decided to leave at least something unorchestrated. If it were a girl, she'd be either Amelia or Juniper—the latter in honor of Maureen's sister, who had been named Jennifer after Donovan's "Jennifer Juniper" was a hit in 1968 and who had died in a car accident in 2000. If it were a boy, he would be Graham, which seemed just unusual enough and would honor Julia's Gram.

They began a baby book. It included sonogram photos of embryos, their list of possible names, photos from the Hawaii trip, including one of Maureen on the beach reading *What to Expect When You're Expecting*. It included the wedding photos Maureen had so wanted to be part of the story. It included letters from the grandparents written just after they learned of the pregnancy and original poems they'd written a few months later, such as this one from Maureen's mother:

> You're starting to show and that's a great sign.
> Soon you'll be feeling just fine.
> Baby will be kicking, moving all around,
> Exciting times coming, no comparison to be found.

Their baby book made no mention of sperm donors or fathers. Its central male figure was Dr. Szymanski, kindly looking and white haired, identified as "the man who helped us have you."

■ ■ ■

The fetus never did turn around, in part because Maureen's anatomy didn't offer him extra room, so it was going to have to be delivered by C-section. The doctor wanted to schedule the delivery for June 6, 2006.

"I'm sorry, but the lesbians just cannot have a baby born on 6-6-6," Maureen argued, thinking back to Julia's monster-child terrors. The doctor agreed to move it a day earlier.

A nurse summoned Julia into the operating room when it was time for the baby to be born. It was about four in the afternoon. When they got the baby out, Julia announced it was a boy. The baby was crying hard and steady, but when Julia started talking to him as the nurses were cleaning him up, the pitch of crying suddenly dropped. *He knows her*, Maureen thought through her fog of drugs. The nurse swaddled the newborn and brought him over to Maureen, who took a loving look at him and then vomited.

The baby resembled not so much a newborn but a miniature hirsute man-boy. He had black hair on his head and back and Elvis sideburns, and he looked like he'd just come from a tanning salon. The genetic rigging of eye color was a failure; he had, and still has, bright blue eyes framed by long eyelashes.

"Yeah, this isn't Graham," Maureen said, holding him a couple of hours later in the hospital room. Julia agreed. He didn't look or seem like a Graham. They stayed up all night, reminding each other they should sleep, staring at the baby and trying to figure out his name.

"I've got it," Maureen blurted out at three in the morning. Years before, a friend had solicited name suggestions for his new Italian Spinone dog. Maureen had suggested Aldo, though the friend wound up choosing Romeo instead.

"Aldo," Julia said. "That could work." It would be a nod to the Barzini side of the family—not enough to satisfy her mother, perhaps, but certainly Italianate. Done.

In fact, Aldo is, more than most kids I've met, stacked with family names on top of family names: the first name indicating his mother's mother's Italian mother, his middle name the same as his mother's mother's father's Polish last name, his second middle name the same as his other mother's mother's given last name, and his last name the same as that mother's given last name. Maybe because the calculated technological combination of the two families is hidden from view; maybe because they had to fight hard for a place on the family tree; maybe because ethnic background was such a big part of their own families' lore; maybe because the aura of an unknown man, at once central and irrelevant, was hovering on the edges of their story: Aldo is marked by names designed to make his belonging, and by extension his mothers', an incontrovertible fact.

In the wee hours of the morning after the day he was born, though, the freshly named Aldo was an unbelievable creature. He was supposed to be denied them and would have been had they successfully refused their desire for each other way back when. He was just what they had planned, made from a piece of each of their bodies, but the elaborate science had come to feel sometimes like an impossible temptation of fate. They could not believe what they had done. They could not believe that they had gotten here and that he had gotten to them. They could not believe how hairy he was.

We fooled Mother Nature and got away with it, Julia thought. Maureen felt more like a cat burglar, as if they had walked into the Smithsonian, stolen the Hope Diamond—this precious, gorgeous jewel—and walked on out without anyone noticing a thing.

▪ 4 ▪

THE KIDS IN THE PICTURES

Tess and I call each other best-friends-in-law, and our kids call each other cousins. She and Richard first met in the Dominican Republic in the late 1980s, when she was a nurse and he a medical student. At thirty, Tess had found herself newly single and suddenly living in Madison, Wisconsin, caring for her mother, who had been diagnosed with breast cancer. The only way she could stay sane in Wisconsin was to leave Wisconsin; and she generally prefers to do good works, so she had gotten herself on a medical mission to the Dominican Republic.

Tess is pale and freckled with bright-red hair and thus not terribly hard to pick out of a crowd of Dominicans; she and Richard quickly found each other. There was not a lot to do in their mountain village, so they told stories about themselves with, it turned out, secret nuggets tucked inside. Tess said she was a feminist, and Richard insisted this meant she was a lesbian; she protested that it most certainly did not mean that, that assuming one could be equated with the other was simply willful ignorance. Richard insisted he had a girlfriend named Charlene, although Tess found that confusing, since she was sure he was gay.

One day, they descended the mountain together to take a shower and go out on the town—which just barely qualified as a town, really, but did have a restaurant, a nightclub, and a casino. At the nightclub, a few beers in, Richard pulled Tess in close on the tiny dance floor.

"I have to tell you something because I really like you," he said nervously. "Charlene is actually a guy named Chuck."

Tess laughed. Now he made more sense.

"Okay," she said, leaning back in, "let me tell you something, too. Feminist and lesbian are two different things. But I'm both."

They became best friends.

A year later, after her mother had passed, Tess was preparing to move out to California from Wisconsin, and Richard offered to drive with her. On one long, flat stretch in Nebraska or one of the Dakotas, they began to talk about their desire to have kids. They both wanted daughters. They bandied about their favorite girl names. It was theoretical, a way to pass the time—especially for Richard, who is five years younger than Tess and for whom parenthood still seemed fantastical—but it stuck with Tess. If she wanted to get pregnant, she was going to have to get going pretty soon. It was not lost on her that sitting next to her in the car, with his big foot perched on the dashboard, was a man whose genes and soul she adored.

In another life, in another story, Richard might have wound up the biological father to Tess's children, but not in this one.

■ ■ ■

When Tess was eight, she had set sail with her family for India, where her father, a mime and theater teacher, was on a Fulbright Fellowship. She spent her second-grade year in New Delhi. It was the late 1960s, after British rule but before Americans had begun trekking to India looking for spiritual enlightenment. Everywhere the family went in India, Tess stood out. Crowds formed around her, some of them touching her orange hair to see if the color would come off in their hands.

The place left an impression on her that lasted well into adulthood. She was old enough to say to herself, "I want to remember this," and she did. She remembered it when her family moved from there to Jackson, Tennessee, where the racial inequities around her made even less sense than ever after her experience as an exoticized, suspect minority in India. She remembered it as she returned to the middle class from a country without one, where her family of modest means had lived as super-haves while witnessing the incomprehensibly deprived conditions of the many have-nots around them. Even then, Tess had an incorrigible need to fix things, to caretake, to nurse and tend to the world. For years, she begged her parents, who had no interest in more kids, to adopt a child from India. *Please, please, please, we have to do this,* she'd repeat. When that didn't seem likely to happen, she instead imagined it for herself. She saw herself with two children, one that she carried and one adopted from India.

She knew that was unusual, but she had never really felt much of a draw to normal family life. When your father is a mime, Methodist minister, and theater professor who wanders from Wisconsin to India to Tennessee, and your parents eventually divorce, you might find normalcy either a comforting draw or a dull repulsion. For Tess, it was the latter. Though she didn't know where she'd be and with whom—aside from these two kids she'd dreamed up—she had a hard time imagining a husband and a house in the suburbs. When as a precocious teenager she came out as lesbian, in part as a political declaration of female solidarity and strength, a normative heterosexual life appeared not just unappealing but impossible.

■ ■ ■

In 1997, Tess, then a triage nurse manager finishing her nurse-practitioner degree, took a trip to Greece as part of a mythology course she was taking. Sitting next to her was a man named Walter, a friend of the trip's leader. Somewhere over Kansas, as they were talking, Walter happened to ask Tess what her father did. Tess paused and gulped. For reasons that might be obvious, she dreaded the moment when she told people her father was a mime. Walter's reaction was different—no jokes, no sudden simulating of pretend walls in front of his face.

"Well, isn't that funny," he said. "My daughter's a mime. Jo."

Although Jo lived in Washington, DC, Walter wanted Tess to meet her, in part because of the miming coincidence and in part because he just really liked Tess.

A few months earlier, in the midst of a difficult breakup in Washington, DC, Jo had gone to a psychic. He'd told her a number of things, among them that she would meet someone new in the near future and that this someone would have red hair. The following Memorial Day, Jo went to San Diego to visit her father and his wife, who had a party, to which they invited Tess and her red hair. When Walter introduced them, Jo couldn't suppress a cringe. *Here we go*, she thought. *Another friend of dad's who wants to talk about miming.* By the end of the party, they were friends. Jo wasn't sure Tess was a lesbian, and she really didn't care; she liked her. A few months later, after some e-mail exchanges, she got a card from Tess. On the front, a 1950s comic-book girl says to a 1950s comic-book boy, "Don, I'm a lesbian," to which the boy replies, "That's great! We can go over lines together," to which she replies, "That's lesbian, not thespian." On the inside was a note from Tess saying she would be in DC in a couple of weeks. "You're the only other thespian lesbian I know," Tess scribbled. And so began a long-distance friendship, on its way to becoming a relationship.

Very early on, Tess told Jo that she was planning on having children. She was looking for someone who could be a partner with her in that endeavor, and she thought Jo might be the person. Jo was honored by the idea, and she was falling for Tess, so she went with it; and it was fun and exciting to fantasize about a life with Tess, in a sweet little house with a garden, with kids pitter-pattering.

They moved in together, into a sweet little house with a garden, and Tess quickly became serious about bringing children into the mix. When things started to get real, though, Jo began to get nervous. Jo, whose last breakup had made her skittish, just wanted to get used to being together. Also, though she spent a lot of time around kids—nieces and nephews, children in the classrooms where she taught movement theater—she had never intended to have any of her own. It was less that she disliked children than that she didn't like some parts of herself. She saw herself as flawed enough that she feared any child she might give birth to would be deformed. She worried that she simply wouldn't know what to do.

When Jo and Tess got a cat together, that itself was a lot for Jo. Nervousness turned into full-on fear. Jo hadn't had a pet since 1983, when her family dog died, and embracing another creature likely to die before her brought up her most primal fears. At three, her grandmother had told her that her mother would die if she kept working so hard, and Jo had taken that literally; she lived in constant fear of the death of those around her and with the irrational sense that she was responsible for the impossible task of keeping those deaths at bay. The thought of having children, of loving people so much while knowing they might die while she was still there, of being responsible for people whose endings she could neither predict nor control, was terrifying.

Jo wanted to help Tess realize what was clearly a lifelong dream, but at the same time, she kind of hoped Tess would forget about it. When the topic came up, Jo would fight the impulse to beg off and run errands, yet she was also convinced, despite Tess's protestations to the contrary, that if Tess had to choose between her and children, Jo would be on the losing end. Eventually, she simply decided to say yes. *I don't know the first thing about being a parent*, she told herself, *but Tess will know what to do.*

■ ■ ■

In the late 1990s, facing forty, Tess decided it was time to try to get pregnant, one way or another, even though she knew her odds weren't great. She was looking for sperm—she and Jo joked about the cute waiter at their favorite Thai place—but more than that, she was looking for collaborators. For a while, after Tess's parents had divorced, her mother had been a single parent, and Tess thought that looked way too hard and lonely. She resolved that she would not do that to herself. If she could, she would surround herself with parents, the more the merrier.

In particular, she wanted a man to be part of the endeavor. The children of some of the lesbians she knew seemed kind of disoriented around men. She didn't want to share legal rights with a father, but she and Jo did want father figures who were actual people, in the hope that men would not appear to them a bizarre, mysterious species.[1]

With Jo's agreement, Tess wrote Richard a long letter that said as much. She told him she would love for him to be the biological donor for her child and to have a father-ish role in their kid's life, and she asked what his thoughts and feelings were. He did not respond. Hurt as she was, she is not one to push too hard, and anyway silence was its own answer; he clearly wasn't ready. So she and Jo started to look around for other possibilities, half waiting for Richard to become ready.

A couple of years passed, and they could not wait any more. She asked her friend Michael, the recently divorced ex-boyfriend of a close friend, to brunch at a place called Hash House A Go-Go. They had met at the Buddhist Center, where Tess and Jo had been going for several years, steadily integrating Buddhist practices and beliefs into their lives. Michael comes from a family of North Dakotan spiritual seekers—mostly strong-minded Christians—and while he was ending his heterosexual marriage, he'd also begun a spiritual search. The ex-boyfriend had introduced him to the Buddhist Center and to Tess and Jo, and both the place and the people sat well with him. He, Jo, and Tess all had fathers who were interesting, good, and sometimes a bit flaky and wise mothers they worshiped. He and Tess were both scientists and hard workers, solid midwesterners, optimistic and pragmatic, who had become Buddhists.

Michael had always wanted to have kids, and for quite some time, the conditions had been there: he had been married to a soul mate, for nearly a decade, both of them with good jobs—he at Hewlett Packard, she at a university—and decent resources. His wife had been ambivalent about having kids, thinking she might regret not doing so yet not really wanting to either. He was certain about kids but ambivalent about heterosexuality. He'd thought, and hoped, that his feelings for men would go away, but at forty, he'd decided that was not a way to live. He'd embraced being gay and split up with his wife, painfully but amicably. He took with him the assumption he'd grown up with in Fargo in the 1970s: gay people don't have kids. As he mourned the loss of that dream, he'd sowed some wild oats and then had settled into a new relationship with a man fifteen years his junior named Joaquin.

"So, listen," Tess blurted to Michael over brunch. "I was wondering. Okay, I'm just going to say it. I was wondering if you'd consider being the father of our child?" It was clear from the outset that she wasn't just asking for a bucket of sperm but was instead asking him to make a major life decision about parenthood. By that time, they had a strong bond. Michael could not believe that the desire he'd finally let go of could be revived so effortlessly, over bacon and eggs.

"I'm in," Michael said quickly when he recovered from the shock. "I should probably talk to Joaquin, though."

Joaquin grew up in Tijuana, in a big, traditional Mexican Catholic family. There were no openly gay people in his family; the idea that gay people existed, let alone could become parents, was almost entirely unfamiliar. Across his childhood and over the many years in San Diego, where he'd moved at seventeen mostly to explore being gay, the thought of becoming a parent still hadn't crossed his mind. He had plenty of experience with kids—nephews, cousins, his own little brother—but simply never pictured himself raising any. He had been with Michael less than a year when Michael told him of Tess's proposal.

Still, perhaps because Joaquin has given so many new things a try and life had mostly rewarded him for it, he tends to meet new situations with a why-not shrug and a smile. What he hadn't ever considered an option suddenly was, and it seemed to him that this was his one and only chance to experience something like fatherhood.

"Let's do it," Joaquin said. "Let's give it a try."

Month after month, over more than two years, Michael provided semen—sometimes harvested with Joaquin's help—in a little cup, and the two of them would drive it over to Tess and Jo's place, where Jo would inseminate Tess using a syringe. Once, with all of them lost in the spirit of collective effort, Jo, surprising everyone including herself, even tried insemination. They had fun with it. Jo, then in film school, made a short movie in which Michael, playing a waiter, serves Tess and a Jo stand-in a cup of sperm to make a baby. They could show you a picture of the four of them, proudly holding a specimen cup with semen, gazing at it like a little newborn. It's yucky and sweet.

After a while, though, when all that kept happening was nothing at all, the pregnancy pursuit got less fun. Still, with each attempt, Tess, Jo, Michael, and Joaquin grew more and more serious about having a kid and more and more invested in one another. For years, they had been studying together weekly at the Buddhist Center, learning the Kadampa Buddhist tradition. Their shared Buddhist practice, combined with the monthly pregnancy attempts, had built attachments and trust between them. They had no model or handbook for making this kind of four coparent family, but somehow that didn't seem to matter much. They had come to believe that creating a family together was their karma— the intentional moral action in the present that affects both the future and the past.

The Dharma, the Buddhist teachings that they had studied, offered not just a philosophy—that life is painful; that the pain is caused by attachments to our desires and to worldly things; that we can eliminate suffering by following the Four Noble Truths—but also a set of practices to focus, clear, train, and concentrate the mind. They meditated to see life peacefully and clearly, to let go of the desires that were causing them pain, to accept the impermanence of life and the karma that followed them from previous lives. As the months passed without a pregnancy, they also did some Buddhist prayers together around fertility. They meditated, as their tradition's founder, Geshe Kelsang Gyatso, taught, on patience. Becoming parents had gone from an idea to a practical task to a prayer.

They only tried the fertility route for a hot minute. Tess took Clomid for a month and hated the way she felt. The fertility doctor told her with cheery confidence that he could certainly help her get pregnant. She'd just need to take this test, then that one, then that one and that one, and then they'd need to retrieve her eggs, fertilize them in the laboratory, and then introduce embryos back into her body. If that didn't work, they could find an egg donor, as he put it, "like you." He showed Tess and Jo charts and estimated the fees, which were in the tens of thousands of dollars. Tess looked at the doctor, then at Jo, then back at the doctor. She tilted her head, thinking about his assumption that what they wanted was to reproduce her genetics, which was never her thing. She imagined all the poking and prodding, the injections and hormones and ultra-sounds, which she might endure at great expense with no guaranteed outcome. She looked at the pictures of babies on the walls, almost all of them white and many of them twins or triplets.

What is this place? Tess thought, suddenly spinning in spiritual dis-orientation. *What am I doing here?*

"I'm not interested in any of this," she declared, rising. It had taken years, but it turned out to be an easy decision.

"I think we need to adopt a child," she said, turning to Jo.

The doctor said Tess hadn't gotten pregnant because of a fallopian-tube problem, but she knew something different, and it was suddenly clear, as if she'd put on glasses after a period of vision loss. She knew that it was because her children, their children, were born to other mothers. She suddenly felt more urgency than her biological clock had ever set off. *Jesus*, she thought. *They're there, and they are probably wondering where I am. Shit.*

■　■　■

If Tess and Jo were doing it now, they might easily have adopted a domestically born child, if they could. At the time, the thought made Tess too nervous. As a nurse, she had seen too many mothers give up a child for adoption and then change their minds, and the thought of going through that freaked her out.

Tess and Jo set quickly to work on international adoption, and as for many people, the wide range of different adoption rules quickly limited their choices. There was no country, including the U.S., that would accommodate an application from a lesbian couple planning on raising a child with a gay male couple, neither couple able to marry even if they wanted to, and with no legal ties between them, so Tess would have to adopt as a single parent. This already knocked off many possibilities. To adopt from Haiti, Tess would have to say she was Christian. To adopt from Russia, she'd have to sign an affidavit affirming her heterosexuality. They could lie. After all, although she was a Buddhist who had long ago left Christianity, her father was a Christian minister, and although she was a longtime lesbian, she still thought of herself as bisexual. Lying was neither Tess's nor Jo's top choice of a starting point for building a family, though. Guatemala and China were serious possibilities—and they had lesbian friends who'd adopted from those countries, before Guatemala shut down adoptions after corruption and baby-selling scandals[2]—but Tess kept feeling the childhood pull to India. Adoption had seemed like the right idea in principle, but in practice, it was beginning to seem to cut them off at every turn.

One evening, overwhelmed, having spent the day surrounded by sheaths of adoption information brochures and printouts, Tess sat to meditate in front of the shrine in her San Diego living room (cushion, incense, Buddha statuette). *I don't know*, she said in her head. *But then also, I really do know.* She clarified this to herself. She was certain there was a kid out there for her, but she had no idea where. So she asked the universe, *Please help me. Please guide me. Please guide me to my child.*

That night she dreamt of a tiny, beautiful baby in bright, colorful, striped clothing. The baby was being held by its mother, and just beside the mother was the baby's grandmother; and behind them, along a path heading up a mountain, was a whole village of people. They were handing the baby to her. She could not tell if they were happy or sad. The location—the mountains, the color, the clothing—looked familiar, like India but not quite. In her groggy, postdream state, she recognized the place: her child must be in Nepal. She opened her eyes and saw Jo looking at her.

"Nepal!" Tess said.

The next day, Tess contacted agencies that handled adoptions from Nepal. That she and Jo made their decision on the basis of a dream may sound absurd or like a comforting psychic invention, but Tess is not a person taken to self-delusion. She might willfully overlook other people's foibles out of kindness and conflict aversion, but she isn't very good at lying to herself. So that leaves this: either the dream was some sort of coincidence, or the universe really did answer her back. Either way, she wasn't about to ignore it.

■　■　■

When Tess and Jo asked Michael and Joaquin if they'd be dads to a future adoptive child from Nepal, the men were stunned and confused. They had figured their opportunity to parent had disappeared just as quickly as it had arrived. They'd tried to get pregnant, and it hadn't worked. They had each tucked the dream away again and gone on with their lives. But the move from insemination to adoption did not mean, for Tess, that the dads were out of the picture. The pursuit of a father had never been, for her, about the sperm.

Michael and Joaquin said yes without much thought or conversation. They were already aligned, their hearts already fully in it. Michael was deeply moved and, in a way, deeply relieved. He'd been concerned about the imbalance in a family in which two parents were biologically related to a child and the other two were not. This way, none of the family members would be biologically linked. *A baby is a baby is a baby*, Joaquin thought. When it turned out that Tess and Jo were zeroing in on Nepal, Joaquin was even more certain. It seemed right for a bunch of Buddhists to adopt from the place where—though most of the population now identifies as Hindu—Buddha was born.

Neither Michael nor Joaquin really expected to be part of the adoption decision-making process, and they weren't. Tess never imposed anything—she's a consensus builder who can't stomach the thought of pushing people around—but she had been the initiator of this family-making project and, with Jo on board, remained its forewoman. Tess did the vast majority of the voluminous adoption paperwork, while Jo collected supporting documents. Although Tess and Jo planned on becoming legal domestic partners and did so a few years after California law allowed it, the Nepali government only allowed single-parent adoption. Tess would be—still is today, in fact—the sole legal parent. (Jo began the process of second-parent adoption, which will give her legal parental status, in 2014.) All that the four of them had established up front was that Michael and Joaquin would have the girls at their house one night a week and that one other night each week they'd all have family dinner. That's it. Joaquin and Michael were written into Jo's and Tess's living wills as the custodial parents should both women die, but aside from that, they had no legal documents delineating rights and obligations while they were all living. That didn't seem to matter to any of them.

They considered trying to find one big house together, but at least some of them knew they would drive each other crazy in such close proximity. And that's probably true. You can have as many shared values as you want to, but it seems likely that the more parents you try to have in your family, the more difficult and complex things can become. Parents screw you up in one way or another, and becoming one almost inevitably brings that to the surface. That's hard enough with two parents, but try confronting invisible demons with four, all with their own communication habits, all of them coughing up, with varying levels of self-awareness, the gunk from their own upbringings. It's even harder if some of the parents are only going to be on duty part-time and feel only partly authorized to fully parent. No amount of shared history or shared values, not even Zen tranquility and wisdom, can take care of that.

Perhaps the newness of what they were doing protected Tess and the other three parents-to-be from worrying about such things, or maybe the fact that Tess was the de facto leader seemed to settle the question of what would happen in a dispute. In any case, their location on the edges of the institution of the family no doubt shaped the dynamics between the four of them, generating creativity, strain, excitement, and silences. Families with two parents of the same sex were just beginning to be recognized as culturally legitimate—it was several years before *Modern Family* ratified that notion on television—and they had every reason to assume that a four-parent family would be unfathomable to even many of their own friends. Legal recognition was then, and remains still, nearly nonexistent for multiparent families. Even as courts "have expanded their definitions of 'parent' to include more people and encompass adults parenting in less traditional families, including same-sex families and families created with the use of assisted reproductive technologies," the legal scholar Deborah Wald noted in 2007, "they have maintained the rigid idea that a child can have only two legal parents."[3] Under those conditions, the struggle is not simply to create a family against conventions but to create one that is recognizable to others as a family—and not, say, as a couple of moms and their kids' nice gay uncles.

In the absence of institutional structures that could recognize and regulate them, though, they were at least left to their own devices. They were liberated from scripted family roles and could even make up their own version of what constitutes a parent, despite the confusion this sometimes generated for others and even at times for themselves. They were also nudged by the existing structure, which required that they present the façade of single-parent adoption translated into legal reality, to centralize the family-making power, albeit in Tess's benevolent hands.

■ ■ ■

The agency that Tess and Jo chose said the adoption process would take from six weeks to six months. Tess sent the paperwork off in February 2003, and they waited. Tess made the grave error of joining an adoption listserv, where people who had entered adoption at the same time as her were giddily announcing the arrival of adopted children into their families. Her heart was slowly sinking. She figured they were being delayed, or rejected, because she was, on paper, a single mother. She could hardly respond to the delay by suddenly announcing that actually she was just one of four eager parents, including her girlfriend and their homosexual friends, awaiting the arrival of a child into a family whose structure most closely resembled, by design and from the get-go, that of a divorced couple and their second spouses.

The first time a social worker came to the house on behalf of the adoption agency, Jo and Tess put away pictures of their life together. Tess asked Jo to be somewhere else during the visit. The next time, they agreed that Jo would be introduced as Tess's roommate—an old-fashioned cover story, to be sure, but good enough. Jo, already stung by being absent on all the paperwork and frustrated by the waiting, did not like making herself invisible. She did it, but not without planting within herself seeds of resentment that could later sprout, despite her attempts to bury them. Hiding who you are in order to get what you know you deserve from a system that devalues you can have a subversive kick, but mostly it's alienating and exhausting. It throws toxin into what feels like a heart-opening process.

Tess developed her own antidotes. In the many months of waiting, Tess would go outside most nights and look up at the moon from their backyard in San Diego.

"Take my love to my baby," she said to the moon.

Once, Jo overheard this prayer.

"Can you please say 'our baby'?"

■　■　■

A year after Tess's dream, in February 2004, she got a call from the agency one morning at work.

"Go to your computer," said the woman on the phone. "I have your baby. Go look at the picture."

When Tess opened the picture, she swears to this day that what she saw was the baby from her dream. The voice on the phone, chattering about how Tess would need to leave for Nepal on Thursday, sounded distant. She had thought that the point of the dream was to guide her to her kid's country, but now she concluded it had been guiding her to this particular child. She forwarded the e-mail to Joaquin and Michael and called Jo to tell her they had a baby. Jo jumped in the car. When she arrived, she found Tess surrounded by excited coworkers, who had crowded around Tess's computer to ooh and ah at the baby photo. Jo joined the crying already in progress.

While Tess worked on trip planning, Jo focused on fixing up the house. They had already transformed a guest room into a baby's room, so Jo set about painting the dining room and then repainted it when the color wasn't quite right. She had a new heating system put in. She knew very little about Nepal, except that the Himalayas were there and the Buddha was born there, but she figured they'd need supplies. She bought soy milk, bottled water, snacks, and orange juice from Costco and packed them with kids' clothes and toys in a big suitcase for the trip to Nepal. She consulted with her doctor about possible food- and water-borne illnesses and shoved in bottles of antibiotics and lotions just in case of infections or scabies.

The closer they got to Nepal and the baby who was to make them a family, the less Tess, Jo, and Michael could openly display or talk about becoming a family. (Joaquin, a bit overwhelmed by the prospect and costs of traveling to Nepal, stayed home to get his and Michael's house ready for a baby.) They would have to inhabit the roles of tourists. Jo, who had decided that the trip might make a great film-school thesis project, the story of a pioneering four-parent family traveling to a far-off land to meet their baby, took the public role of photographer, friend of the mother-to-be—a far cry from coparent, but then that was what the situation required. She invited a good friend, a talented photographer named Jackson, to come along. At least that way, at least in private, she could experience becoming a mother, the thing that had once terrified her more than any other.

■ ■ ■

Nepal's political history had left it among the least developed and poorest countries in the world. Nepal, which sits in the Himalayas between China and India, was ruled by a series of dynasties until the eighteenth century, when it was unified under the rule of King Shah; his successors later battled for power with the Rana family, who for over a hundred years inherited from one another the role of prime minister. In 1950, the king, Mahendra, took over all political authority and declared the country a constitutional monarchy; within a decade, he'd banned political parties and dissolved the parliament. In 1972, King Mahendra had a heart attack on a hunting trip and died, and his son Birendra took over. Birendra ruled, as his father had, through *panchayats*, "rubber-stamp local and regional councils," a system he tried to maintain through the 1980s by having adversaries arrested;[4] it's safe to say he was not well liked by most Nepalese. Under pressure from a prodemocracy movement, King Birendra lifted the ban on political parties in 1991. A small Maoist guerrilla insurgency had gained strength by 2001, when the king's son killed his own mother, King Birendra, some other members of the royal family, and himself. Birendra's successor, King Gyanendra, quickly dismantled the government and cracked down on the Maoist insurgents, leading to fierce, violent conflict.[5] In 2006, the monarchy was dismantled and Nepal declared a democratic republic, but when Tess and her crew were flying to Nepal in search of their child, they were flying into a civil war with long, deep, tangled roots.

The other parents did not seem to be thinking too much about that— one of the privileges of Western status being, perhaps, a certain sense of distance and protection from the troubles of the Global South—but for Tess, the Nepali political struggles were inseparable from the way their family was coming into being. Without poverty and war, she thought, it seemed unlikely that their baby would be waiting for them there in

Nepal. What brought them and a Nepali baby together, at least in part, was their relative positions within a global stratification system in which the United States remained dominant, always a receiver and not a sender of adoptive children. *So be it*, Tess thought. She did not see herself as a virtuous child saver but as living out a decision made by the parents and the child—with larger forces, karmic and political, swirling around them—before this particular lifetime. She could face a bit of danger to get to her child. She was protected not just by relative privilege but by the certainty that she had always already known this child.

■ ■ ■

Once they arrived in Nepal, the reality quickly asserted itself. They arrived in a relatively calm period between the murder of an anti-Maoist leader and a series of antimonarchy rallies involving violent clashes with police and felt safe inside their hotel, but outside in the city, they were often on edge and sometimes fearful. Several general strikes shut down the whole city. One day, a bomb exploded in the commercial district. On other days, they did not leave the hotel compound. People wandered the streets with machine guns. Bodies were being ritually cremated at a cemetery by the river while sacred cows walked the streets. When they did go out, Jo was scared to cross the chaotic streets, in which the drivers appeared to use horns instead of brakes.

At least for Tess, some of their three-week trip to Kathmandu was like a spy flick. In order to adopt the baby and leave the country, Tess would first have to get documents from the U.S. embassy. She would have to do it alone, too; they had all agreed that Michael, Jo, Jackson, and their cameras would stay behind closed doors, lest they undermine the claim that Tess was a single mother-to-be. Tess had no idea how she was going to do this in the midst of a civil war or how she could get from the hotel to the embassy in a city in turmoil. Jackson, a gregarious sort, had made a friend on the plane ride from Bangkok to Kathmandu, when he'd sat next to a lovely Nepali man, a professional tour guide named Sanjay. He'd introduced Sanjay to the others and, maintaining the necessary pretense, explained that Tess was headed to Nepal to adopt her child and that he, Jo, and Michael were there to support her. Sanjay had offered to help in any way he could, so Tess now gave him a call and explained her predicament.

"Don't worry about it," Sanjay said. "I'll get you there." Tess protested that the risk would be too great to him, but he dismissed her.

Sanjay instructed her to cover up as much of her body as she could—her pale skin and freckles were a dangerous attention getter—and to meet him in front of the hotel. Tess rode through the city on the back of his motorcycle, only her eyes visible through her helmet, to the U.S. embassy. They zipped through the busy streets of the city on his motorcycle, its license plate covered. When they arrived at the embassy, he drove his motorcycle into the bushes, and Tess ran across to the embassy. It took her hours to get her documents. When she emerged, she thought, *Oh God, I'm here by myself. Now what?* Suddenly, out of the bushes popped Sanjay and his motorcycle; she hopped on the back, and they zipped back through town to the hotel. That was day one in Kathmandu.

On day two, documents in hand, Tess and Jo went to meet their child. Jo carried her cameras, passing easily as a supportive friend called along to film "the moment." The car ride to the orphanage took them through destitute neighborhoods and then landed them in front of a dilapidated former palace. Through the gates was a big yard, in which children were chasing after soccer balls and each other. Across the commotion of the children running amok, a Nepali man waved to Tess. She and Jo followed him to an office, where he made tea and chitchat, gave them a detailed history of the orphanage, and then called for a staff member to take them on a tour; they absorbed it politely, although Tess felt the urge to run through the hallways opening doors and screaming for the baby. Finally, as the tour was winding down, Jo spotted a woman waving to Tess. "Baby room, baby room," the woman called over the din. Tess and Jo followed her over to the baby room.

They watched as several *ayas*—nannies—fussed over a baby in the corner of the room, changing her clothes, then changing them again, trying to get her into the exact right clothes for the moment. Tess looked at Jo, pointed, and mouthed, *That's our baby*. The child was almost a year old, but she was tiny, about sixteen pounds, and still could not sit up by herself. When the women saw Tess, they picked up the baby, raised her over their heads, and chanted, "Sujita! Sujita Balika! Sujita!" The women handed the baby, finally, their chants subsiding, to Tess, while Jo snapped photos of the moment.

The name Sujita means "great conqueror." Tess and Jo worried that in the United States people would call her Sue, which would diminish the sense of being in the presence of a great conqueror. So they added Maia, meaning "love," ahead of the name: Maia Sujita.

"Oh, my God, we have a baby," Jo said to Tess back at the hotel. "This is my daughter," she whispered to herself, to see what it sounded like, a lump in her throat. She hadn't planned on being a mother, had feared it even. And here she was.

"What's that smell?" Jo asked Tess.

The baby reeked of something nasty but unidentifiable. After Tess took a bath with Maia, the stink was still there. A couple of days later, making use of a bit of social capital—Jo's sister, who worked for the State Department, had a close friend at the U.S. embassy in Nepal, who found them a pediatrician—they learned that the putrid smell was coming from a terrible ear infection. Tess gave Maia antibiotics, stuck her in a sling, and accepted Sanjay's offer to show her, Jo, and Michael the sights of Kathmandu. Two at a time, they climbed into a Buddha Air plane that took them over the Himalayas.

On the other days that the city was not shut down, while Jo and Michael took care of the baby in the hotel room, Tess went out on her own to complete her tasks, ticking off items on the list of government offices from which she needed to pick up or deliver a document—the Ministry of Women and Children, the Ministry of Family, this ministry, and that one. The more Tess rushed, the slower everyone seemed to move. At each stop, they wanted to sit with her and have tea. When she had to make photocopies of a document, she would find that there was just one copy machine in the building, which was under lock and key, which required filling out another form and waiting for hours for the copier. It was like a very warm and friendly obstacle course, and Tess had to watch herself lest her impatience turn her into a demanding, entitled, ethnocentric American.

On the way back from another day trip, Sanjay offered to take them all to the spot where Maia Sujita, a bundle on a police-station doorstep, was last seen by her birth parents. Jackson thought that was a great idea and wanted to take video.

"No," Tess said firmly. "I'm sorry, I just can't." She began to cry. She could not visit the exact location of another family's heartbreak, could not hold in her head the image of a lost baby, of a lost family, of the pain that launched the fulfillment of her own karma.

■ ■ ■

The orphanage did not have much information on Maia Sujita's first family. She had been left on the doorstep of a local police station, they said. No one knew why, but looking around at the poverty and turmoil, it wasn't difficult to imagine many things that might lead a person to such a despairing act. The police, as required by law, had posted announcements in the local papers showing the baby's picture, listing where and when she was found, and inviting anyone with information about the baby's family to come forward. No one did. The following year, Tess and Jo went to a Nepali monk in San Diego for a spiritual reading—he read rice the way some fortune-tellers read tea leaves—and Tess asked about Maia's family. Her mother, he told them, was Tamang and died young. Her father was Gurung. She was born, he said, on July 10 at eight at night in the mountains, though that was four months later than the date on her orphanage documents. That's as close as they came to knowing more and as much as they will ever know.

If they did know more, the baby's story could easily prove to be much uglier. A child left at a police station by a family wishing for her a better life—abandoned and thus orphaned—seems an innocent and sad tale, but the realities of international adoption in Nepal and elsewhere are much more complex, if no less sad. Technically speaking, all babies up for adoption in Nepal at that time had that same story of abandonment, since Nepalese law only allowed adoption if a child had been abandoned. According to the Schuster Institute for Investigative Journalism, though, until 2000, Nepal had only a few international adoptions because Nepalese children weren't typically abandoned but were passed along to extended family if their parents were in distress. In 2001, when "some international adoption agencies and facilitators discovered Nepal," international adoptions jumped from 8 in the year 2000 to 394 in 2006.[6] Quickly, it appeared, there was a suspicious increase in the discovery of the "healthy infants and toddlers that Westerners most wanted to adopt."[7] Concerns began to be raised—culminating in investigations both by the U.S. State Department and the government of Nepal, which for a period then shut down international adoptions—about "baby buying, fraud, coercion, or even kidnapping."[8]

Tess, Jo, Michael, and Joaquin knew none of this in 2004, but it is there now, part of the story of their family, a question mark that could not be erased even if they wanted it to be.

■   ■   ■

When Richard and I got married that summer, while Jo videotaped, Tess held baby Maia with one arm and a chuppah pole with the other. She didn't tell anyone, but even though she was in the thick of new parenthood—she called taking a quick shower "Mama's little vacation"— Tess knew then that she wasn't done having kids. She had known since she was a little girl that she was going to have two kids, and within months of Maia's arrival, she'd gotten the nagging sensation that she had another kid out there. She needed to talk to the other parents.

The messages from the universe she was picking up on were surprisingly specific: *Your second child is older. And a girl, most likely.* These messages from the universe dovetailed with the structures of adoption, too. For one thing, older children are in much lesser demand as adoptees, devalued in circumstances that already devalued them. Nepal also then had a rule that you could adopt two children but not of the same gender and not a second that was older than the first—probably to make sure people weren't just trying to adopt a nanny for their baby. If their kid was a girl and older, Tess reasoned, it made sense that she wasn't in Nepal but in India. *I know you're out there somewhere*, she said to the girl.

A few weeks later, she received an e-mail from the agency through which she'd been connected to Maia. She hadn't unsubscribed. In it was a picture of a fine-featured, petite five-year-old girl. "This child is available," the note said. "Her name is Priya. She lives in an orphanage in Mumbai, India." Although Priya was disarmingly pretty, the expression on her face was not really what you'd call sweet. It was more unapologetic and goading, as if to say, "What? Yeah, that's right, here I am. What?" Tess thought, *My God, I think that's my child.*

When Tess forwarded Jo, Michael, and Joaquin the e-mail with Priya's face and said she wanted to adopt this child, it threw them all for a loop. Jo was still in film school, she'd started a new job selling cars, and things with Maia were solid and getting easier. She just hadn't imagined another child, and nor had Michael or Joaquin; the family had just seemed to be settling into itself, the women adjusted to their nonstop parental duties and the men into their roles as what they sometimes called "weekend daddies." Many people they encountered didn't seem to be able to make sense of a four-parent family, but they had stopped bothering to care.

"We're just getting used to this child," Jo said. *I went this far in my evolution of self for you that we got this one child*, she thought. "Can we just leave it at that?"

"Yeah, can't we just enjoy this one?" Joaquin said.

That weekend, after Maia was asleep, the four parents held a family meeting on the deck of Michael and Joaquin's house. Tess made her case. This was a girl in India, a country that did not value and protect girls very well. With four parents focused on Maia, she could use a little diffusion of attention, and they all knew she'd love having a big sister. Most of all, Tess said, she just had a really strong feeling about it.

Jo fought it inside, but she saw the direction this was headed; and maybe it wouldn't be so bad. The dads knew that Tess's energy for being a parent would, as it had already, be forceful enough to carry them all through. They'd been through it all once before. They'd turned themselves into parents. They had the equipment. They were confident. They were older, with the resources to handle another kid.

"Sure, Tess," Michael and Joaquin said. "Let's do it."

"Let's do it," Jo said. Jo returned to the picture, again and again, until the girl became of a real person to her, not a symbol of another overwhelming responsibility and potential loss. The picture became Priya. Within a few weeks, Jo had recalibrated. Later, she said that she had tried to fight her karma but that her karma had prevailed.

When Tess mentioned the plan to Richard, he inadvertently activated Tess's somewhat buried concerns about adopting an older child.

"You just don't know what kind of damage has already been done," he'd said, in his signature style of loving pragmatism, which gives him a rare talent for saying precisely what people don't want to hear.

"Like what?" Tess had asked.

"Well, what if she smears feces all over the wall?" Tess doubted very much that this would be the case, but still.

■   ■   ■

Tess set aside her fears of shit smearing, called her contact at the adoption agency, and told her she wanted to adopt Priya. The woman was relieved. It turned out there was a family in Kansas, whose kids were all boys, that was interested, too. *She can't grow up in Kansas*, Tess thought, *the youngest of a family of boys, the dark girl in the white town, with her name changed to Faith or Tiffany*. Tess took it as another sign and started the paperwork.

For reasons no one still seems to be able to determine, it was two years and several months before Priya met her new family. In that time, Tess could not be in contact with her or be known to her; the risk of devastating a child, if the adoption did not pan out for any reason, was too strong. Priya was just a picture to Tess, Jo, Michael, and Joaquin—a strong concept and a constant presence but a snapshot of a girl—and they were nothing at all to Priya.

The agency had procured a few more pictures of Priya for Tess. Most days, while waiting for Priya, Maia, Jo, and Tess put the framed pictures in the breakfast nook so Priya could join them for the meal. Sometimes Maia put a plate of food in front of the photo. On evenings in the backyard, they'd send kisses up to the moon, instructing the moon to send them back down to India and onto Priya. In Hindi, Priya means "beloved."

Finally, in 2006, the adoption was cleared. Tess flew by herself to Mumbai, while Jo stayed with Maia. Tess landed at three a.m., slept at a hotel for a few hours, put on a sari, and took a taxi to the orphanage at seven that morning.

As the nineteen-year-old taxi driver stood nearby, Tess waited in the office. In bounced Priya, then eight years old, like a pixie just released from a spell. The office had always been off-limits to her, as it was to all the children, and she regarded it with excited disbelief. She ran her fingers along the table, touched each of the items on it. She bobbed over to Tess, looked up. Tess was terrified and overjoyed.

"Mama?" she said. It was a matter-of-fact question, spoken with the distance of a child who'd spent five years raised within an institution. Tess was relieved to be recognized. Once the adoption had been approved, she had sent pictures of herself, though not of Jo, Michael, and Joaquin, which of course would have risked undermining the adoption.

"Yes," she said in Priya's dialect, Marathi. "I love you." That pretty much exhausted her Marathi.

Priya nodded. She looked over at the taxi driver in the corner.

"Daddy?" she inquired.

Tess laughed. "No, no," she said. "Absolutely not." This child literally had not a clue of who her parents would turn out to be. In fact, the adoption structure—and, one might say, a heterosexist world more broadly—itself had made such confusions likely. There was no way for Tess to reveal ahead of time, or even in that moment, the family that awaited. The notion that Tess might be one of two mothers, let alone two mothers and two fathers, was not something the adoption bureaucracy or orphanage ever allowed to surface. No wonder Priya could imagine a forty-something white lady who spoke another language was adopting her with a nineteen-year-old Indian man.

■　■　■

They left Mumbai for New Delhi less than twenty-four hours after Tess's arrival. As a way to take care of Tess and Priya from afar, Jo had reserved a room at the fancy Oberoi Hotel. Tess had objected to the price and to a life of luxury in a site of extreme poverty, but what with the long plane ride and intensity of meeting Priya, she relaxed into it. Priya had no such ambivalence and took immediately to the place, delighted by the huge bed, the soft linens, the swimming pool, the little soaps. In Delhi, they went to get physical exams and documents from the embassy. Sipping tea with bureaucrats, Tess looked over at Priya, who smiled and looked back at her. Priya's expression reminded Tess of the first photo she'd ever seen of Priya. It said something like *I told you so.*

In between chores in Delhi, Tess took Priya to visit places she had known as a child when she'd lived there with her family. Tess had bought Priya sunglasses, and she wore them everywhere they went. That somehow both tickled and broke Tess's heart. Tess's emotions were jumbled and stewed: hazy memories of India as a child and the hazy feelings that went with them, mingled with sudden and uncontainable love for Priya, combined with the memories that they were already beginning to make; her past and present converging through this child, now the same age as she was when she first visited India, a stranger with whom she could barely communicate, and also her daughter.

Everywhere they went, they attracted attention, the pale Anglo woman walking beside the skinny, gorgeous Indian girl, in matching sunglasses. "I will protect you," Tess often said to Priya amid the crowds and hubbub, hoping that even though Priya didn't understand the language, she'd get the intention behind the words. When people started to approach, though, Priya would grab Tess's hand and wedge herself between Tess and the curious stranger. Priya seemed to be thinking that it was Tess who could use her protection, and that might have been so.

Priya spoke maybe three words of English. She had been removed from everything she had ever known and was bopping around town with a woman who didn't look a thing like her, with whom she could not speak, who claimed to be her mother. Sometimes, on those days and into the coming months, Priya would hold tight to Tess and sit across her lap like a baby. Sometimes, when she was scared, she would curl herself into a tight ball and sit, unmoving, behind a piece of furniture. Walking on the streets of Delhi, Tess thought this was probably the bravest person she had ever met.

■　■　■

Tess called the rest of the family from the hotel room in New Delhi. It was Joaquin's birthday, and they were all out at a restaurant, celebrating. Jo, Michael, Joaquin, and Maia each said hello and chattered at Priya in English. Priya stayed quiet, smiling and looking out the window at the city. Priya now had an inkling of who they were—Tess had shown her pictures and tried to explain—but Tess could see it was barely that.

Priya puked a lot on the plane ride from Delhi. They arrived in Los Angeles at the same time as five Yemini Air flights landed and had to wait several hours to get on their commuter flight to San Diego. While they waited, Tess tried to explain to Priya just who would be there to meet them. She showed Priya pictures of the family again.

"I'm Mama," she said, "and then there's Mommy. There's Daddy. There's Daddy. There's Sister." She went down the list of grandmas, grandpas, aunties, and uncles who couldn't wait to meet Priya. Priya absorbed the information with a combination of fantasy and flexibility. She smiled at the pictures of Maia but opted to believe, until face-to-face with the actual Maia, that she would be an only child.

Two full carloads of family members went to meet Priya and Tess at the airport. Some were related by law or biology, and others had been deputized by Tess, though nobody really spent much time distinguishing between those statuses. This was not a kinship world in which biology was more powerful a marker of family membership than choice; none of the members of the immediate family had any biological link, and the whole thing was created mostly on the fringes of family law. At the airport arrival area, the three other parents held a "Welcome, Priya!" banner with Grandma Betty and Aunt Amy—Richard's mother and sister, who had both moved to San Diego around the time Maia arrived—joined by Jo's father, Walter, and his wife, Maria. The only person Priya recognized was Maia, and she lit up when she saw her.

As they pulled out of the airport to head for home, Priya stuffed into the backseat of a Subaru with a bunch of strangers, Michael caught a glimpse of her as she looked out of the windows, her first glimpse of the United States from the ground. She was beaming, as though this was exactly what she'd been planning all along.

That night, the new sisters pushed together the beds that Jo had bought at Ikea. Priya stood in awe of the stuffed animals, toys, and clothes that she couldn't yet believe were really hers. Then the two girls took a bath together.

"So where is Priya going to live?" Maia, by then three years old, asked Tess and Jo. Priya had finally conked out on her new bed.

"Well, she's your sister, honey," Tess said. "She lives here with us now."

"Don't be silly," said Maia. An abstract, photo-in-a-frame sister is one thing, but sharing your toys and your parents is another thing altogether.

■　■　■

A couple of months after arriving in the States, Priya looked at her passport, which said "Priya No Last Name." She handed the passport to Tess with a sniff.

"I have a name, Mama," she said to Tess. She was quickly picking up English. Her tone was matter-of-fact and her eyes flinty. Her earlier life might have built this toughness in Priya, but it was hard to know, since there was almost no remaining trail to her past. All anyone knew was that Priya was relinquished in Pune into an orphanage where many of the children's mothers had been sex workers and then transferred to an orphanage in Mumbai.

"I have a name. My name is Priyanka Rai, and my mother's name is Kalpana Rai." *I must remember this*, Tess thought. *This is crucial information.* It made the needle in the haystack look just a bit bigger.

"Oh, I lived in a really big house with my mother and a whole bunch of kids, but I was the only one that was hers," Priya continued. "And my father was white." It's uncertain what, if any, of this is true. Sometimes she made mention of a "bad man." She also used to say she was from Nepal, had a big brother, and rode on a motorcycle. Kalpana Rai is also the name, it turns out, of an old Indian movie star. Within a year, Priya was unable to recall this conversation. The memories of memories had long since faded along with her Hindi, a language she had more or less refused to speak since her arrival in the United States.

Like her sister's, the gaps in Priya's story hold possibilities that—given the way closed international adoptions, in which the birth parents and adoptive parents are unknown to one another, operate—are as unsettling as they are unknowable. In 2003, India ratified the Hague Convention on the Protection of Children and Cooperation in Respect of Intercountry Adoption, which set international standards for international adoption. Still, like Nepal—not a Hague Convention signatory—the Indian international adoption system has been rattled by stories of "children kidnapped from Indian slums, sold to orphanages, and funneled into the global adoption stream,"[9] and high-profile "corruption and baby-trade" scandals.[10] Priya may not be a movie star's daughter, but there is no telling how she came to be in the orphanages in Pune and Mumbai and no denying the possibility of a bad man somewhere along the line.

Sometimes, even now, the girls say, "I wish I could meet my mother." Tess is undisturbed, though she still has to take a breath. She is not one of those who would suppress the fact that they have other mothers. She doesn't point out that biology does not necessarily a parent make, which she knows they already know, or try to compete with the ghosts of mothers past. It's a moment of sadness for all of them, an acknowledgment of a loss made all the more sad because its details are imperceptible.

"I wish I could meet her, too," Tess usually says. "I wish I could thank her. I wish she could see you, because you are so beautiful and so wonderful. Your mother and father would be so happy with who you are. They would be so happy to see you." And also, "I wish I had been able to hold you up when you were a tiny baby and feed you and kiss you and love you up."

Tess also has a mother who has died and yet is still very present. She knows. And so she says, "I have a mom who died. You have a mom who died. Now this is our family." And she hugs her children to her.

■   ■   ■

On Priya's first Father's Day in her new family, Michael was out of town on business. The girls got up early and made Joaquin breakfast in the kitchen of their dads' place. He decided to take them to church, even though the kids thought it made no sense for a secular Buddhist to insist on taking his kids to Catholic Mass. At church, he was stirred by the rituals of his childhood. Priya put her arm around him. Joaquin saw himself in Priya: like her, he had grown up in a different country, with very limited resources, no running water, no electricity or indoor plumbing, speaking a different language. Still, he never expected her to call him Dad. She'd already had parents, wherever they might be.

"You know I love you, Priya," Joaquin whispered. "I'm so happy that you're my daughter." He was having an epiphany or maybe a flashback to a past life. *I know why she is here with me. I know why I am here with her.* It wasn't a reason. It was a knowing.

"Don't cry, Daddy," Priya said. "You're going to make me cry." Priya did not like to cry, at least not in front of others. Joaquin's breath caught in his throat, as it had the first time Maia had called him Daddy.

After church, Joaquin took the girls down to the San Diego harbor for a bit of air.

"Go pick a flower from somewhere," Joaquin told the girls.

"I feel like a thief," Priya said, but Joaquin assured her that taking one flower from someone's garden would be okay.

Joaquin walked the girls over to the water. He had an urge.

"I have this thought in my head," he said to his daughters by the waterside. "I want to honor your birth fathers. Both of them must have prayed for you guys to be cared for when they were no longer there. I think their prayers were heard, because you guys are in our lives and you're being loved and cared for, and I'm really happy and joyful for that." He paused and pointed to their flowers. "The whole world is connected by water, so somehow we might all be connected. Throw your flower in the water, for your fathers."

■ ■ ■

In some ways, the absences in the children's stories have come as a relief to all of the parents sometimes and to some of them all the time. The silences have freed the girls to create stories about their origins that were likely to be much less painful than what they would remember if they could. But they also risked erasures, as if their stories only really began when they left their birthplace. There was nothing you can do but refuse to erase the past that makes the present story possible, even if it is a series of nearly blank pages. There are other silences, too, chosen ones, just as there are in any family's story: the power struggles between couples and individuals, the everyday vulnerabilities and resentments, that making a family, especially a new kind of family, elicits.[11]

Some nights at the weekly family dinner, Tess looks around the table and imagines herself floating above them and looking down. This is her family, such as it is. In some ways, surrounded by three other parents, she still feels like the single mother she swore she'd never be; she also knows she is not. They found their children, both of them, and these children found their adults; and here they are, a somewhat motley crew. It is an unlikely family—not easily imagined, not like many others—with its own rhythms of normalcy.

The parents often speak of their children as their karma. It is tempting to see that as a means of negating the power differences between nations and between parents in which their family is rooted. But it really isn't that or at least not mainly that. It is a philosophy of acceptance of what is and of positive action in response. The spiritual explanation doesn't so much erase power relations—though okay, really, it can divert your attention away from them—as answers them with loving action.

Here is what Maia and Priya's parents tell them: our stories all began before we were here, and now we are a family. We were brought together by love. Each one of us is different, and we all come from different places. We came from where we came from. We can't change the past; it is what it is. Every action, every karma, is like a seed; it bears its fruit, the *vipaka*. All we can do is make positive actions. Those actions are called love. That love is what led us to each other. It is what holds us together.

Also, Mama was not going to take no for an answer.

MY NEW KENTUCKY BABY

Richard and I conceived our second child in a booth at the Cache Creek Casino buffet, although that probably sounds more impulsive and risqué than it actually was. When we were getting ready to welcome Reba, Richard and I had agreed that we would leave open the question of whether we would have another child. One of us was already then becoming a biological parent, so we agreed that when the time came, if the other one really wanted that same chance, his desire would carry extra weight. We tend to work like that, negotiating even far in advance, even with something unpredictable and momentous, even with something that doesn't lend itself to weighted voting, to make sure that neither of us gets what the other one might also want.

We had taken Reba, then about two, with Richard's mother as a babysitter, to the casino, and they were asleep in the hotel room. Richard and I were taking a break from the slot machines to scarf down a smorgasbord meal. Somehow, conversation turned to the question of another child. We'd written up the pros and cons before—I'd begun as a definite no but was trying to be a decent fellow—and we tossed it around again. What a relief it was not to have an infant, to have a bit of our selves back, and also how sad to no longer have a baby. Reba was thriving, but we also suspected that a second child would dilute the attention she'd been getting in a healthy way. We had gotten a late start on being parents, which meant it would be best to quit before we were too decrepit and also that Reba needed a companion for the big part of her life that could be left after we were gone. We couldn't possibly afford the process again, but then again money is just money. We were already in parenting for an inch, so we could just as easily be in it for a mile.

By the end of dessert, we agreed to try to have another child. Maybe it was the way casinos distort your sense of money's value or maybe the way love pushes you to set yourself aside or maybe the power of bread pudding, Richard's favorite dessert. Maybe the one who had no biological progeny played his trump card. In any case, we agreed to try and then dashed back to the slots.

How to implement this scheme was the big question. We had given Tamar right of first refusal. Much as she had appreciated the Reba experience, the memories of gestational diabetes, thirty-seven hours of labor, a C-section, and the detachment process, along with the simple fact of aging, led her to decline. The odds of another friend offering to carry a baby for us seemed at best slim. The process with Reba had been beautiful and majestic but also emotionally complex and exhausting: the weird combination of guilt and gratitude toward Tamar and Andy and the egg donor, Jane; the intense period of group marriage and then the abrupt, painful separation; the ambiguous boundaries of familial relationships; the practical hassles of organizing such an elaborate production, including the medical and legal maneuverings. The thought of doing that again, while parenting a preschooler, just when we were beginning to get some sleep, was overwhelming. So when Richard and I discussed the possibility of market-based surrogacy, it brought both of us a surprising sense of relief. Hiring an agency to help set us up with paid strangers, working with an egg donor and gestational surrogate to whom we had no past relationship, now seemed not so much unsettling, cold, and overly mercantile as sensible, clear, and clean.

Still, when I looked into surrogacy agencies that had specialties in same-sex family building, I found myself again uncomfortable with the glossy brochures and high fees, which themselves reminded me that our way of becoming parents was really only available to us because we had the earning capacity, borrowing power, and family financial support to afford it. When I looked at the profiles of egg donors on various websites, I still could not feel a connection to any of them. "They're all smiley and young and blue-eyed," I complained to Richard. They seemed lovely, but in an Up with People way that I can't bring myself to fully embrace. Where were the black women with attitude and the neurotic Jews or, better yet, the Jewish women with attitude and the neurotic African American women?

Thankfully, we knew some of those. So we asked a close friend—a woman with a very sweet, deep, ongoing attachment to Reba who'd known her since birth and sung her to sleep—if she'd consider providing eggs for our next child. She said she'd give it some thought.

■　■　■

We'd avoided some of the more troubling aspects of market-based reproduction when we'd had Reba. Although egg and womb were "outsourced," they belonged to women with whom we had long pasts and strong connections. Although our own class advantages made the venture possible for us, the class differences between those of us involved were almost nonexistent. We were able to operate as a self-regulating team, confronting or making use of legal, medical, and financial systems rather than having our intimate relationships generated and managed by them.

With our decision to enter the fertility industry more fully with child number two, we would have a much harder time avoiding the unsettling facets of commercially assisted reproduction. We would likely wind up with an agency that saw us as body parts, with little concern for the full people housing them. I knew this already, from conversations with our friends Doug and Eric, who'd had twins through the most famous agency serving same-sex couples, Growing Generations. I bought a book about assisted reproduction in which Doug and Eric were featured. The common separation between "traditional surrogacy" (with a woman carrying a baby made from her own egg) and "gestational surrogacy" (with a woman carrying a baby made from someone else's egg), the journalist Liza Mundy explained in *Everything Conceivable*, was to lessen the chances of a successful legal claim to motherhood from the surrogates, to decrease the bonding between the "carriers" and the fetuses they carried, and to increase the pool of potential surrogates.[1] The head of Growing Generations put it this way: "It's a lot easier to divide those two bodies."[2] Dr. Vicken Sahakian, a fertility doctor who worked regularly with Growing Generations, among others, expanded the point:

> If you're looking at beauty or physical features you're not going to find that in the surrogate pool. It's a fact. Most surrogates I come across are not typical donor caliber as far as looks, physical features, or education. Most egg donors are smart young girls doing it for the money to pay for college. Most surrogates are—you know, they need the money; they're at home, with four kids—of a lower socioeconomic class.[3]

Ick, I thought. We had no apologies about our desires to conceive our own child, to approximate what our own genes would look like if mixed together, and to have sisters who looked like sisters. But could I really stomach—and pay into—a system in which people found dividing women's bodies "easy" and glibly separated them into pretty, smart girls with the class qualifications to contribute to the gene pool and poor, homely homemakers whose class qualified them only to be paid vessels?

Where I was uneasy, Richard was grateful: grateful for the science that made it possible for us to reproduce biologically, grateful for the possibility that others might help, grateful that we had the means to make it happen, even if that meant home equity loans and mortgages and credit cards. For him, it was about participating in ontogeny and phylogeny, about continuing a bloodline; until men could get pregnant, this was as close as people like us were going to get, and it was nothing short of amazing. My concerns about class privilege smacked of class privilege, and he met them with what you might call an invisible eye roll.

Poking around online, I thought maybe I'd found a way to balance my politics with the goal of baby making: a small agency in Massachusetts, run by an openly gay lawyer, which presented itself as a different kind of operation. "We think long-term and encourage building meaningful relationships that will continue to exist throughout the life of the child," said the Rainbow Surrogacy[4] website. The agency's "relationship-focused approach" seemed to view surrogates as people rather than as means-to-an-end containers and to encourage rather than cut off bonding between the women carrying children, the people who intended to parent those kids, and the kids themselves. Richard liked the idea of Massachusetts, thinking that maybe we'd have a better chance of another birth there, where we had already once established legal parentage. Rainbow Surrogacy was cheaper than some of its competitors, too.

We met with the agency's president and one of his colleagues a few weeks later at the Fairmont Hotel in San Francisco, where they were attending a conference. The president wore a smart suit, northeastern manner, and round-rimmed glasses. He told us that some other agencies—by which I assumed he meant his main competitor, Growing Generations—do not like the surrogates and the clients to have too much contact, and monitor any contact they do have, for fear that they will become too bonded. He did not get that, he said. At Rainbow, they believed contact should be encouraged, since making a baby together can and should be an intimate bonding experience. My political anxieties about commercialized reproduction were quieted, and I left the meeting relieved that I could have my baby and my politics, too.

That desire was strong enough that at first I could hardly see any evidence that punctured it. The first Rainbow e-mail to us, in early 2008, announced that the president of the agency is "one half of a gay couple and the proud dad to two boys through traditional surrogacy" and then mentioned that the agency's fees had just increased, but if we signed on by the end of the month, we'd be under the previous fee structure. A twenty-one-page contract was attached. The contract referred to one of us as the "Adopting Father" and the other as the "Natural Father" and required us to cover the "Carrier's" legal fees, insurance, medical costs, and a mental health professional for up to two months after the birth. It insisted that we not agree in writing to allow the carrier or egg donor visitation or breast-feeding ("breast pumping is ok"), not attempt to find a carrier on our own or have a physical relationship with the carrier ("including not sleeping with, offering to sleep with or having any form of sexual relations with the Carrier"), not engage in unsafe sexual activity until "confirmation of pregnancy," and allow the agency to "monitor the relationship" between us and the carrier. Violating these terms would mean sacrificing the initial agency fee.

I read all of that, chalked it up to legalese, reminded myself of the meeting at the Fairmont, and rationalized that one couple opting out of commercialized reproduction would make no dent in that commercial system. Plus, we already knew how long this could all take, and we weren't getting any younger. So we rustled up the money, taking and borrowing from my parents, pulling from our retirement funds, signing up for new credit cards. We prepared to apply for a home equity line. We forked over the $11,500 "agency fee," along with $6,500 for legal, social worker, office, and "coordination" fees and signed on. And those were just the "initial" fees.

Paperwork and e-mails flooded our way. There was the Timing of Payments notice, the lengthy Explanation of the Matching Process, the Parenting Questionnaire, and the separate Father's Questionnaire. We had to send them our wills, choose a plan for purchasing insurance for a surrogate, and look for a psychologist to evaluate us. The social worker wanted to talk to us, and then her successor did, and then hers did. The case manager, and then her successor, offered to answer any questions we might have. We had many.

▪ ▪ ▪

In March, as I was resignedly narrowing the pool of people-person egg donors, we got a call from the friend we'd asked to consider egg donation.

She'd decided, after serious and careful deliberation, that she couldn't do it; among other things, she was concerned that in order to keep her non-familial relationship to a future child clear, she'd need to distance herself from our children and us. That's not something she wanted to do. She said we might get a call from a mutual friend, Chloe, from whom she'd sought counsel while thinking it all through. Sure enough, that very evening, Chloe, who was finishing a Ph.D. in environmental economics and had a son a few months younger than Reba, called and said she wanted to get together.

She came to our house a couple of nights later and offered us her eggs.

"Are you fucking kidding me?" I said, recalling the brochures at the fertility clinic that handled Reba's creation. "A doctoral donor! Do you know how much your eggs are worth on the open market?" Chloe laughed.

Richard asked her if she would feel weird knowing that her son had a genetic sibling, and she a genetic child, living nearby.

"That's not how I think about it at all," she said, in the direct, self-possessed, and no-nonsense manner I'd often admired. "An egg is made up of some cells. I am offering you some of my cells. Very special cells, but that's it. Of course, I'd want to know and love any child that comes of this. But that's not my child."

Chloe came to the table with her thoughts fully formed and a decision made. She had at first been mad at us for not adopting, what with all the kids who needed parents, but had already worked that through; she'd asked herself why she reserved this anger for us and not for herself, realized the answer had to do with unexamined heterosexual privilege, and the anger had dissipated. She figured she had pretty good genes and might as well share them. She'd consulted an obstetrician who had used IVF herself and discussed egg donation with her husband, her mother, and our mutual friend. Her biggest fear was that the child would later come to her insisting that she was its mother, but she confronted that fear with a Zen-like shrugging off of control: she would allow the story to unfold however it needed to.

Chloe's own life had prepared her well for the decoupling of biology and parenting. Her biological father had been abusive, and she had been raised by her biological mother and a stepfather who was somewhat checked out of parenting. This experience had long since led her to reject the idea that the people whose sperm and egg made a baby were necessarily parents and to embrace the idea that families are fluid entities. Both the men who had claimed to be her father were pretty screwed up, and here were two fathers whom she already knew to be conscious parents. It seemed to her like a chance to fix something broken in her universe. She was, as she put it the first night we spoke of it, "complete with it."

Richard and I could not believe our luck—or, rather, the kindness of our friends. I don't even recall deliberating about the offer before accepting.

Chloe knows her own mind, and it is a sharp one. Dr. Szymanski, our go-to local fertility doctor, made the mistake at their first meeting of offering unsolicited information about her uterus and her hormones and told her that if she wanted to have another child, she should get pregnant right away. He seemed to see not so much people as body parts. Chloe was not pleased. To the doctor, the process was one of physiological maneuverings—indeed, that no-nonsense, results-oriented approach was exactly what appealed to Richard. To Chloe, the physical process of making a child was simply the final step in a spiritual one, where things we cannot see and cannot understand transpire, where, she was certain, the spirit of our child was saying, "This is my place in the world." She was willing to put up with the shots, probes, anesthesia, and condescension in order to be, as she put it, "an instrument of love."

The night Chloe came to offer us her eggs, Richard had dreamt that we already had a second baby and had woken up laughing. The dream baby looked and talked exactly like the old-timey movie and television star Jimmy Durante.

■   ■   ■

A few weeks later, I received an e-mail from a Rainbow social worker named Katherine. "We have found a potential carrier that we think will be a great match for you two! Gail is a thirty-five-year-old single mother of three children, living in Kentucky. She is very excited about helping a couple to create a family as wonderful as hers. She has a very strong support network in Kentucky and feels ready to embark on this journey with the support of her mother, siblings, and close friends." She attached Gail's profile and a few photos. Gail, pale with shoulder-length light-brown hair, smiled alone and then with a baby and then with a baby and an eight-year-old boy. She liked "reading, playing games, spending time with family, going to movies and concerts, doing crafts, swimming, many outside sports, and of course shopping." She was of German descent, a high school graduate, and a widow. Her father was an alcoholic. "I have a really easy pregnancy and I love being a mom but for some people they aren't able to get pregnant so easily," she wrote. "I think if someone wants to be a parent then why shouldn't I help them when it's so easy for me. My family is complete and it wouldn't be my baby. I'd just be carrying it for someone else. It would be my job to protect it until it's born and then they can protect it." She listed her base fee as $20,000. She'd found the agency through a Google search.

Another Rainbow staff member had expanded on Gail's profile, on the basis of a phone conversation. She grew up in Indiana and "recalled having a good time with her friends in her small town where they would play hide and seek and outdoor activities such as baseball in the neighborhood." Her parents divorced when she was eight, and her mother remarried when Gail was twelve and then divorced again. Her stepfather molested her two sisters during postdivorce visitations, and when they told their mother, she pressed charges and he served time. Both her father and stepfather had since died, and Gail remained close with her mother and sisters. She met her husband when she was eighteen and had her first child the next year. They married a few years later.

Gail's husband was diagnosed with cancer shortly after they married. Before Gail's husband started treatments for his cancer, they froze some of his sperm. They didn't want their daughter to be an only child, and the doctors said the drugs could make him sterile. Gail's husband died when she was twenty-three. Her second child was conceived from that sperm.

Several years later, dating another man, she became pregnant again, but that man, the social worker's write-up said, "is not involved in her life as he did not wish to be a father and had not been in touch." She'd told her two older children about surrogacy, and they "are excited about the process and think it is an honorable thing for their mother to do." She hoped "to create and hopefully continue a friendship" with the intended parents but figured she'd talk to them and see how it went. She sounded much like the "average surrogate" described by Liza Mundy: "[she] tends to have children of her own; to value family deeply; to have begun her own family at a young age; to enjoy easy pregnancies; to live in a conservative, heartland-type community; and yet to be a bit of a nonconformist, an individualist who enjoys tilting at the status quo."[5]

Notwithstanding Katherine's enthusiastic exclamation points, there was nothing in particular that made Gail a "great match" for us beyond the fact that she had completed a form and we had completed a form. She was in a state whose laws were unsympathetic to surrogacy and hostile to same-sex relationship recognition. As it turned out, no one at the agency knew much of anything about Gail beyond her profile and the single phone interview, and it later became clear that they had no intentions of ever meeting her. Still, however careless the matching process, there she was: a woman in Kentucky who would consider carrying our child, who wanted a friendship, a tilter at the status quo who had herself used a form of assisted reproduction.

We talked to Gail on the phone the next week. She was nervous and giggling. We mostly made small talk about kids and movies. Toward the end, I asked her what she thought it would be like to carry a child that she wasn't going to raise.

"It's kind of like a babysitting job," she said, giggling. "I figure I'd be babysitting your baby for nine months." I reckoned it might be more emotionally complicated than that, but I liked that. She would be our fetus sitter.

We flew Gail out to meet us in person. She had never flown before, and no one at Rainbow had thought to walk her through the details of the process. She didn't tell us at the time, but she had been petrified— not of the actual flying but of all the unfamiliar parts of the process. She didn't know that there would be a security line or what she would need to do in that line or how to check her luggage and where and how to pick it up later. She didn't realize how long it would take to park at the Nashville airport, and she missed her flight. She laughed about it later when I picked her up, but inside she was overwhelmed and already missing her children.

Within a few hours, Gail had lost much of her nervousness. She was funny and fun loving. I thought maybe that was part of the appeal for her, besides the money and the "why shouldn't I help?" motivation: a taste for something new, different, bigger, and weirder than her everyday life in Bowling Green. We introduced her to Chloe, and they seemed to appreciate each other. By the end of the trip, we'd all agreed to try to have a baby together.

Gail had very little experience with gay people—she knew not one gay man in Kentucky—and she described a lot of people, including her own mother, as "kind of old-fashioned"; but the fact that we were two men didn't faze her at all. Her daughter Nicky, who actually had a gay friend, was positively lit up by the idea. She told everyone at school, with pride and maybe a bit of teenage defiance, that her mother was going to carry a baby for two guys. Gail's middle child, a boy, had been skeptical, though not because we were two men.

"You're not going to have to bring the baby home, are you?" he asked. Sandwiched between a teenaged sister and a baby one, he had no interest in another sibling.

Gail's sisters were not surprised to hear about her plans.

"That sounds like you," they said.

■ ■ ■

The agency, despite the sales pitch, did little to facilitate a relationship between Gail and us, aside from taking over financial transactions. We fought with them over nearly everything, even as staff members disappeared and new ones—young, enthusiastic, rarely up to speed—popped up in their places. The agency wanted Gail's emotional support to come from a long-distance phone relationship, at a fee of $3,000, with a social worker who was authorized by signed waiver to report to the agency if "there is any threat to the health of the surrogate, if there is any threat to the health of the child, or if the surrogate is thinking of changing her mind." We insisted that she have access to face-to-face support by a mental health professional in her own locale, whose sole loyalty would be to her. The psychiatrist the agency required us to see assured us that was the standard of care according to the American Society for Reproductive Medicine.

"We believe our success in having the highest success rate in surrogacy and having every surrogate relinquish the child is in large part due to [the outside social worker's] extraordinary ability to provide support over the phone and to build a relationship of trust and understanding with the surrogates," the agency's president wrote to us in an e-mail. He offered the example of a surrogate who "developed intra partum depression taking a whole box of Tylenol, trying to kill herself when she was six months pregnant." The social worker had "jumped to the rescue": "She got in touch with a psychiatrist, who prescribed the one type of antidepressant that was not dangerous for the baby and we jointly (and nicely) threatened the surrogate with a locked institution if she didn't take her medication every day and show up for every consultation with the psychiatrist we set up. She did both, and delivered a healthy child three months later." He told another cautionary tale of a surrogate who changed her mind about "releasing" the baby inside her, revealing this in a "chat room for unhappy surrogates," some of whom were part of the social worker's "remarkable cadre of loyal surrogates." They reported her disclosure to the social worker, who reported it to the agency, and through an "incredible intervention, the surrogate agreed to release the child." He suggested that while a local therapist might be "by the book," it would "compromise the surrogacy" and could cost much more. "I fear greatly," he said, "that we will lose control."

I was not comforted. To him, this was a goal-oriented business transaction; to me, it was an intimate process. And this was not an environment that was exactly conducive to feminist values.

To the agency, Gail was a service provider, and not one who could opt out once she opted in; to me, she was a person who, much as I hoped she would carry our baby, should remain in control of her own body and destiny. The notion that threats, cadres of chat-room tattlers, and incredible interventions would build trust and understanding seemed unlikely; the notion that all that mattered was the "rescue," "control," the "relinquishing" of a healthy baby, and a high agency "success rate" seemed to undermine claims that Gail herself was a priority.

We would have to work on trust and intimacy on our own.

■　■　■

It made the most sense to do the egg donation and fertilization in California—logistically, financially, legally—and on each of Gail's subsequent trips, we all relaxed around one another. We were all regulars at the Alta Bates fertility clinic, where Gail, Richard, the doctor, and a nurse, Patty, who seemed as invested in our baby as we were, would cram into a tiny laboratory room and wait for the tall, skinny, eastern-European-accented embryologist to present the needle that might contain our future child. On Gail's three visits, we took her to see the sights: the grand foyer of San Francisco City Hall, the crooked Lombard Street, the DeYoung Museum, the TV-famous Painted Ladies in San Francisco, the Golden Gate Bridge. She stayed at a bed-and-breakfast and then at a Marriott; she had never stayed at a hotel before. We were there when Gail's children touched an ocean for the first time in their lives.

When the first embryo transfer didn't take, Richard and I were disappointed but not surprised. We had already ridden this roller coaster. When the second one didn't take, the doctor adjusted Gail's medications, and we adjusted our expectations. For what we thought would be the third and final pregnancy attempt, we invited Gail to bring her kids, and we took them and Reba on a road trip to Monterey. Chloe and her family were, coincidentally, staying in a house in nearby Carmel Valley, celebrating the visits of two of Chloe's brothers from Israel, and invited us for dinner. We drove up a long, winding road to the house. The dinner was raucous and fun, freed up by the knowledge that this constellation of people would never be together again—Kentuckians, Jerusalemites, Oaklanders—and by the serendipity.

Our relationship with Gail was comfortable but also strange: inherently familial but also most likely short-term; starting and to some degree set to end with a market transaction but also somehow much more; at once superficial and deep. It was a bit like a friendship you might make on a train ride or stuck in an elevator or on jury duty—we chose each other, but we were also tossed together by circumstances rather than some sort of organic affinity. We had very little in common beyond our common goal, and we knew our paths would never have otherwise crossed. She was, after all, a single, small-town mother with limited income and high school education, being paid by two highly educated, citified men, a doctor and a professor, to conceive and carry a child whose oocyte was provided by a woman finishing her doctorate. Gail once told me that she wanted to take the money from the surrogacy, quit her job at the amusement park / campground, and become a home health aide.

We had managed to produce the exact arrangement from which I had sought to dissociate myself—a "doctoral donor," a working-class gestational surrogate with a high school education, and a for-profit surrogacy agency—but somehow it was more complicated on the inside than it had looked from the outside. Not surprisingly, at the center of our relationship with Gail, both unspoken and glaring, were our class backgrounds and differences. They brought us together and also kept us apart. Of course, there was the very fact that Gail was essentially in our employ, using her body and its reproductive capacities to make money. Bighearted as she was, if she had more resources for herself and her family, she probably wouldn't have chosen to carry other people's kid, especially not some strangers'. She later told me that she had been shocked that we chose her—though in our minds, she was choosing us—given that she was not college educated. She saw herself as less desirable because of her social class.

The impact of social class was also more subtle and unspoken. There was, for instance, the sudden experience of entering another class culture and its various new but no doubt previously imagined pleasures. What must it have been like to be flown, your first time on an airplane, like a businesswoman on her way to an important meeting; to sleep, all expenses paid, alone in a hotel room, after so many years of kids, overtime, and shared spaces; to drink freshly squeezed orange juice and order lattes, like a lady who lunches? And, from our side, there was the pleasure of "giving" someone a first-time experience—of ocean, of fresh-squeezed juice, of everyday life in a yuppie-ish neighborhood—made possible by different class locations. Some of that was probably simply a self-satisfied reminder of what we had that others did not, a sort of status self-flattery. But it was also warmer than that and nicer than noblesse oblige, in which privilege obligates generosity. Because we were meeting across class, we had the gratification of seeing someone do and have some things that weren't open to her before because of social class. For Richard, who grew up not so differently from Gail, it seemed to trigger memories of his own move out of one class and into another, and treating Gail to things seemed like an outstretched arm. For me, it was a weird mix of discomfort and relief, paying for the removal of class barricades and seeing our class culture through the eyes of a visitor to it who, for all of her excitement and gratitude, seemed pretty eager to return to her own comfort zone.

Like many unconventional family-formation arrangements, ours also brought into being its own temporary web of power with its own un-

usual dynamics. It involved, for one, something of a short-term, local-
ized reversal of power. If Gail's relatively disempowered position on a
class hierarchy got her there in the first place, once on the team, she
gained considerable power. We had financial and social power afforded
by our class, gender, and professional statuses, but we were also aware of
our own vulnerability and the costs of alienating Gail. Even our generosity had an edge of self-interest. She could, despite contracts and agency
threats, torpedo the whole endeavor at any point. She could dictate
terms to us if she wanted or just quit. Gail didn't have that in her, and
years as a worker on the margins made it unlikely she'd suddenly turn
into an entitled boss; but the potential itself must have been novel and
heady.

Oddly, for a relationship with so many unusual components—the
crossing of lines of class, sexuality, race, and ethnicity; the project of
creating a baby that Gail would not raise—the friendship seemed to rest
on our embrace of conventional gender and class roles. We took on the
role of benevolent class guides, exposing Gail to new experiences that
she absorbed like a game-show winner on an all-expenses-paid trip to
a foreign land, delighted and certain that she would never return. As a
single working mom, she spent most of her days taking care of others,
and although on her visits she missed her kids terribly, Gail also enjoyed being taken care of. We were also like doting husbands, helping
her with her luggage, checking her into her bed-and-breakfast, whisking
her off on sightseeing outings, picking up the bill, and relieving her of
the anxieties that come with navigating unfamiliar worlds. She was, she
said later, relieved that we knew what to do. We were her guys.

We could have let the relationship be purely transactional and medical, which in some ways would have been much easier. We could have
treated Gail like an employee, and she could have treated us like clients.
None of us seemed to consider that possibility. Some of that, no doubt,
was discomfort with treating the making of life as if it involved no more
relational intimacy than you find at Burger King. We were also driven,
I think, by the love of a future child, who deserved a story in which

we watched out for each other, in which we did things together on our way to making her, not just doctor visits but trips that made memories together, to places she would later see, a story in which we touched the ocean together with our toes.

■ ■ ■

In October 2008, Richard and I took Reba to Nevada to campaign for Barack Obama for president. We plucked Reba away from her day-care provider, Madeline, who was having a goiter removed that weekend. Until a few weeks before, Reba had gone to Madeline—known to pretty much everyone as Granny—five days a week. Granny combined the strictness and heart of a traditional African American matriarch with a mischievous sense of humor. She had never had a same-sex couple in her brood, but when we'd come to her, she'd quietly taken herself to a workshop on alternative families. Madeline had told us, despite our protestations and in no uncertain terms, that we ought to have a second child.

When we arrived in Reno, we got a call from Madeline's daughter saying that after the surgery Madeline had a bleed that had not been tended to in time and had been without oxygen for an extended period of time. She had not yet woken up. When she was still not conscious the next day, we turned around and drove back to Oakland and straight to the hospital. After a calm, professional conversation with the neurologist, who suggested that there was little hope if Madeline didn't wake up within twenty-four hours, Richard threw himself on Granny, crying to her to wake up, wake up, wake up.

Granny's whole family was in the hospital over the next few days, as it became increasingly clear that she had lost oxygen for too long after her surgery and was not going to revive. The family dealt with their grief with loud conversations and waiting-room picnics. They were shushed a lot by hospital staff. We visited daily.

When Madeline was still on a respirator, Richard and I told the family that if we had a baby, and if it were a girl, we would name it after her.

"You're going to name your baby Granny?" one of Madeline's daughters said.

Madeline died later that week, and we will never fully recover.

■ ■ ■

After three attempts to get pregnant, we ran out of eggs. We had already decided that if that last transfer didn't work, we would throw in the towel. Chloe, though, told Richard she did not believe it was over and that she was willing to try again one more time after the semester ended. She had been to a psychic who'd told her a pregnancy would happen the "second time."

"There is going to be a child," she said.

Chloe did not go easily into this decision, but she was firm in it. The first time had not been fun. Indeed, she had recently taken a "medicine journey"—hallucinogenic mushrooms under a therapist's supervision—in which she experienced egg donation from the perspective of her ovaries. On that journey, she had no idea who she was or where she was, but she felt her body being invaded: some alien was going in and taking parts, and she was petrified. A voice told her that she had agreed to do the invasion. *What? I let someone do that?* said her dream voice. *Why would I do that?* Then the words "Josh and Richard" began repeating, like a chant. *Who the hell are Josh and Richard?* she thought. Then the word "love" came into her head, and she remembered: *Oh, that's right. I allowed someone to go into my body and take parts of me so that there's going to be more love in the world.*

We figured we could squeeze one more embryo transfer onto our credit cards. We wound up with four viable embryos. The doctor suggested that this time we might consider being more aggressive, transferring all four rather than two. We decided to go for it. We booked a flight for Gail.

The embryos were transferred on January 20, 2009. Hopeful signs were all around. It was Gail's birthday and also Inauguration Day. We went from the lab directly to Reba's preschool to watch, on a grainy old TV borrowed from the church upstairs, the swearing in of Barack Obama.

Later that week, the news broke that Nadya "Octomom" Suleman had given birth to octuplets conceived through IVF with an unusually large number of transferred embryos. *Oh fuck*, I thought. *We could be the Octodads.* When we got the call that Gail was pregnant, the first thing we checked was the numbers, which to our great relief suggested just one fetus.

■　■　■

Unlike Tamar, Gail's approach to pregnancy was unworried and unde-tailed. She had done it before, and it didn't seem to require much extra attention beyond going to checkups. She would work, as she had with her own kids, until the day before giving birth—if she didn't, she could easily be replaced at her job. She was nearly impossible to reach, and we went slightly crazy wondering what might be going on with the pregnancy. On the rare occasions that someone from the agency spoke to Gail, we'd get a sunny, exclamation-point-ridden, information-thin e-mail from a caseworker in Boston.

Richard and I both certainly felt the call to micromanage the pregnancy—Richard was briefly unhinged when after an insemination Gail walked a mile and a half down Telegraph Avenue to Taco Bell (too much walking! Taco Bell?)—but backed away, partly because of our vul-nerability to Gail and partly out of respect for her. I couldn't allow myself to be that guy who, by virtue of class, gender, education, and the nudg-ing of a commercial reproduction industry, treated Gail's body as mine to control and myself as more competent than she. I reminded myself that she'd already been pregnant a number of times, had carried three healthy babies, and obviously knew what she was doing.

Gail, she told me later, had read to the fetus and talked to her. "It's Nanny Gail," she would tell her. "I'm babysitting you until your daddies can meet you." Once she began showing, coworkers and strangers in grocery stores had started making comments and asking questions, until eventually she explained the situation.

"How can you do that?" people would ask. "You're carrying it. You're feeling it kick. Its heart is beating inside you." Gail was patient with them. "She's not mine," she would say. "They trust me to take care of her. It's not my baby." For Gail, this was just common sense, and she claims to never once have considered the baby her own.

"But how can you leave that hospital without that baby in your arms?" people would ask. *Because it would be kidnapping*, Gail would think, *and I wouldn't want somebody kidnapping my kids*. She'd smile her placid smile and say, "I know it's going with parents that love it. They're her parents." *And I will get to sleep all night*, she would think.

In the meantime, the monthly checks for the surrogacy lightened up her everyday life. They were larger than her monthly paycheck from work. She used them to live beyond necessities. She took her kids out to dinner and to the movies and later bought her daughter a car.

Before our trip to Bowling Green for the twenty-week ultrasound, Gail called us in a panic. She had an unfamiliar pain, and the doctors had diagnosed, by sonogram, a placental abruption, in which the placenta had separated from the uterus—which in the worst case would be life threatening for the carrier and the fetus. Richard and I were also panicked. We had put a good woman at risk. Our baby might be dying, in Kentucky, without its family. In addition to devastating loss of life, we could be facing financial ruin. We'd purchased simple pregnancy insurance but nothing covering catastrophic events requiring lengthy intensive care.

The Rainbow Surrogacy staff, none of whom had ever laid eyes on Gail, were little help. Over the course of the pregnancy, they had seemed unable to determine whether Gail had been going to her medical appointments, whether she had any prenatal screenings, and if so, what the results had been. Richard called an ex-girlfriend, an obstetrician, who told him that this did not sound like a placental abruption and that neither intensive care nor bankruptcy seemed likely. We flew to Kentucky and accompanied Gail to her next ultrasound. The radiologist reported that there had been a confusion of terminology—what they were trained to call an abruption other doctors knew as subchorionic hemorrhage, a much less serious condition. Everything was fine.

Also, it's a girl.

We received short periodic updates from Gail every few weeks. In July, she reported that "little Maddy" liked to kick at night, so she was up in the middle of the night with her legs hurting. Richard asked if she needed anything.

"Yeah, more sleep lol," she wrote. "Maddy and me are doing good. Are you getting all the shopping done for Maddy? I feel huge already but I know bellies gonna be alot bigger by the end. People at work are joking with me that I'm going to have to get bigger work shirts cause Maddy is really filling out mine but I keep saying no these will work til the park closes then I can wear my own clothes lol. Well, gotta go hope your all doing good tell Reba I said Hi!"

That was about it. It really was like having a babysitter for our fetus.

▪ ▪ ▪

If we'd dodged medical and financial disasters—unless you counted the massive credit card debt we were rapidly amassing—we still had to contend with the law. The surrogacy agency had recommended that we pursue second-parent adoption, in which a nonbiological parent adopts after the baby's birth, but neither of us liked the idea of adopting our own child. We hired a lawyer to pursue a prebirth order in California designating us as the parents, as we had done in Massachusetts.

In our attorney's petition on our behalf to the Alameda County Family Court, she cited California Supreme Court cases that had "expanded the concept of a (natural) parent . . . to include a person who intentionally causes the birth of a child through the use of reproductive technology," and that had established the legal approach of looking "to the parties' intentions" to determine parental rights. She noted that it was the intention of all involved, including Gail and the egg donor, that Gail carry our child as a surrogate and that all of us believed that we, "the Petitioners," were equally parents to the child Gail was carrying. If the court didn't enter a judgment in our favor, she argued, Gail "could be forced to take parental responsibility and be named as the 'mother' on the child's birth certificate by hospital staff, despite the fact that she has no genetic connection to the child and has never intended to raise the child." This would violate California law, on top of being unfair to everyone, including the child. This particular court had to take action, she said, since "California Family Code Section 7620 provides that an action shall be brought in the county in which the child resides," which is determined by the residence of its parents, which everyone involved intended to be us.

It was not lost on me that our lawyer also emphasized the normative markers of stability: we had "resided together in a primary, family relationship for approximately ten years," "own a home together, were married in Massachusetts," had one kid already, and are a professor and a doctor. Ozzie and Harry. It wasn't her legal argument—after all, we'd presumably also have the right to be parents if we were unmarried renters or a waiter and window cleaner who'd just met—but I guess she figured a dose of normativity couldn't hurt.

Three weeks before the baby was due, after many forms and fees, we were legally deemed her parents by the Alameda County court. A couple of days later, Richard and Reba flew to Bowling Green, Kentucky. Reba, then three, called it Green Bowls. I would join them a week later, when I could get away from work. My parents made plans to pop over from an event they were attending at their alma mater, Antioch College, in Ohio, and Richard's mother, Betty, booked a flight from San Diego.

■ ■ ■

I was not keen on an extended stay in Kentucky, which I figured would be full of homophobia, guns, and fatty foods and maybe not so safe for a biracial man, a Jew, and their black-Jewish daughter. Richard's reports from the scene had not dissuaded me. He and Reba were staying at a Hampton Inn on a strip of chain motels and chain restaurants and eating at Cracker Barrel and Red Lobster.

Richard had gone with Gail to meet the obstetrician when she was already three centimeters dilated and brought with him the court order and the Surrogacy Delivery Plan our lawyer had written up for the hospital staff. It spelled out everything that would typically be taken for granted in a hospital birth: who the parents are, who should be in the delivery room, whose insurance should be used, who should be invited to cut the umbilical cord, into whose room the baby should be delivered for care and feeding, whose names should be on the birth certificate, who should sign discharge papers. It requested a private room for Gail. It offered tips on terminology and sensitivity, such as avoiding the term "mother" or "mom" to refer to the surrogate ("she does not consider herself a parent to the baby that she is carrying") and not confusing this situation with an adoption ("the emotional and logistical details of surrogacy are not at all similar").

The doctor, pale skinned and dark haired, turned quickly hostile. He claimed to be caught off guard by the presentation of legal documents. Richard had called several times to request an earlier meeting, but the doctor had not returned his calls because, he now told Richard, it would be a violation of the Health Insurance Portability and Accountability Act (HIPAA) to talk to him about Gail's case—although Richard pointed out that Gail had authorized such conversations. The doctor flatly rejected Richard's claim to being the baby's parent.

Richard was unflappable during the meeting, insisting that the doctor seek legal and medical counsel so that he could be an effective doctor for Gail and for our baby. Alone with Gail after the meeting, though, Richard wept. To have what had been such a concerted team effort in California now become such a battle in Kentucky, to have such a significant life event be tainted by disrespect—another white man talking down to him, another straight man denying his relevance, not even a speck of professional courtesy—was crushing. He felt suddenly vulnerable and threatened. Gail comforted him as best she could. At the next checkup, the doctor was more cordial, although he did not shake Richard's hand. He scheduled labor to be induced on what later turned out to be a day he would be on vacation.

Richard distracted himself and Reba with the available attractions nearby: Dinosaur World, the Corvette Museum, and the Mammoth Caves. When we were all assembled in Bowling Green, we got rooms for us and the grandparents at a Hyatt, and Reba ran back and forth between them and played in the pool. A friend whose twins had refused her breast milk—she'd pumped and frozen bags and bags for them, in case they changed their little minds—had saved it for us. I had shipped it to the hotel and arranged for it to be stored in their walk-in freezer next to vats of ice cream.

Halloween had been coming up, and Reba and her best friend had announced that they both wanted to be Dorothy. We and the friend's parents had been trying to divvy up the rest of the *Wizard of Oz* characters among ourselves but then decided we should all be Dorothys. Richard got costumes at Walmart—one little, two plus size—and we three Dorothys dashed down the Hyatt hallway and sang "Over the Rainbow" to my parents.

■　■　■

Our California lawyer had been working with a Kentucky lawyer, whose job would be to present the court order to the local family court, requesting that the judge order that the hospital and the Department of Vital Records abide by the California judgment. His first contact had not been encouraging.

"One thing the hospital's attorney mentioned to me," he wrote to us a few days before the due date, "is for everyone to, of course, remember that Gail (and the baby) is their patient, not either one of you, and while they will certainly attempt to accommodate you, whatever Gail says goes as far as the hospital is concerned." Our California lawyer politely explained to the Kentucky lawyer that he was exactly missing the point.

Not long after my arrival, while Richard and I were in a matinee of *Zombieland*, our lawyer called. Richard dipped out of the theater and was gone for a long enough time that I knew it couldn't be good news. The local family court had declined to even review the California court order, leaving things in legal limbo. Our lawyer said she would threaten to sue Kentucky for violating the Full Faith and Credit Clause of the Constitution and instructed us to get out of there as soon as the baby was born.

I felt vaguely unsafe and out of sorts. People seemed to stare at us. One night, I dreamt that the baby was born healthy and then abducted. Richard dreamt of an alien invasion of earth.

A few days later, while Reba ate bad hospital lasagna with my parents and Richard's mom, we were in the delivery room with Gail and her mother. The obstetrician on call was not especially chatty, but she had a comforting air of competence. The nurse assisting approached the event as business as usual, giving Gail instructions in a tone indicating that noncompliance was not an option, with a hint of compassion for our unusual situation. We were allowed to stand behind Gail and her mother, Joanne.

I was teary eyed and oblivious. Richard, however, knew that the baby was in distress. It turned out that Gail had a cervical lip—a portion of undilated cervix blocking the baby—and the baby's heart rate was decelerating. Every time the doctor tried to manipulate Gail's cervix, she moaned in pain; Joanne held her hand.

Richard ducked out and called his little sister, Amy, who had been a labor-and-delivery nurse.

"Don't let them fuck it up," Amy said.

The doctor was giving it one last try before considering an emergency C-section, and suddenly she looked up at us.

"What color hair were you hoping for?" she said, with an edge of relief. There would be no need for a C-section.

"Hair?" I said. Reba had been bald for two years. "She has hair?"

Madeleine Blanche emerged at noon with a full head of black hair, long eyelashes, and her tongue sticking out. Richard cut the umbilical cord. The baby cried just as she was meant to and was whisked off to the maternity ward as the new-baby song—"Brahms's Lullaby," I think it was—played over the hospital PA system.

When all was calm again, we said good-bye to Gail and her mother. It had been a painful delivery until the epidural had kicked in, and after Maddy was born, Gail had to push out the placenta, which had gotten stuck; she later said it was like having another little baby. The drugs, exhaustion, and relief had clearly overtaken her. She mumbled a goofy "see y'all later," already drifting off into what was to be a twenty-hour slumber.

We went off to a room in the maternity ward to be regularly awakened by a hungry baby, who took quickly to the breast milk I had pulled from the Hyatt freezer that morning.

Our presence at the Bowling Green medical center seemed to send the staff of women into southern-hospitality overdrive. They dispensed diapers, advice, and coffee cake. We chatted about four-year-olds, work, and the costs of preschool. A nurse named Kristy brought a button for Reba that said, "I'm a big sister!" Unfamiliar heads popped in and out, sometimes with some excuse to check on us, sometimes without. Not homophobia but a kind of homocurious buzz was swirling around us, turning us into objects of gossip but also of generosity and attention. Anxieties about discrimination were one thing, but my assumptions about homophobia now seemed glib and snobbish.

The problem was getting out of there the next day. One sympathetic young clerk had been instructed by hospital lawyers not to put our names down on the birth forms as parents, but Gail had refused to sign anything that gave her legal or financial responsibility for our baby, insisting that she was not the mother. The clerk tried the form with just a father's name, but the computer spit it back, saying it required a mother. So she sent the forms, along with a copy of the California court order, to the Kentucky Office of Vital Statistics with neither father nor mother listed. Her small act of administrative disobedience was, to me, touching. The hospital, not knowing what else to do, released us and our legally parentless baby.

On our way out, we went to visit Gail, who had finally woken up. She was dressed and out of bed. She looked refreshed and ready to get back to her post-fetus-sitting life. She'd called to get help from Richard, since the hospital staff was asking her to wait to be released until, they said, "our lawyers get back to us." Gail knew Richard would know how to address this.

"You're not refusing to release this patient, are you?" he asked a blank-looking administrator. "Unless she is on a psychiatric hold, you cannot detain her against her will. Get her a wheelchair, please. Now." Minutes later, a wheelchair arrived.

We chatted with Gail, her mother, and her teenaged daughter about Madeleine and exchanged a few small gifts. Gail held Maddy for a minute. We kept to light chitchat and laughter, but beneath it, I felt something heftier. We had been brought together by an industry of commercial reproduction, itself dependent on the inequalities of class and status that distanced us from one another, and we had maneuvered through subtle dynamics of power between us. We were neither strangers nor people whose closeness would extend much beyond holiday cards. Yet there was no denying the intimacy of the occasion: here, being passed from person to person, was a new human we had all been part of making.

At the Nashville airport the next day, the Southwest Airlines agent refused to allow us to fly with the three-day-old baby without a note from her pediatrician. "I'm her doctor," Richard said. I watched him dig around for his medical license and then scribble something on a piece of paper. When we boarded the plane, with only a release document from the hospital to identify Madeleine, going home with our children felt like some sort of escape attempt.

■ ■ ■

In January, when Madeleine Blanche was a few months old, we traveled to Boston for my nephew's bar mitzvah. We still had no birth certificate.

We took the opportunity to arrange two blessing ceremonies in my parents' hotel room at the Newton Marriott. Richard is a Rev.-James-

Cleveland-gospel-music-loving spiritual atheist, and I'm an agnostic Jew, but we both believe in the power of ritual, especially if conducted by people we love. First, my father's sister, Mary, a devoted Wiccan known to us as Mimi, led a ceremony she'd designed that combined pagan traditions she knew and ones she'd found online. "By the earth that is her body, by the air that is her breath, by the fire of her bright spirit, by the waters of her living womb, we cast a circle," Mimi spoke, as my parents, Richard, Reba, and I circled the baby three times. She called on Gaia and Pan; she solicited blessings from the North, South, East, and West and from each of us.

Richard blessed Maddy with health and love. I touched her nose and then her mouth. "May you smell beautiful aromas," I said, "and taste beautiful things." My father blessed her with humor. My mother blessed her with something to believe in and also with the hope that the hair on the back of her head, rubbed off from her constant lying-down position, would grow back in.

"I hope we will be friends forever," Reba said, while bouncing on the bed.

"The circle is now open but unbroken," Mimi recited. "Merry meet, merry part, and merry meet again. Blessed be!"

Later that morning, our friend Margot, who was starting rabbinical school, led a Jewish ceremony for the baby—*brit banot*, in Hebrew—in which the girl would be blessed, washed, and given a Hebrew name, Miriam Batya. We began by singing "This Little Light of Mine," then one of Reba's favorite songs, as we passed the baby, wrapped in her cousins' prayer shawls, from person to person. The Torah, Margot told us, relates that three strangers appeared one day at Abraham and Sarah's tent, and as a sign of hospitality the couple offered them water and washed their feet. According to the *midrash*, the rabbinic interpretations of the Torah, because of this eager welcome of strangers, God provided the Israelites with special waters from the well of Miriam, which quenched their thirst, physical and spiritual, on their journey from slavery to freedom. "In the Torah," Margot said, "water is the only substance that preexisted all of creation. It is the substance from which all life is thought to have begun."

As we washed the baby's feet, Margot turned to Reba. "Reba, by participating in this ritual, you are also taking on the very special job of becoming a big sister," she said. "This means that you agree to watch out for your sister, to protect her, to play with her, to teach her everything you know, and to be her friend. It also means you get to wear the big-sister boa. Are you ready to take on that job?" As Reba nodded, Margot placed a pink boa around her neck.

Margot invited us to say a bit about the women for whom Maddy was named. Richard talked about her first namesake, Madeline Knox, and how Reba would not be who she was without her and how much we wished that she had been able to meet and help raise Maddy. I talked about her second namesake, my father's mother, Blanche, with help from Mimi and my father. Blanche Weintraub Gamson drank black coffee, smoked cigarettes, and had a deep voice and a flair for the dramatic. As a child, she would tell people she was born on the Fourth of July, although her birthday was actually the fifth. She wore black to my parents' wedding. She had been an actress in the 1920s, once appearing in a Broadway ingénue role opposite Humphrey Bogart, and sat at the periphery of the Algonquin Round Table. She quit to marry my grandfather—her second husband—and have a family. "Joshie," she used to say to me when I'd caught the acting bug in elementary school. "once an actor, always a sonofabitch."

Margot told the stories behind Maddy's Hebrew names. Miriam hid her baby brother Moses by the side of the Nile to evade the Pharaoh's order that newborn Hebrew boys be killed. As she watched, the Pharaoh's daughter, Batya, discovered the infant and adopted him. Miriam then suggested that Batya take on a wet nurse for her child and recommended Yocheved, her own mother. As a result, Moses was not only saved but nursed by his own mother, who taught him his background as a Hebrew. Miriam: clever girl, rebellious, refusing to be set aside. And musical, too. Miriam, it is told, composed a brief victory song after Pharaoh's army was drowned in the Red Sea, the first instance of music in the Bible. Batya: she who saves the cast-aside.

"In her names and identities," Margot said, "she embodies harmonious contradictions—both the one who casts off and the one who receives, the spirits of two strong women who were seemingly on different sides yet invested in the same cause. I also want to acknowledge the particular significance that Madeleine is being blessed and named today while she is still without a birth certificate that reflects who her family is. The strength and defiance her names represent will serve her well."

Margot filled a cup, *kos Miriam*, and we each drank from it. "May you be blessed to find Miriam's well whenever you need it," we repeated, "and may its never-ending blessings sustain you on your journey."

■   ■   ■

Our lawyer had drafted a letter, to be signed by the heads of the National Center for Lesbian Rights, for the Kentucky lawyer to take with him to a meeting with the Kentucky Department of Vital Statistics, the agency charged with legally recording births and deaths. The letter cited cases (*Finstuen v. Crutcher, Adar v. Smith*, and on and on) in which the Full Faith and Credit Clause was applied by courts, and it threatened court action if Kentucky refused to recognize the California court order. The U.S. Constitution, our lawyer wrote to the Kentucky officials, "does not permit states to pick and choose which judgments from other states they will honor." The implication was that the agency's recalcitrance had to do with the fact that we were two men. It did seem likely that had we been a heterosexual couple with such a court order, we would have left the hospital with documents listing us as legal parents.

Back and forth it went, with conversations and e-mails between our lawyer and a cast of characters including the general counsel of the Kentucky Department of Vital Statistics and the nominee for U.S. attorney for the Eastern District of Kentucky. In the end, the problem for Kentucky officials turned out to be much duller than antipathy for gay people. They didn't believe that California had jurisdiction to determine the parentage of a child born in Kentucky. Kentucky officials were wary of setting precedents in how to handle interstate surrogacies—especially since surrogacy was legally and socially controversial there. Since there was no federal surrogacy law to guide them, the various parties were dealing with the complexities of interstate surrogacy law by, as our lawyer put it, "frankly making it up as we go along."

Kentucky officials mentioned as evidence that they were not discriminating against us on the basis of sexual orientation that if we were adopting, there would be no problem accepting our legal parentage. The next week, calling what Richard and I thought was a bluff, our lawyer returned to them with an amended order from the court in Oakland, stating that under California law, a judgment of parentage is the "functional equivalent" of an adoption. Jurisdictional feathers smoothed, the Vital Statistics office issued a birth certificate saying that Gail was the mother, then sealed it—making it inaccessible to public review—and issued an amended one.

One Tuesday in March, the official birth certificate arrived. Somehow, with all the lawyering and money that preceded it, I was surprised that it was just a piece of paper. Looking more closely, I saw that, although the California judge had directed Kentucky to list Richard or me as mother and the other as father, Kentucky officials had refused. Instead they labeled us "parent" and "parent." Kentucky had out-liberaled California.

We picked up Reba from preschool. She was uninterested in the news but happy for the celebratory dinner, through which our five-months-old baby slept, big eyelashes fluttering.

■　■　■

I didn't see Gail again until several years later. She had since carried a baby for a woman she knew from work and her husband, who were unable to conceive. Her sister and niece were interested in becoming surrogates. Her eldest daughter, who now also had a daughter of her own, had just signed up with a surrogacy agency, too.

"I really didn't have a desire to go to college," she told me over coffee at Starbucks. "The main thing was I wanted to be a mom. That's all I ever wanted to be. You always hear how you're put on earth to do something, and I kind of thought maybe that would be something great to contribute to this world is to help someone else. If someone asks what's the greatest things I ever did, of course, have my own kids and to help two couples have a baby. That's the best things in the world I've ever done."

I was suspicious of the relief it brought me to hear that. I believed her, though. I asked her how she thought of her relationship to Maddy, who was four years old by then but whom Gail had really only just met and who had taken to calling her Gaily.

"I always picture myself being an old woman and her coming to visit me, like me having an eightieth birthday party and her being there," Gail said. "And she'll be like, 'This is the one that carried me.'" That does not even seem far-fetched.

QUEER CONCEPTIONS

A couple of years after Chloe donated the eggs that helped beget Maddy, she went through an amicable divorce from her husband. Before long, she started to show up at events with a new girlfriend, Dee. They moved in together, opened a coffee shop in Berkeley, and announced that they would be getting married at midnight on the 2014 spring equinox.

They'd rented a house in Marin for the weekend and set up tables in the large dining room. At the table with Richard and me were the contractor who had done the work for Dee and Chloe's coffee shop and his wife and another couple who introduced themselves as Min and Max. Min was small with Asian features and wearing a sharp suit. Max had hair dyed pink and an open, easy manner.

"Is that a man or a woman?" Reba, then eight, whispered to me, looking across the table at Min. It was neither an unreasonable nor a weighted question. Reba was weaned on the idea that gender is something some people change and most people play around with, rather than a fixed and stable characteristic. She had evidence to back that up. Dee, who has a friendly, midwestern, rugby-player style about her, was standing nearby in a tuxedo; Reba has known boys who enjoy wearing dresses, and no one makes a big deal out of it. She's seen the pictures from my drag birthday party.

"I'm not sure," I said, shrugging. "Maybe a mix. Be patient and I'm sure they'll let us know." That satisfied Reba. She returned to buttering her dinner roll while Richard and I began small talking with our tablemates.

After the wedding toasts, Max and Min had their own special clink of glasses.

"Our adoption was just finalized," Max explained. Their son, Aiden, she said, who was almost eight months old, was at home with his first-ever babysitter. We began the usual swap of sleep-deprivation and sleep-training stories. Richard talked medical-system stuff with Min, who was a health care consultant, and I talked academic-world stuff with Max, who taught art at a local university. They complimented the adorableness of our daughters and showed us pictures of their baby, whose adorableness we also affirmed. Over the din of the wedding party, we began to trade family origin stories.

■　■　■

The question of family came up very early for Min and Max. They had gotten together fast and furiously, joking along the way that they were simply following the lesbian handbook. After they met—also at a lesbian wedding weekend, this one in Santa Fe in the fall of 2008—they talked on the phone and online daily for weeks, and then Max stopped dating other people and Min broke off the relationship he was in, and then Min came to visit Max in San Francisco for Halloween and then again for Thanksgiving, and finally, just after Christmas, they rented a U-Haul and moved Min from Santa Fe into Max's San Francisco apartment. In the midst of getting to know and testing each other, they agreed that they wanted to have a family, which raised the stakes even higher.

Like many couples who adopt a child, Max and Min's route to making a family was a circuitous one that did not begin with adoption. Yet you might say that adoption was, for them, somewhat overdetermined. Even as a high schooler in small-town Florida, Max had imagined she'd be a mother, though she didn't think that much about how. As she got older, she never really developed a yen for pregnancy and childbirth, and by the time she was really ready to consider it, she was in her late thirties, her odds of pregnancy much diminished. Min was an adoptee himself, born in Seoul, South Korea, and adopted into a white family in South Dakota during a wave of Korean adoption that began after the Korean War and lasted through the 1980s. Also, Min was a transgender man who had been born female and was preparing for a full transition. Min had considered pregnancy at various times but had polycystic ovarian syndrome, which made that unlikely. Pregnancy and transitioning from female to male didn't seem like the most comfortable combination, anyway.

All told, you'd think if any couple would go directly to adoption, Min and Max would be the one.

The legacies of a lifetime behind you, though, rarely make for a direct path to much of anything. When Min and Max met, Max had already decided that it was time to try to start a family, even if that meant doing it on her own. Max is a pragmatist, drawn to the efficient and the economical, to showers rather than baths, and had determined that donor insemination made the most sense. Years before, she had asked a friend who was going overseas to donate sperm for her to freeze before he left. Pregnancy and childbirth still seemed unappealing and painful to her; but the sperm was bought, paid for, and banked, and she figured she'd give it a try. Her age was not a disincentive, really; her parents had dropped out of high school when they had her, and somehow being pregnant as a thirty-seven-year-old professional with a master's degree and a doctorate in education seemed like karmic balance.

Min's experience with adoption had been enough of a mixed bag that it wasn't an automatic go-to, either. He knew almost nothing of his own origins until his late twenties, when, in Seoul for a Korean adoptee gathering, he'd visited the orphanage from which he was adopted and read his file with the help of a kind social worker named Mrs. Kim. His parents had been told, and had told Min, that as a baby girl, he had been found on the orphanage's doorsteps. This turned out to be a lie. In fact, the file said, his mother had given her baby up to an adoption agency, signatures and all.

Min's parents had also understood their job to be one of erasing the signs of their children's origins—his older sister was also adopted from Korea—in order to Americanize them. As a young girl in the Midwest, it wasn't until the third grade, when the girl-who-became-Min could see herself in the bathroom mirror, that she realized she didn't look like her parents. When she put that together with the teasing of some of her schoolmates, who called her "chink" and "gook" and "Connie Chung," the girl-who-became-Min began to experience the confusion, alienation, and pain over racial difference that is often reported by transracial adoptees.[1] By the time Min was a teenager, she'd layered over her status as an "outsider within" by turning it into a joke: "It's an Asian thing" had become one of her go-to punch lines. Min had weathered all of this and come out strong, and he knew now how wanted a child he'd been; but he didn't see much reason to choose that path for the next generation.

Max had clearly made up her mind already, anyway, and Min knew that resistance was futile. Max would try to get pregnant, they agreed; and since Max wasn't that gung ho about carrying a baby, and Min was still living in a woman's body, Min said he was even willing to give pregnancy a shot.

Min insisted they get married first, though. Perhaps because of his experience as a transracial adoptee, an Asian woman in a predominantly male industry, and a transman, Min was particularly sensitive to the need to be officially, legally recognized. It was law, after all, and not nature that made him recognizable as his parents' child. Law, and his own constant demonstrations of competence, had helped protect him from the devaluing assumptions about Asians and women that he'd confronted on the job. And it was law that would establish his gender status and provide a basis for combatting the hostility, stigma, discrimination, and derision that still follow trans people pretty much wherever they go. For all of the crossings of cultural and gender boundaries he embodied in his life, for all his queerness and tattoos, Min had also inherited from his parents a traditional South Dakota streak. Marriage seemed like a necessity to him.

Max, not so much. She is not a religious person, for one thing, so the covenant arguments for marriage held no sway for her. She also grew up in an environment where staying married was hardly normative; almost everyone divorced, including not just her parents but her grandparents, aunts and uncles, cousins, and neighbors. She didn't see much evidence that being married had much to do with being a good parent, either. After her parents split when she was a teenager, her mother decided she hadn't really lived her life, staying out late dancing and going on dates, leaving Max to fend for herself and watch out for her two younger siblings. Her father had more or less checked out before the divorce and seemed to prefer fishing to parenting. Even if she were a person interested in social conformity rather than a queer-identified artist with bright-pink hair and "Homo Bound" tattooed on her arm, she would have had a hard time seeing the point of marrying.

It was so important to Min, though, that he presented it as a prerequisite to having kids, which Max wanted and wanted right away. Negotiations began. Min wanted a violinist and guitarist to play classical music. Max would not wear white, she said, and the ceremony could not be religious. Min agreed, so Max contributed some of the money she'd been saving for years to buy a house and became the marrying kind.

■ ■ ■

Max and Min got married for the first time, on the one-year anniversary of the day they'd met, at an old fire station by the waterfront in San Francisco's Fort Mason Center, classical music and all. Max was surprised at how fun and moving the day turned out to be. She wore a red dress, and Min was in a tux.

Everyone knew that Min understood himself to be a man, but technically theirs was a marriage between two women. Though same-sex marriage had been legal for a hot minute, it was no longer recognized by the state after Proposition 8 passed in November 2008 and was deemed valid by the California Supreme Court six months later in *Strauss v. Horton*. So Max and Min had the ceremony in San Francisco but then high-tailed it across the country the next month to get married in Vermont, one of the handful of states that then recognized same-sex marriage.

Almost as soon as they got married, they sprung into baby-making action. Min had arranged to start his transition a few months later and withdrew his offer to get pregnant. Max never had an issue with Min's desire to be a man—her younger sister had also married a transman and was building a family with him, and she had always dated people whose gender was unorthodox—but she was annoyed that he'd gone back on a promise. Some of Max's friends told her it was a classic bait-and-switch, but she couldn't very well argue that reneging on a pregnancy promise because you want to start testosterone treatments was merely the culmination of an elaborate ruse. It wasn't likely that Min's uterus would be able to sustain a pregnancy anyway, so it had to be up to Max.

The first time they tried to get Max pregnant, using the sperm donated by Max's friend (a dark skinned, haired, and eyed Mexican and German mix), they had a midwife come to their home to help with the intrauterine insemination. That seemed uneconomical to Max, though, whose latch-key upbringing had instilled in her a frugal, do-it-yourself streak.

"You have to learn how to do this," Max told Min. For the next attempt, she downloaded YouTube videos with step-by-step insemination instructions, bought some sterilized equipment, and had Min do the inseminations. There was no romantic ritual, as some inseminating couples have, no candles or make-out session to make the conception seem a more meaningful outcome of love and sex. Max had read that an insemination takes better if it occurs just after an orgasm, though, so in the name of efficiency, they always made sure she had an orgasm first.

Neither of them was all that thrilled with the situation. Max didn't love trying to get pregnant while not wanting to actually be pregnant. Min, for his part, wasn't happy about a known donor who wasn't Asian and was also a lot taller than he. It wasn't that he wanted to be able to pretend that he'd reproduced his own genetics but rather that he really wanted his child to be able to experience what he had not: an identification with his parents that was visible on the body.

The sperm from Max's friend, as it turned out, wasn't perfect—low motility, they were told—and after several failed attempts, the stash was used up. Min and Max chose a sperm bank and searched the database for Asian donors. They chose a Korean American donor who seemed funny and lighthearted. When they used up his sperm, they found a Vietnamese donor whose smile in the sperm-bank photo looked a lot like Min's.

After more than a year without a hint of pregnancy, they consulted a fertility doctor.

"Looks like everything is working fine," the doctor said, puzzled. Max's test results came back as "Unexplained Infertility." Max thought maybe she was the explanation. She suspected that her psyche was whispering to her body that she didn't really want to be pregnant. Yet among the things being raised by struggling young parents had generated in her was a fierce independence and stubbornness, and she was prepared to barrel though whatever she had to, including her own guilt, in order to win what now seemed to be a battle with her own body.

Min, who is a bright-side kind of guy, was having trouble holding on to his optimism. "Hang in there," he told Max after each failed attempt. "Next time, for sure." His words started to sound tinny to Max. She turned for support to an online forum called Queer Conceptions, where lesbians and transfolks and assorted others discussed their family-making ups and downs, and she started injecting herself with estrogen and other hormones. When that didn't work, the fertility doctor recommended in vitro fertilization. They tried that, too, once, even though they'd sworn they never would. When that didn't work, even the fertility doctor seemed hopeless.

They were emotionally and financially drained, and Max had to admit that there had to be a better way to make a family than torturing themselves. When they gave up trying to get pregnant, Max and Min were not so much despairing as relieved. It was as if they had been driving down a road, not knowing for sure whether it was going to take them where they were trying to go, driving and driving in the dark until they dead-ended, and then saw above them a flashing arrow pointing toward the road that would finally take them there.

■ ■ ■

When Min and Max first introduce themselves, people often think that they are kidding or that they changed their names after they met to make them match. Min likes to say that the coincidence of their names works well, since they are like the opposite ends of a volume knob: Min's dial goes from gregarious to quiet diplomacy, while Max's turns from understated to impatient assertion. The truth is, though, that neither of them was born with the name they now go by. In a sense, going into the process of making a family, they already had a great deal of experience in conceiving a human being: each, at different times, in mirroring ways, had conceived a new self, embraced a new identity, and taken a new name.

Max had been asking herself questions about identity for as long as she could remember. Once, when she was ten years old, curious about race but uncertain how to ask about it, she broke into the stash of makeup her mother sold for Mary Kay, covered her skin with brown makeup, tucked her hair up in a hat, and walked around her mostly white neighborhood in Juno Beach, Florida. She wandered across the dirt road to a trailer park and felt people's unfriendly stares, as though a shift in her skin had suddenly made her an outsider. Many years later, working on her master's of fine arts in the 1990s, she picked up where her ten-year-old self had left off, in a month-long performance piece. She had already embraced a queer identity—was consumed by it, really, celebrating it as often as she could in the days and nights of queer San Francisco—and wanted to push the notion that identities are fluid, flexible, and multiple into her art. She'd developed five characters, each representing a part of herself, each with a different name, each embodying a different constellation of gender, class, and sexuality. They included a mohawked queer kid, a grandmother, a hip artist, and an upper-middle-class, conservative, straight businesswoman. She rotated through the characters across the month, inhabiting their different clothing, values, and mannerisms, and each persona showed up to the art gallery at a scheduled time to write in her or his journal.

By the end of the project, she had decided to rename herself. She was not close to her parents, to put it mildly, and disconnected herself from them further by dropping her last name. She took her given first name and made it into her new last name and took the first name Maxine. Maxine, her father's mother, was her closest relative, and she was Maxine's "little girl." Unlike her parents, Maxine wanted to expand her horizons, took her on road trips and gave her books, and never turned away from her, regardless of what identity she was trying on at the time.

When Max changed her name legally, her grandmother was happy for her, seeing in it, as Max did, the power of self-determination. Her parents were pissed, but Max could not call up any sympathy. She knew that if she had married a man and taken his name, they would not be the least bit upset, and anyway, she thought—thinking back to their absence at her high school graduation, to the times when she was more parent to them than they were to her—they had not earned a say in the matter. Naming herself felt like a baptism. It was almost as if she had adopted herself.

■　　■　　■

By the time Max and Min met, Min too had renamed himself, and in some ways it had been more effortless. He'd spent much of his adult female life in lesbian communities that had been talking for years about gender fluidity and hotly debating "whether the gender binary should be expanded or only resisted."[2] The notion that gender is a spectrum, rather than a pair of fixed statuses, had become a given among his crowd; nobody got too bent out of shape anymore when you took whatever place you wanted on the gender spectrum. He knew what place he wanted to take. He'd found a partner who knew who he was from the get-go and supported him. He knew his way around the health care system. California in general and San Francisco in particular had protections against discrimination on the basis of gender identity.[3] In the world at large, Min was often read not as trans but as a little Asian gay dude, and he only sometimes bothered to correct that impression.

In his family of origin, not surprisingly, things had not been as smooth. When Min first told his parents in 2009 that he was going to be transitioning from woman to man—he wasn't sure when, but he wanted them to know that it was going to happen—he'd gotten a text message from his mother saying only, "We can't talk about this." The next year, his father was having heart surgery, and Min had returned to South Dakota to help out. He had been on hormones for nearly a year, and his chest surgery was scheduled for the next week.

He'd gone to South Dakota determined not to talk about it, since his parents had made it very clear that was the only way they could handle it, and he just couldn't see turning his dad's heart surgery into a family drama focused on him. The whole week he'd listened while they talked with what seemed like every person they came into contact with, everywhere they went, about "our daughter this" and "our daughter that." They were bragging about him, but it had still stung. He'd allowed that maybe he was oversensitive to it, and maybe the testosterone was throwing him off, but all he could hear was *daughter our daughter girl she's a girl she's our daughter.*

The day before he was leaving, his mother heard him banging around the house. "Are you okay?" she'd asked.

"Yes," Min said. "Wait, no. I'm not. I just feel like I'm hiding, and I don't know what to do." His mother sat in silence. "I love you, and I'm here for you and dad, and you don't want to talk about it, and it's hard for me. I mean, my voice is changing, and there's things about my transition that are so obvious and undeniable, and I feel like you don't want me here. I feel like I'm not okay with you."

Min's mother, who was Dutch and married a man of Norwegian descent, is not prone to emotional displays or nurturing acts, but she'd walked over to Min and sat down next to him, and they'd cried together.

That was more or less the end of it. His parents adjusted to Min's transition with remarkable speed; there didn't seem much point doing otherwise. The next year, Min helped them move into a new place in a new city. It was a fresh start: no one knew them or their family. Everywhere they went, his mother and father proudly introduced him and told anyone who would listen how amazing and successful he was, their son Min this and their son Min that, what a good son he was and had always been, and what a good father he would eventually be.

Becoming a parent and becoming a man had by then become intertwined for Min, too, not because one had anything much to do with the other but because they were happening at the same time. He'd started on testosterone around the same time Max had started, as part of the pregnancy attempts, on estrogen. The following September, three days after he and Max had bought a house, which they chose in part because it had a perfect room for a nursery, Min had his first sex reassignment surgery, a hysterectomy. He'd flown to Baltimore two months later for chest surgery, arriving home on Thanksgiving with drains on the side of his chest and his chest bound tightly enough that when he tried to move his arms, he looked like a tyrannosaurus. A week later, he went to court to get his name and gender legally changed. Six months later, in the summer of 2011, Min and Max got married for the third time, this time as man and woman. A month after that, they signed on with an adoption agency.

In many ways, within themselves, they had finally become whom they had chosen to be. On paper, though, they were a heterosexual couple, when they saw themselves as a queer couple. In public, unless they made a point of saying something, people hardly knew what to make of them. It they were by themselves, people seemed to think they were a gay man and his BFF; if they were with another male-female couple, people assumed Max and the woman were a lesbian couple and Min and the man were boyfriends. Max, in particular, was disturbed by the sense of her own erasure. Having fought so hard for her queer-dyke identity, to claim a name for who she was, she found herself suddenly being misidentified by others. There was no name, she thought, for who she was now and no name for the family she and Min were making.

■ ■ ■

Min and Max had looked first into Korean adoption but quickly taken it off the list. It was very expensive, for one thing. For another, the first thing the Korean agencies they contacted asked for was their bank statements and a picture of their house, which was a turnoff. It turned out that one of the requirements was also that a couple be married for five years, and waiting four more years to get started was unfathomable. They also suspected that if a Korean agency found out Min was trans, the whole thing would go down in flames.

Their friends had recently adopted a baby, quickly and happily, through the Independent Adoption Center, which had a reputation for LGBT friendliness. A month after their final marriage—which had magically and disconcertingly transformed them into a heterosexual couple—Max and Min paid their deposit and, a bit hung over, went to a weekend intensive workshop put on by the agency.

They already knew that the agency had a firm position in favor of open adoptions, in which the birth family is known to the adoption family, shares information with them, participates fully in making a birth plan, and has contact with them over the coming years. As the agency's materials put it, open adoption gives kids not just important information about their genetic and medical histories but also important pieces of a story and their own place within it. Open adoption gives "answers to basic questions that all adoptees wonder about, such as 'Who do I look like?' and 'Why was I given up?'" The agency suggested, too, a particular narrative that could displace "the frustrations of the unknowns and feelings of rejection that are inherent in closed adoption": "Through open adoption, the adoptee knows he/she was placed for adoption out of love. He/she is aware, on an ongoing basis, of his/her birthparents' love. As a result, the adoptee is able to feel good not only about where he/she is, but also where he/she came from."[4] Birthparents could also have more control over the process and work through their "normal feelings of grief much more quickly and easily," and adoptive parents could feel more "entitled to parent," since they are specifically chosen by the birth parents to do so.[5] The story of the family can be extended to include, rather than write out, the people whose bodies made the child.

Although open adoption made Max a bit nervous, it suited her well, but Min—the product of a closed adoption—was less enthusiastic about muddying the boundaries of the family. As a kid, he'd witnessed the distress of his parents when his older sister had received, out of the blue, a letter from her birth parents. Still, he was convinced that open adoption would give his child things he had not had, including a story that was not a lie.

Sometimes Min still had his doubts, though, in part because he didn't totally trust the source. He'd found himself, for instance, at that weekend adoption intensive, the only adoptee in a room full of people weighing in on the adoption experience. Being the only this or that in the room was a familiar thing, to say the least: he'd been the only Asian American, the only woman, and the only transman. Rarely, though, were the people in that room also lecturing him about the damage that being Asian, female, or trans did to a person. And yet here he was, listening to a discussion whose main point seemed to be "closed adoption bad, open adoption good."

The facilitator had presented a few adoption scenarios and asked people to consider the pros and cons. Looking at one of the cases, a man raised his hand.

"Well, that person was adopted through a closed adoption," the man said, teacher's-pet style, "and everybody knows they will never be a productive part of society, because they're angry and they'll never be able to fully function in the world." People nodded. The facilitator did not disagree. "Then, since it was a transracial adoption," the man added, with a need-I-say-more gesture, "you have a whole other set of issues."

Max looked over at Min, whose face had gone red, expecting to see steam come out of his ears. It wasn't so much that Min disagreed that transracially adopted kids have identity struggles that others do not or that closed adoptions leave kids with unanswered questions about their origins that could haunt them for a lifetime. He was stuck, like many transracial adoptees, between "conflicting accounts" of race and adoption, one of which emphasizes the damages done to adoptees and the other asserting that the most important factors for a child's development are "'love' and swift placement into stable families."[6] As the ethnic studies scholar Julia Chinyere Oparah and the writers Sun Yung Shin and Jane Jeong Trenka, all transracial adoptees and activists, put it, "On one hand, we resist being defined as victims condemned to half-lives between cultures, without meaningful connections to our families or communities. . . . On the other hand, our experiences of racism, isolation, and abuse and our struggles with depression, addiction, and alienation indicate that adoption across boundaries of race, nation, and culture does indeed exact a very real emotional and spiritual cost."[7] This is a struggle, though, not a sentence to a life of angry, unproductive dysfunction.

Min raised his hand and took a breath. "I am cross-culturally adopted," he said, his voice rising. "I'm from Korea, and I was adopted through closed adoption." Some people shifted uncomfortably in their seats. Min took a breath. "And I'm angry, that's for sure, but only because of what you're saying right now. I'm pretty high functioning. I'm married, I have a career, I'm educated, and you really don't know what the hell you're talking about."

"Well," the facilitator said, trying to move on, "there are definitely different perspectives."

■　■　■

In the adoption world, the "Dear Birth Mother" letter, which presents the parents-to-be to expectant women who might consider placing their baby with them, is central. It is to adoption what the personal essay is to college admission. A quick web search turns up advice like "8 Simple Ways to Make Your Birthmother Letter Stand Out" (among them, "bring the reader into the action," "put yourself in her shoes," and "use good design")[8] and "5 Tips for Writing a Dear Birthmother Letter" (among them, "paint a picture of how you live," "be positive," "become the solution").[9] There's a lot of competition, especially for newborns, so a kick-ass letter is deemed essential.

Max, who has a background in graphic design and web design, saw this for what it was: a marketing document. She spent many months on it, playing with different colors and different fonts, choosing and re-choosing pictures. She hired a photographer to come to take photos of her and Min in their backyard with their dog, and they changed clothes a few times so that the pictures looked like they were taken on different days. She referred to it as "our brochure," though the agency's staff—perhaps because if a brochure is a parent-marketing tool, the agency might be seen as a baby broker—insisted she call it a "letter."

It's never easy figuring out how to present yourself to people who are in a position to totally change your life—employers, parole boards, and so on—and even harder when you have no information whatsoever about your audience. For all the advice about standing out, the sweet spot of adoption self-marketing is distinctive ordinariness. You do want to stand out but not in ways that might appear likely to screw up a kid. You don't want to get too political. You want to be authentic, but you don't want to play up the real parts of you that a pregnant woman might see as scary or off-putting. If you're a formerly lesbian couple, and one of you is a transman, you face some tough decisions about how exceptional and authentic a Dear Birth Mother letter you're going to produce.

Also, the adoption agency had to approve the letter, and like most organizations, this one tended toward caution. Max, who wears black every day, was told that she could not wear black in any of the photos accompanying the letter; sometimes the agency would send back pictures on the grounds that the smiles looked inauthentic or with no explanation at all. The agency rewrote and edited the text. Its forms had boxes for heterosexual and gay people to check off, as though those were the only two possibilities. There was little room, within the rules of this particular game, for Min and Max to present themselves matter-of-factly as who they were.

Min and Max decided to market themselves as open and a bit "alternative." They showed their tattoos but at enough distance that you couldn't make out the word "HOMO" on Max's arm. They mentioned Min's experience as an adoptee, the excitement of San Francisco, and the house they own in a diverse, "open and accepting" neighborhood. They talked about game nights and theme parks. They posted a photo of Max holding her baby nephew and another of her at Great America hugging Snoopy. They included pictures of the two of them with their friends' daughter, in front of Christmas stockings and holding their dogs Ollie and Charlie, with Max's grandmother Maxine in Las Vegas, with Min's family at Mount Rushmore and at a Minnesota theme park, and with their mixed-race godchildren and a four-foot chipmunk at the opening of the *Alvin and the Chipmunks* movie.

Min was not finished transitioning at the time, so in the photos, he looks softer jawed and smoother than he was to later on; but the couple offset that a bit through pronouns and pictures: in one photo, he is "showing off his new tie at work," and in another, he is in black T-shirt and beret "playing Wii with a friend." The gender story they told, in fact, was a pretty traditional one. Min wrote about how he admired Max's "kind spirit, her nurturing patience, and her honest nature," about how she "will go to the ends of the earth to help a lost kitten"; next to a photo of Max at the front of a classroom, Min says, "as much as she loves to teach, she is looking forward to being a stay-at-home mom for a few years as we start our family." Max wrote about Min's "outgoing personality," about how he "loves to rock climb," and how "he will be the most wonderful father when our time comes."

This image of Min and Max as an alt-heterosexual couple—San Franciscans, on the creative side, a mixed-race pairing, an adoptee in the mix, with an affection for Disney and kittens—is not inaccurate, but it did involve a strategic dequeering. This was neither sneakiness nor personal preference but a gradual, sometimes imperceptible set of decisions made in response to the realities of the adoption process and its structures and a trans-unfriendly world:[10] the Dear Birth Mother letter, which requires smart spin and bet hedging; the adoption agency's counselors, who did not recommend putting black clothing, let alone queerness, out front; the fact that most women who are giving up their babies are themselves experiencing social stigma and disapproval and aren't eager to send their baby into a family that also might attract disapproval. The fewer the limits, the greater the odds. Max and Min were already limiting themselves to babies with some Asian background, and neither they nor the agency saw much point in limiting themselves further to people who would appreciate and understand a transman–queer woman pairing.

That would have to come later.

■　■　■

Some people Max and Min met at the weekend intensive finished up their paperwork, Dear Birth Mother letter, home visits, and background checks and "went live" on the agency website within a few weeks. It took Max and Min a year. Just three weeks after their profile went live, though, they got a call from the agency telling them there were some birth parents who wanted to talk to them.

The next day, Max and Min Skyped with the birth parents, eighteen-year-old sweethearts from Las Vegas. They wanted to have a family some day, the teenagers said, but they were nowhere near ready. The young man was Asian American and looked like he could have been Min's little brother; they had similar smiles. The young woman was white and looked like she could have been Max's little sister, complete with the same style of tattoos. They told Min and Max that they chose them because they seemed "really open," which probably had something to do with the tattoos and pink hair.

Min booked plane tickets to Vegas for the next week, while Max called the agency in Los Angeles—which was handling the Vegas contacts—to touch base before the trip.

"Sounds exciting," the counselor at the agency said. "And yeah, just so you know, you guys have until Monday to share with them that Min is trans." Max was thrown into a panicked rage. This was not how they'd planned to approach the disclosure. They'd understood from earlier conversations that they could take time getting to know, and getting to be known by, birth parents before talking about it; any prejudice could be forestalled by the reality that they were actual humans and excellent ones at that. It was Thursday, and a weekend didn't seem like a lot of time to connect with strangers who might consider making them parents.

"Well, do it by Monday, because I'm going to call them then," the woman replied.

When Min found out, he was unperturbed. It had to be a misunderstanding. They were going to be at the adoption agency that night anyway, and he was sure the executive director, a licensed clinical social worker named Linda, would clear it all up.

"Yes, that's right," Linda said that night when Max and Min pulled her aside. "You have until Monday, and then we need to call them and see how they feel about it." Min objected that this was not what they had been told earlier. The maneuver was disconcertingly familiar: institutions casually appropriating the power to define identity to others while framing gender diversity as some sort of scandal to be managed.

"Look," the agency's director continued, "this is very important. It's like if you had HIV, you would have to disclose that to them. Or diabetes or cancer." Max's jaw dropped, and Min put his hand on her arm to stave off an explosion. He calmly explained that being trans was nothing like having a life-threatening chronic illness to begin with, because it is neither an illness nor chronic. It was a transition, and his was in the past.

"Okay, yeah, you're right, that's a bad analogy," Linda said. "It's like if you had bipolar disorder and were on lithium, you'd need to disclose that."

Min and Max had, of course, encountered the view that trans people suffered from a disease, but they did not expect to encounter that view in this setting. *Here we go again*, Min thought. He pointed out that Linda probably knew that trans people had been treated as mentally ill, second-class citizens for far too long and that she might do better to take that transphobic assumption off the table.

"You're right, you're right," Linda said, clearly uncomfortable. "Let me explain it this way. We would tell anyone who had a major surgery to disclose that fact." Max asked her if she would say the same thing to any woman in the room who'd had a boob job or a hysterectomy. Linda, flustered, said that was different.

"It's not different!" Max yelled, now unwilling to control her outrage. "It's absolutely not." She let loose the frustrations that had built for months over how much she had made herself invisible as a queer person in order to qualify as a parent. "No one asks the heterosexual couples to announce that they're in a heterosexual relationship!" she shouted. "No one calls birth parents and asks them if they're okay with a dad who was born a man." She pointed out that both straight and gay people had the privilege of being a category on the agency's forms, and therefore no one required of them that they have awkward conversations with potentially life-changing strangers about their gender or sexual identities. "I would have liked a box to check just like everybody else," Max said.

Linda took a step back. "Look, if they find out after the adoption, it can be grounds for them to go to court and take back the baby," she declared. "It's our job to make sure that doesn't happen. If you don't disclose it by Monday, we won't be able to continue to work with you."

In the car, Min vented about filing a discrimination lawsuit and writing articles about the agency's discriminatory practices; Max was still so mad she could barely speak. After they'd cooled down a bit, though, they came up with a disclosure plan that would be true to their own experience of Min's gender and not freak out the Vegas kids. They'd embed it within a bigger Things You Might Want to Know about Us conversation.

"We've been thinking about things about us it might be important for you to know," Max said on their Skype call that Monday morning. "So we see that you're Catholic, and I'm not. I don't identify with any religion."

"Okay," the young woman said.

"And I'm Buddhist," Min chimed in. "We were both raised Christian, so we understand Christian values and don't have anything against them, but that's not where our values fall."

"No problem," the young man said.

"And I'm forty, so I'm a little bit older," Max said.

"Yeah, that's not a big thing for us," the young woman said.

"And also, I was born a girl, but we fixed that," Min said. It was a clever phrasing, at once recalling the dominant, digestible, trapped-in-the-wrong-body trope and slyly asserting that biology is as reliable a vehicle for gender as an old car.

There was a pause. Min and Max held their breaths as they watched the couple take that in.

"Oh, that's interesting," the young woman said.

Min and Max asked if they had any questions.

"No, not really," the young man said.

"When does your flight get into Vegas?" the young woman asked.

Min and Max visited the young couple in Las Vegas four times, sampling different casino hotels. It was like hanging out with younger, taller versions of themselves. They met some of the couple's family members, accompanied them to the hospital and met the nursing staff and social workers, came up with a birth plan. They built a big-sibling–little-sibling kind of friendship. They felt like poster children for open adoption.

"Dude," the young man said to Min on one of their visits to the hospital. "Some day, in like ten years, I'm going to be in this hospital waiting to have my baby, and I'm going to need your support and your advice."

"Dude, I'll be there," Min said.

In December, a month before the due date, Min had surgery. The doctor promised he'd be recovered in time for the baby, who was due on Martin Luther King's birthday.

The weekend before MLK Day, Max got a text from the birth mother saying that she was uncomfortable but that everything was fine with the baby. They were having a girl. She'd text again when it was time for Max and Min to get on a plane.

The next day, they heard nothing. They spent their time getting the gear they needed for their baby, whom they had, after much tense negotiation, named Avery. Her room was ready for her. The next day and the day after that, the due date, they again heard nothing. On the way to work the next morning, Max got a call from the adoption agency, and she asked if they knew what was going on.

"Oh, she didn't tell you?" the agency counselor said. "They decided to place with a family member." In a daze, Max pulled over and called Min, who was at home packing their bags. Min, with the denial that is sometimes required of optimists, asserted that this couldn't possibly be true.

"The baby was born on Saturday, and they've already placed her," Max said. The words sounded like they were coming from someone else's mouth or like they were in a different language. It seemed an impossible betrayal.

Max and Min spent the day walking around in a cloud of despair and disbelief. They called their parents, whose heartbroken responses broke their own hearts again. It felt like their baby had died. They knew the baby was fine, that they had no claim on her, that they really shouldn't think this way, but they wished the Vegas couple ill. They took the week off from their jobs and blew all the money they'd saved for their final trip to Vegas on a trip to Napa. It did not ease the pain.

The next week, a text message arrived from the birth mother in Las Vegas. "I'm really sorry," it said. That was the last Min and Max ever heard.

At Min's urging, Max bought an angel trumpet tree, and they planted it in their front yard, where it still grows, a tribute, a memorial really, to the child whose name is not Avery. Still, now, Avery is a present absence, a faceless, rustling sorrow.

■ ■ ■

When Min was recovering that May following another transition-related surgery, he turned to Max in the car one day. He had been thinking about *The Secret*, Rhonda Byrne's 2006 power-of-positive-thinking self-help best-seller. Years before, he'd listened incessantly to the audio book repeatedly and even gone to the movie. His friends mostly thought it was snake-oil salesmanship, but Min had come to believe the tenet that we attract the things that we want to have happen in our lives.

"If we're going to adopt," he told Max, "we have to make the decision to really be back in it. We need to put the energy out into the universe." Max nodded indulgently. She had already proposed to remove the restrictions on race from their profile, and Min had finally agreed. Now, Min suggested that they start making space for the baby, so that they could visualize a baby occupying that space, implementing *The Secret*'s "Law of Attraction," in which energy draws like energy. That weekend, they bought a crib mattress at Babies R Us; the next weekend, a combination dresser and changing table; the following one, a video baby monitor on sale. The day after they got the monitor, Max got a call from a counselor from the adoption agency. A birth mother, she said, had been trying to reach them.

"So someone called," Min said, unable to call up his usual good cheer. "Let's see what happens."

Max spoke with the birth mother, a Texan named Vanessa, that afternoon.

"Yeah, so I think I want you guys to raise my baby," she told Max. Vanessa was Latina, midtwenties, raising two boys on the outskirts of Dallas on a limited income. It turned out she had received more than two hundred Dear Birth Mother letters from the agency, but Max and Min were the only couple she'd contacted. She was friendly but not especially talkative. She didn't really know the baby's biological father, she said, or where he was now. The school district had told her that both her kids were autistic. It was already more than she could handle alone.

"So when is the baby due?" Max asked.

"Two weeks," Vanessa said.

"Jesus Christ," Max said. She was relieved, though. The thought of befriending another birth mother for months and wondering the whole time if the adoption would fall through was more than she or Min could take.

Vanessa didn't have access to a computer, so she couldn't Skype; and she didn't have her own phone, but she said she would call again soon on her sister's phone. When they talked to her the next week, two days before Vanessa's labor was scheduled to be induced, they went through the same casual trans disclosure as they had with the Vegas couple— Max has no religion, Min is Buddhist, Max is past forty, Min was born a girl but we've since fixed it—and asked if Vanessa had any questions.

"No," said Vanessa. The counselor from the adoption agency later asked Vanessa if she knew that Min was transgender and whether she had any questions about it. She knew, Vanessa said, and she had no questions.

It wasn't entirely clear whether she fully understood what "transgender" meant, but neither the counselor from the adoption agency, who spoke with all of them for several hours to hash out the terms of the adoption, nor Max and Min pushed it any further. It felt a little tricky, letting Vanessa's relative lack of education possibly work in their favor, but they also did not want to create a problem where, as far as they were concerned, none actually existed.

Vanessa appeared to have her own disclosure to make. Once not too long ago, she told them, Child Protective Services had been called when her older son had fallen into her parents' backyard swimming pool and nearly died.

Max asked her how she came to choose them as possible parents from all the contenders.

"I liked the chipmunk," Vanessa said.

"What?" Max responded.

"The chipmunk. On your letter. I really like the picture of you guys with those kids and the chipmunk from *Alvin and the Chipmunks*. My boys love that movie." Max thought maybe it was more than that, that Vanessa saw in their faces that they would not judge her or saw in the picture brown-skinned godchildren who looked like her own kids. This much was clear: after all the pregnancy attempts, the adoption that almost was, the negotiations and expenditures, it seemed that their family might owe everything to a giant replica of a cartoon chipmunk.

■　■　■

On Tuesday, the day Vanessa's baby was due to be born, Max was beside herself with anxiety. At work, while she was on the phone with an agency social worker, she shushed a coworker who was watching a video. When he got mad, she started crying and screamed, to his great confusion, "You have no idea what's going on right now! Someone could be giving birth to our son!" She went home early.

"Just don't think about it," Min told her, which was no help. They tried pretending it was a normal night, ordering pizza and watching a movie. At around eight o'clock, Max got a text from Vanessa's eighteen-year-old sister, Gabriela, telling them the baby was born.

"Big deal, so he was born," Min said.

A little while later, another text from Gabriela dinged above the movie soundtrack: *He is healthy and we cant wait for u to meet him and take him home.* A few minutes later, another text: *Do u want a pic?*

"Do we want a picture?" Max asked, wanting a picture very badly. Min shrugged. When the picture arrived—chubby brown face under a little cap, skinny legs poking out of a diaper, chipmunk cheeks—he couldn't help but let down some of his defenses. *Oh, my God*, he let himself think, *that's a real baby. Maybe that's really him.*

"We'll see," Min said. "I am not going to book tickets until the agency calls and says everything is a go."

They got the call from the agency the next morning, flew to Dallas that afternoon, and went directly from the airport to the hospital just before midnight. The hospital was in Arlington, a predominantly white city that had the hospital closest to Vanessa's hometown, where nearly half the population was Latino living on modest incomes.

Vanessa was awake with the baby when they got there. It was a lot, meeting Vanessa and wanting to be good to her, strangers in an intimate moment, meeting the baby and wanting to hold him. They were gentle with each other. Vanessa passed the baby to Max and Min. They tried to play it cool—it seemed intrusive just to be there in the first place, and nothing was official yet, and and and and—but Max knew it was obvious she was holding back tears. Two weeks had passed since the first time they learned of Vanessa's existence.

They decided to call the baby Aiden. It had no special meaning to them, but it reminded them of the last-hurrah vacation they'd taken to Ireland the year before, several months before Avery had been born. The name came into Min's head, and Max liked it, end of discussion. Aiden: Little Fire.

■ ■ ■

When Min and Max arrived at the hospital the next morning with flowers and a teddy bear, they were intercepted by a counselor from the adoption agency named Tammy, who had driven to Houston to help with the adoption. She asked them to wait in the hallway waiting area while she and Vanessa finished up the paperwork with the hospital social worker. She came back twenty minutes later with a concerned look and empty hands.

"She's feeling really confused right now," Tammy said. "She doesn't know if this is what she wants to do." Vanessa was alone in the hospital room. Her parents, who were watching Vanessa's two boys, opposed the adoption and refused to come to the hospital. Her only real supporters were Gabriela, Gabriela's boyfriend, Teo, and an aunt, and they were all at work. The hospital social worker had been pressuring her to sign the hospital's adoption papers, and that had only created more confusion and doubt for Vanessa, who had thus far only been dealing with the adoption agency.

While Min was responding to worried texts from his mother, Tammy reported that Vanessa's sister had arrived. For an hour, no one spoke to Max or Min, and they sat, dumbfounded, in the waiting room, trying not to think about what seemed to be happening, until the hospital social worker came out in tears. The agency counselor, Tammy, had insisted that she back off and that Vanessa was not going to be signing any paperwork under duress.

The social worker sat down across from Min and Max in the waiting room. She was in her sixties, white, with what looked like a rather expensive haircut and a pained expression. "I'm so sorry she's putting you through this," she said. "Obviously the best thing for her to do is for you guys to adopt this baby. I can't believe this. I have family members who were adopted. It's not right what she's doing to you."

She clearly meant her words as comfort and recognition, but they landed on Max and Min like a much-needed wake-up slap. What they heard was *she is less valuable than you* and *her baby is better off with people like you than people like her* and *she is a perpetrator and you are victims*. They saw the class situation that led them to this baby—they, who owned a home, who could fly to Texas on a moment's notice; Vanessa, who didn't own a phone let alone a home, raising two kids solo, barely scraping by—reflected back to them by the social worker as some sort of birthright. They felt suddenly protective of Vanessa, who was vulnerable in ways they were not simply by virtue of where she'd landed on race, class, and gender hierarchies. They could live more easily with the painful sensation that Vanessa might change her mind than with the implication that they were entitled to the baby she'd borne. They met the social worker's sympathetic look with steely stares.

"Well then," the social worker said, dabbing the wetness around her eyes, and left.

Another hour passed before Tammy emerged and invited Max and Min into the hospital room. They introduced themselves to Gabriela, who was standing by the door, and hugged Vanessa, who was holding the baby. They gave Vanessa the teddy bear and flowers. The small talk came in awkward fits and starts.

"Do you want to hold him?" Vanessa asked Max after a few minutes. While Max held the baby as though it was not a big deal, the counselor started to talk about what happens next. Vanessa could not legally terminate her parental rights until forty-eight hours had passed, but the hospital would release Vanessa and the baby that day. The day after, they would sign papers. Then Min and Max would stay in Texas for two weeks, which was required by the state, before going home to California with Aiden.

Min and Max hadn't had any time to gather anything but their own clothes when they'd left San Francisco, so they rushed off to a mall to buy a car seat, diapers, and formula. A few hours after they got back to the hospital, a nurse arrived at the hospital room with discharge papers and a wheelchair for Vanessa and Aiden. Outside the hospital, the nurse unceremoniously removed the baby from Vanessa's arms and handed him to Max. It was nothing like either Max or Min had imagined. There was no pause in which to mark and take in the momentousness of Aiden's transition from Vanessa to his parents. They put the sleeping baby into the car seat.

"See you tomorrow," Vanessa said with a small, tired wave as Gabriela helped her into the car driven by Gabriela's boyfriend.

Max looked behind her at the baby.

"What do we do now?" she asked.

"Um, I guess now we have to raise him, right?" Min said.

"I guess so," said Max, grinning.

Min called his mother. She and his father had been waiting for the call, their car already packed, and began the seventeen-hour drive from South Dakota to Texas to meet their first grandchild.

At the hotel the next morning, the signing of paperwork became, for Min and Max at least, the meaningful moment they wanted and needed,

the ritual marker of the beginning of their new family. It was just signatures, and it just took a few minutes; but watching Gabriela and Teo
support Vanessa in what she was choosing to do and feeling the confidence that Gabriela, Teo, and Vanessa had in them as parents, it felt like
a holy act.

They spent almost every day over the next two weeks with Vanessa and
her family. Mostly they hung out in the hotel suite, Vanessa's kids jumping on the bed and the adults making chitchat, with an occasional outing
to the nearby Steak 'n Shake. Min enjoyed himself, but it also was taking a lot of energy for him to get excited about extending and loosening
the boundaries of his family. For him, the adoptive family had been the
only family; the person who gave birth to him was and would always be
very much outside the family's boundaries. He could handle it a couple of
times a year, he thought, and it was already becoming easier; and he was
glad that these folks were a part of his child's story, but he longed sometimes for the clarity of a family border that could not be transgressed.

Max, though, found herself excited to see the beginnings of a fluid,
not-quite-nameable sort of family—Vanessa, her two kids, her sister,
her sister's boyfriend; Max, Min, Min's parents—brought together by
the baby being passed around from person to person. She was firing
motherliness on all cylinders, and she began to see Vanessa, who was
about fifteen years younger than she, as a little sister.

■　■　■

On Max and Min's last visit, as they were preparing to head off with
Aiden to the airport, Vanessa pulled them aside. Despite what she'd told
them, she confessed, she actually knew the birth father and his family
well. In fact, she had been in touch with him a bit and had texted him
from the hospital when Aiden was born. In fact, his mother and sisters
had just shown up at Vanessa's parents' house claiming, on his behalf,
that she had no right to let some strangers take the baby out of Texas.
They were demanding to know where the baby was and threatening to
have Vanessa's other children taken away from her.

"This woman is bullying you," Max told Vanessa, a protective arm around her, after she'd recovered from the shock. "She has no rights over your kids." She told Vanessa she'd call the adoption agency and that Tammy, the counselor, would talk her through the situation.

"Can we leave?" Min and Max asked Tammy when they reached her, trying not to panic. Tammy said she'd talk with Vanessa, the birth father's mother, and the birth father and keep them posted. They shouldn't miss their flight.

Saying good-bye, Max and Vanessa both lost it. Max wasn't sure why Vanessa was crying, but she imagined it was just her own pain flipped over: one woman in deep pain but also grateful, the other unspeakably grateful but hurt by the other's loss, each longing for her own mother's missing affection, each in different ways driven now by maternal love; the sense, present but not articulated, that something besides love and circumstance, something more like injustice, was what brought them to this moment and made it make sense. They would visit at least twice a year, Max knew, and they'd already talked about celebrating Aiden's first birthday together. Still, Max felt Vanessa's pain the way a parent feels a child's, wishing it could land on her instead, as if such a thing were possible.

Tammy had suggested that Vanessa have the birth father's mother call her on the agency's toll-free line, which she did while Max, Min, and Aiden were at the airport waiting for their plane to board. They had no right to take her grandchild away, the mother had shouted to Tammy over the phone.

"The baby's on his way home with his parents," Tammy had told her, "and I can assure you that this is all very legal. Unfortunately, only the birth father can contest this." When the birth father called the agency the next day, Tammy told him that she was glad he had found them and that they would do everything they could to help him. He said he didn't really believe he was the birth father, which was why he hadn't come forward before, but that if he was, he wanted a say in the adoption, maybe to choose a family closer by in Texas. In order to contest the adoption, Tammy explained, he would need to get a paternity test, and the agency would make sure that the baby was brought to the hospital for a DNA test. Then he would need to hire an attorney to prepare the legal challenge.

"The investment is pretty high," Tammy told Min and Max. "We usually see it stop there." The class hierarchy, she implied, would once again work for them, as the cultural and financial capital needed to hire a lawyer and challenge the adoption were most likely beyond this young man's reach. It came as an unsettling relief that she was right.

■ ■ ■

"What was it like to suddenly realize you were a father?" Min's father, Robert, asked him a few months after Aiden was born. By the time Aiden was born, Min's trans status no longer grabbed much of Min's parents' attention, but parenting and grandparenting consumed them. Robert told Min about his own experience of becoming an adoptive father: the sudden arrival of a child you have not conceived, whom you have not watched come into the world but who is now depending completely on you for love, survival, and guidance. That they were both the fathers of adopted children felt even more like a bloodline to Min than had he and Max had a biological child.

Min has probably thought more than most people about what ties a family together across generations. Love is part of it, of course, but not all of it. Min believes in the power of names to connect. He comes honestly by that belief. He had been first given a name that would mark him as unmistakably American in a culture where plenty of people—certainly those he grew up around in South Dakota—still read anyone who looked Asian as a foreigner. When he was transitioning from a female identity to a male one, he not only had renamed himself to mark his gender identity but also had done so in a way that reestablished his Asian identity; indeed, people often mistakenly add an *h* to the end of his name, assuming it to be the Vietnamese name Minh. As his new middle name, he had chosen his father's name, Robert. He wanted Aiden's middle name to be Robert, too. The thing that ties an adopted child to the generations before, Min argued to Max, is your name.

Max didn't especially like the name Robert, but she could see how meaningful it was to Min. She, too, had given plenty of thought to how names mark the self and its relationship to others. Like Min, she had fought for hers, named herself in ways that both connected her to who she had been and marked who she wanted to be.

The year Aiden Robert came to be, Max and Min gave Min's father a picture frame for his birthday. In it was a photo of Min, his father, and Aiden. Max had taken to pointing out how rarely she was in family photos, handing Min the camera to rectify the situation, but she let this one go. The frame says "Three Generations." In some ways, it's the frame of traditional patriarchy: the proud thread of men, connected by the names they share.

The picture inside of it, though, that's a whole other story.

■　■　■

Min and Max sometimes joke about the kind of family stories that Max seeks out. She has long been drawn to obscure, surrealistic films in which a child embarks on an elaborate search for family, such as the flop *North*, in which a nine-year-old child prodigy decides, on the advice of a man claiming to be the Easter Bunny, to divorce his unappreciative parents and search for new ones, or the Japanese film *Kikujiro*, in which a boy finds a picture of his long-lost mother and leaves his grandmother's house to find her, accompanied by a no-goodnik neighbor. Then there is John Sayles's *The Secret of Roan Inish*. In that film, a young girl, Fiona, whose mother has died and father spends most of his time in a pub, is sent to live with her grandparents by the sea. There, she's told by other family members that legend has it they're descended from Selkies, who are part seal and part human, and also that, when her family was leaving the small island of Roan Inish, her baby brother had been carried out to sea in his cradle. Fiona goes to search for her brother, and she sees him one day on Roan Inish, or thinks she does, and sets about showing her family that her brother is alive and that they are not who they thought they were, that their family is made of different stuff.

The love longing, the discovery of new identity, the bringing together of creatures that the world sees as strangers to one another, the confrontation with doubters, the discovery of family and home between fog and waves, the insistence of a child, the power of story: it is all so queer and so familiar.

CONCLUSION

Bedtime Stories for a New Generation

Back when Reba was five years old, I was walking down the staircase into the yard of her preschool. It was the first hot, sunny day after nearly a month of rain, hail, and chill. The kids were too deeply involved in noisy games to notice me. I heard Reba Sadie's voice.

"I don't," she was saying. "No, really!" She was gesturing with her hands and head and raising her eyebrows to emphasize sincerity, the way she's seen some grown-ups do.

"I believe Reba!" her friend Diego announced and then turned around to hang from the monkey bars.

"I don't," I heard someone else merrily chirp, though I couldn't see who.

"I do," said Matteo, whose two moms and two dads are also good family friends.

"Bye, guys," Reba singsonged. "My Abba is here!"

While we were going to collect her lunch box, I asked her what that they were talking about outside.

"Some of the kids don't believe I don't have a mom," she explained, holding my hand. I was disarmed, both by the statement itself and by Reba's smile and skipping, which were telling me how much fun she'd just had.

Just a couple of days before, Reba had asked me if Tamar, our friend who carried and gave birth to her and whom she sometimes refers to as her "belly mommy," was at my wedding to Richard. She already knew the answer was yes—she regularly asked to hear "the wedding story" before bed—but she seemed to want confirmation before she continued.

"So I've known her forever," Reba said.

"Yes," I replied. "Since you were an embryo. Maybe even before that. Hard to know."

"Before that," she said with certainty. "Because I was at your and Daddy's wedding. When I was a spirit. I was sitting on Tamar's lap."

Thinking about all that now, I am reminded of just why the origin stories collected here, and the many others out there being told or not being told or waiting to be told, matter so much. Stories help make things make sense. They put things in an order. This is how it happened. They are also the stuff from which identities are built. Creation stories, in particular, are about selfhood. "In telling the story of our becoming, as an individual, a nation, a people," as the sociologist Francesca Poletta puts it simply, "we define who we are."[1] This is how I happened. *I have known all of you since I was a spirit. No, really.*

In that cheery preschool encounter, Reba was also enmeshed not just in sorting out the mess of information and ideas that surrounded her but in hashing those out with others who might tell her story differently, who might challenge or refuse or applaud her version. Stories, after all, are also inherently interactive and thus unavoidably political. Some stories—safe ones, familiar ones—don't provoke the politics that inhere in them, but the ones in this book certainly do. Even among the five-year-old set, for instance, Reba met up with the everyday negation that nonnormative families often face and responded by developing and asserting her own story. *I sat on the lap of the woman who would carry and give birth to me and watched my fathers wed.*

■　■　■

Scholars have been thinking and writing about the politics of storytelling—often called "narrative" or "discourse" by academics—for quite some time. Stories, this line of thinking asserts, are always deeply and necessarily partial, in both senses of the word: both incomplete and skewed. For one thing, there is always selection involved, and it's the storyteller who is in charge of that selection. Just the telling is an exertion of power. For another thing, the sociologists Patricia Ewick and Susan S. Silbey have written, narratives are told "for a variety of reasons, to a variety of audiences, with a variety of effects," and "with particular interests, motives, and purposes in mind," as "narrators tell tales in order to achieve some goal or advance some interest."[2] Sometimes the interest is overt and conscious, and much of the time it is not. Still, storytelling is always strategic. That's not a bad thing or a good thing; it's just a thing.

Still, much of the scholarly work on narrative has seen storytelling as more strategically useful for groups whose voices are routinely silenced within institutions like academia, media, law, and government. Poletta describes this reasoning:

> Personal stories chip away at the wall of public indifference, scholars argue. Stories elicit sympathy on the part of the powerful and sometimes mobilize official action against social wrongs. Where authorities are unyielding, storytelling sustains groups as they fight for reform, helping them build new collective identities, link current actions to heroic pasts and glorious futures, and restyle setbacks as way stations to victory. Even before movements emerge, the stories that circulate within subaltern communities provide a counterpoint to the myths promoted by the powerful.

In these ways, storytelling has particular "value for disadvantaged groups."[3]

While narratives certainly have that kind of "political potency," Poletta argues, storytelling is also more complicated and double-edged than that. "Stories are differently intelligible, useful, and authoritative," she points out, "depending on who tells them, when, for what purpose, and in what setting."[4] In some circumstances, stories can generate counterstories that elicit hostility rather than sympathy for the less powerful. Certain kinds of stories—for instance, in which protagonists are portrayed as victims with little control over outcomes—can demobilize rather than mobilize those folks for a fight. Stories are used just as often to "articulate and reproduce existing ideologies and hegemonic relations of power and inequality" as to "challenge them," Ewick and Silbey argue, often instructing their receivers in social norms and warning them of "the consequences of nonconformity."[5] New myths created by marginalized groups can generate new forms of "secondary marginalization" inside those groups, in which the "rhetoric of blame and punishment" is directed at "the most vulnerable and stigmatized in [a community]."[6] Also, you just can't control what people will do with the tales you tell. The impact of stories is conditional.

Of course, *how* the stories are told can make a big difference in how that all plays out. Ewick and Silbey suggest that there are two very different kinds of socially relevant narratives. There are those that "efface the connection between the particular and the general" and in doing so "help sustain hegemony"[7] and those that "emplot the connection between the particular and the general by locating persons and events within the encompassing web of social organization."[8] The first, which they call "hegemonic stories," ignore "the cultural, material, and political world," leaving those as taken-for-granteds and telling only the tale of particular individuals. The second, which they call "subversive stories," make those larger forces visible in the telling.[9]

■ ■ ■

The politics of storytelling have ricocheted across this book. There is, first, the micropolitics of family storytelling—hinted at along the way; hiding in the silences, ellipses, and gaps—as both I and the other adults involved have made decisions about how a story should be told, what to disclose and what not to, often with an eye to power dynamics within the family and interpersonal relations outside the family. That's not easy.

Family members often disagree on decisions about disclosure, which itself brings complicated interpersonal politics. As I described at the beginning of this book, the dominance of a One True Family ideology, even in its weakened form, makes secrecy—or at least privacy—about unconventional family creation an appealing option. Making the story public opens you up to shame and judgment, reduced status, and positioning as an outsider; this can make for unpleasant encounters with strangers and tension with intimates. If becoming a parent suddenly raises your status, revealing that you got there in a nonnormative way can suddenly reduce it.

For instance, the writer Melanie Thernstrom, in an account of her path to parenthood via egg donation, in vitro fertilization, and gestational surrogacy, describes the advice of the director of an egg-donation agency. "If you tell even one person that you used a donor, word will spread. But if it were me, I'd tell no one," she added. "Look, I run an agency, so it's in my interest to promote these kinds of families, but to be honest, if I couldn't have children naturally—*God forbid*—I wouldn't want anyone to know!" Thernstrom went the opposite direction but then found that being open about her story invited "a Greek chorus of doleful commentary," as her story became a "perfect canvas" on which people could "project their own ambivalence." "There was a curious insistence that the situation must be darker and more difficult than it actually was and that I must simply be in denial or trying to put a brave face on it all. People were constantly suggesting horrifying hypotheticals about the carriers: drinking, using drugs, disappearing into Denmark, getting HIV or hepatitis C from their husbands or seducing mine (a complicated seduction strategy indeed) and, of course, stealing the baby."[10] Those pitying looks that disclosure elicits—or, for that matter, patronizing compliments for courage and tenacity—placing you below the person in front of you, locking you into their projections, are not always worth the trouble. The parents in this book, in fact, all operated with a heightened sense of storytelling, as though already anticipating how others might see them, their kids, and their family. Decisions about what to tell and how to tell weigh heavily on them.

Family origin storytelling also calls up questions about power relationships between parents and children. As one parent said to me, telling kids the whole story can be like telling them there is no Santa Claus, a replacement of meaningful innocence with a more adult reality. Indeed, many of the silences in this book's stories come from the parents' desire to protect their children—and to protect their own relationship to their kids. Some parents understandably want to shield their children not just from the Greek-chorus commentary but also from details of their own origins. They do not want their child to hear the story in which they were born to someone else or in which they are not genetically related to their own parents or in which they came into their family only after their parents tried and tried to get pregnant. Indeed, one study of secrecy and disclosure among parents of children conceived by assisted reproduction found that about "half the children conceived by egg donation and nearly three-quarters of those conceived by donor insemination remained unaware that the person they know as their mother or father is not, in fact, their genetic parent."[11] The relational stakes of disclosure are high, and for many people, the telling of unconventional creation stories winds up being a delicate, high-risk endeavor. Perhaps it will become less so the more such stories are told.

The relationship between parents, and not just between parents and children, can be roughened by this kind of storytelling, too. Since there is no conventional storyline to fall back on, the story is up for grabs, and the power dynamics between parents are often tested in the retelling. In the retelling of these stories—probably any family story told with a reasonable amount of honesty but even more so when becoming a parent is such a struggle—the power relations can be reactivated as people grapple over how the story ought to be told. That can be difficult to confront. It's even harder when someone else, like me, is telling your story, reflecting back to you the imbalances of power, endemic in any relationship, that the pursuit of parenthood involved. More than a few people freaked out when I sent them the first draft of their family's chapter for this book. Some battled with each other, and me, over control of the story. Parents were divided over who would benefit from this or that sort of disclosure or this or that version of the family creation story and over whose stature would be raised or lowered. Dormant fault lines sometimes cracked open. Sometimes they were closed back up in the writing, covered over in the name of peace and privacy, but these are stories built on small-scale tensions over who controls the narrative.

In some ways, it is easier just to leave it all alone. But silence isn't a great option, either: silences can become secrets, and secrets can tear up a family. Silence is its own kind of politic, in that it leaves it to others to make up their own story about you. This micropolitical situation may be why so many of these stories, including my own, involve dreams, visions, karma, and signs. I believe these are authentic experiences. They exhibit, though, what Thernstrom describes as "the desire to invent a narrative that weaves your lives together in a way that you can read as destiny."[12] As metaphors and plot elements, they can resolve, or head off, some of the difficult micropolitics of unconventional family creation storytelling. They lend the story an immutability, too, that can protect it from others' attempts at rewriting it. Fate is a belief and also a relief.

■ ■ ■

Family storytelling—at least the way I've tried to do it here, by locating the individual paths to parenthood in the larger social structures that shape them—is also political in ways that go far beyond the interpersonal, of course. On one level, the stories in this book confront a core myth of the One True Family: that heterosexual coupling in marriage is the singular, correct way to make a family and that other ways of doing so don't really count, are illegitimate or unnatural or shameful, which serves to justify the denial of equal respect, support, rights, and resources for all kinds of families.

That is a pretty easy one to knock down—a few episodes of *Modern Family* can almost do the trick—and this book has certainly meant to contribute to its shattering. This puts it in line with the variety of social movements that are pursuing the destigmatization and equal treatment of alternative families. The stories here have shown how forceful the will to have and love a child can be, regardless of sexual or gender identity, regardless of relationship status, even in the face of stigma, exclusion, bureaucratic stupidity, legal disarray, social misrecognition, emotional complexity, geographical distance, and astronomical financial burdens. Hyperintentional, inventive, and obstinate, the families wrote their own scripts. The story of heroic transgressors pioneering new paths to parenthood and transforming kinship can be a useful counterpoint to the One True Family ideology.

As the stories in this book have shown, that's only part of the truth. In the short term, it can work well to replace a myth you don't like with one you do; it's not much of a lasting fix, however. The ultradeliberate pathways to parenthood in this book's stories are not so much heroic as revelatory. What they reveal is not just the powerful drive to make family in the face of institutional blockades but also other, harder things: the structural circumstances of poverty and greed that leave some children without parents and some parents unable to raise their kids; the ways market forces facilitate and commodify the intimate relations of family; the normalizing and status elevation that becoming a parent so often brings, like it or not; the unequal distribution of access to assisted reproduction and adoption by class, nation, gender, race, and sexuality. Holding all of those parts of family origin stories is as hard as it is necessary.

You can erase the histories and humans that are part of your family's origins, or you can refuse to do so; the choice is not just a literary one but a political one. I'm hopeful that a refusal opens up new spaces for thinking, and there's evidence from others who've made that choice.

Consider again, for instance, the theme of destiny that has run throughout these and many other family creation stories. Fate seems to tell you that the link between parent and child is out of human control, but looking closer at these stories can encourage a rethinking of what we mean by fate and what role it plays in making family. The sociologist Sara K. Dorow has pointed out, for example, that adoption stories in particular tend to construct "abandonment as an unfortunate and inevitable fate resolved in adoption."[13] If that's the story, one doesn't really need to think too much about the "complicated gendered and racial histories" contained in the family, about the "ghosts of inequality that [the child's] presence evokes."[14] But to bring those histories into the story, to give body to those ghosts, can lead you to a different understanding of fate—what Dorow calls "a politicized fate that is at home with ambiguity."[15] A similar point might be made about assisted reproduction, as what seems like luck or destiny is reframed to include the linked hierarchies of gender, race, sexuality, and class that brought together this sperm, that egg, this womb, and these parental bodies. Fate, here, is not so much a supernatural determination—though it may be that, too—as the social and political forces beyond individual control that brought this child to this parent. That kind of fate is humanly generated and humanly changed.

Family storytelling that connects the fierce, hyperintentional, loving actions that unite parents and children into a family *and* the "forces of market, race, and gender that marginalize and exclude"[16] also makes it hard to stay in the for-it-or-against-it stance. It can help pull you out of the "false dichotomy of imperialist kidnap or humanitarian rescue" that, as the historian Karen Dubinsky describes it, characterizes debates over transnational and transracial adoption.[17] It can help pull you out of the false dichotomy of exploitation or opportunity for powerless women that, as the sociologist Susan Markens found, has characterized media coverage of surrogacy.[18] If there is a position outside of those debates, perhaps the stories here can point in its direction.

Where they point, I would suggest, is toward an expansive view of reproductive freedom. As the sociologist and legal scholar Dorothy Roberts has argued, reproductive liberty must encompass autonomy over individuals' reproductive life—a woman's choice to end her pregnancy, for instance—but must move beyond that. "It must encompass the full range of procreative activities, including the ability to bear a child," Roberts says. "It must acknowledge that we make reproductive decisions within a social context, including inequalities of wealth and power. . . . *Reproductive freedom is a matter of social justice, not individual choice.*"[19] This commitment to reproductive freedom doesn't currently inform reproductive policy. But it could.

Of course, those are the adult conversations. How we tell the stories of our family's creation, though, our kids overhear.

■　　■　　■

The stories our kids tell about their own beginnings draw from the ones we tell, but more often than not, they are new generations, quirky and matter-of-fact. As our stories of unconventional family creation get spoken, they introduce new variables from which kids can generate the stories of their own creation. When my daughter Maddy was four, for example, she wrote a book at preschool called *Maddy and the Little Island*. The words were transcribed by a teacher and were accompanied by scribbly, semidecipherable illustrations by the author herself.

"Maddy bonked into a little girl named Reba," the story opens, "and she said, 'Can I be your sister?'" The answer turns out to be yes, and this Maddy character then asks, "Can I be your friend?"

"Then they loved a man," the story continues, next to some amoebaish orange doodlings probably meant to depict a man. "Then he wanted to be their dad and his name was Joshua Paul. Joshua Paul saw a man that was his boyfriend. He became the other dad of these children." Flip the page. "Maddy and Reba began to walk down the street and they found a house to live in and they loved it. Now Abba and Daddy saw that the house looked beautiful and they wanted to live in it."

From there, the story seems to lose some steam, and the little island of the title never does make an appearance. On the final pages, Reba carries Maddy to the car, and they go "to the carnival" and finally "to

Daddy's hospital that was in New York City." Still, the point is clear and very much in character. Maddy is subject, not object. She conceived her own kin. Our family came to be when Maddy and Reba decided to be sisters, spotted some eligible fathers, and enticed them into parenthood with a beautiful house.

Her book, no doubt, is based on a true story.

NOTES

INTRODUCTION

1. Stephanie Coontz, *The Way We Never Were: American Families and the Nostalgia Trap* (New York: Basic Books, 1992).
2. Ross D. Parke, *Future Families: Diverse Forms, Rich Possibilities* (Malden, MA: Wiley, 2013), 2–4.
3. Stephen Sugarman, "What Is a 'Family'? Conflicting Messages from Our Public Programs," *Family Law Quarterly* 42 (2008): 232.
4. Sugarman, "What Is a 'Family'?," 232.
5. Parke, *Future Families*, 1.
6. See Carol B. Stack's classic *All Our Kin: Strategies for Survival in a Black Community* (New York: Basic Books, 1974).
7. Brian Powell, Catherine Bolzendahl, Claudia Geist, and Lala Carr Steelman, *Counted Out: Same-Sex Relations and Americans' Definitions of Family* (New York: Russell Sage Foundation, 2010), 21. See also Mignon R. Moore and Michael Stambolis-Ruhstorfer, "LGBT Sexuality and Families at the Start of the Twenty-First Century," *Annual Review of Sociology* 39 (2013): 491–507.
8. Todd Parr, *The Family Book* (Boston: Little Brown, 2003), 1–17, 29.
9. "Todd Parr's 'The Family Book' Banned by Illinois School District for Gay Parent Reference," *Huffington Post*, June 1, 2012, http://www.huffingtonpost.com/2012/06/01/the-family-book-todd-parr-banned-illinois-_n_1562989.html.
10. Parke, *Future Families*, 5. See also Maxine B. Zinn, Stanley D. Eitzen, and Barbara Wells, *Diversity in Families* (Upper Saddle River, NJ: Pearson, 2010).
11. Miller McPherson, Lynn Smith-Lovin, and James M. Cook, "Birds of a Feather: Homophily in Social Networks," *Annual Review of Sociology* 27 (2001): 416.
12. See Parke, *Future Families*.
13. Sharon Vandivere, Karin Malm, and Laura Radel, *Adoption USA* (Washington, DC: U.S. Department of Health and Human Services, Office of the Assistant Secretary for Planning and Evaluation, 2009), http://www.aspe.hhs.gov/hsp/09/

NSAP/chartbook/chartbook.cfm?id=13. The class dynamics of adoption are not uniform or uncomplicated, though: the same HHS study also indicates that "nearly half (46 percent) of children adopted from foster care live in households with incomes no higher than two times the poverty threshold."

14. Magdalina Gugucheva, *Surrogacy in America* (Cambridge, MA: Council for Responsible Genetics, 2010), http://www.councilforresponsiblegenetics.org/pagedocuments/kaevejoa1m.pdf, 26.

15. Christina Huffington, "Single Motherhood Increases Dramatically for Certain Demographics, Census Bureau Reports," *Huffington Post*, May 1, 2013, http://www.huffingtonpost.com/2013/05/01/single-motherhood-increases-census-report_n_3195455.html.

16. Rosanna Hertz, *Single by Chance, Mothers by Choice: How Women Are Choosing Parenthood without Marriage and Creating the New American Family* (New York: Oxford University Press, 2006).

17. See Malcolm Gladwell, *The Tipping Point* (Boston: Little, Brown, 2000).

18. Carey Goldberg, Beth Jones, and Pamela Ferdinand, *Three Wishes: A True Story of Good Friends, Crushing Heartbreak, and Astonishing Luck on Our Way to Love and Motherhood* (New York: Little, Brown, 2010). Quote is taken from the publisher's description at http://www.hachettebookgroup.com/titles/carey-goldberg/three-wishes/9780316079075/.

19. Dan Savage, *The Kid: What Happened after My Boyfriend and I Decided to Go Get Pregnant* (New York: Plume, 2000), 196–197.

20. Scott Simon, *Baby, We Were Meant for Each Other: In Praise of Adoption* (New York: Random House, 2010). Quote is taken from the publisher's description at http://www.randomhouse.com/book/167633/baby-we-were-meant-for-each-other-by-scott-simon.

21. Rachel Lehmann-Haupt, *In Her Own Sweet Time: Unexpected Adventures in Finding Love, Commitment, and Motherhood* (New York: Basic Books, 2009), back cover.

22. Peggy Orenstein, *Waiting for Daisy* (New York: Bloomsbury USA, 2007).

23. Anne Glusker, "Misconceptions," *Washington Post*, March 11, 2007, http://www.washingtonpost.com/wp-dyn/content/article/2007/03/08/AR2007030802452.html.

24. Judith Stacey, *Brave New Families: Stories of Domestic Upheaval in Late-Twentieth-Century America* (Berkeley: University of California Press, 1988).

25. Suzanna Danuta Walters, *The Tolerance Trap: How God, Genes, and Good Intentions Are Sabotaging Gay Equality* (New York: NYU Press, 2014), 236.

26. See Susan Markens, *Surrogate Motherhood and the Politics of Reproduction* (Berkeley: University of California Press, 2007).

27. Gena Corea, *The Mother Machine: Reproductive Technologies from Artificial Insemination to Artificial Wombs* (New York: Harper and Row, 1985).

28. France Winddance Twine, *Outsourcing the Womb: Race, Class, and Gestational Surrogacy in a Global Market* (New York: Routledge, 2011), 1.

29. Shellee Colen, "'Like a Mother to Them': Stratified Reproduction and West Indian Childcare Workers and Employers in New York," in *Conceiving the New World Order: The Global Politics of Reproduction*, ed. Faye Ginsburg and Rayne Rapp (Berkeley: University of California Press, 1995), 78–102.

30. Twine, *Outsourcing the Womb*, 3.

31. Diana Marre and Laura Briggs, "Introduction: The Circulation of Children," in *International Adoption: Global Inequalities and the Circulation of Children*, ed. Marre and Briggs (New York: NYU Press, 2009), 17.

32. Arlie Hochschild, *The Outsourced Self: Intimate Life in Market Times* (New York: Metropolitan Books, 2012), 222.

33. Marre and Briggs, "Introduction," 1. See also Laura Briggs, *Somebody's Children: The Politics of Transracial and Transnational Adoption* (Durham: Duke University Press, 2012); Sara K. Dorow, *Transnational Adoption: A Cultural Economy of Race, Gender, and Kinship* (New York: NYU Press, 2006); David L. Eng, "Transnational Adoption and Queer Diasporas," *Social Text* 21, no. 3 (2003): 1–37.

34. E. J. Graff, "The Lie We Love," *Foreign Policy*, November–December 2008, 1.

35. Dorothy Roberts, "Adoption Myths and Racial Realities in the United States," in *Outsiders Within: Writing on Transracial Adoption*, ed. Jane Jeong Trenka, Julia Chinyere Oparah, and Sun Yung Shin (Cambridge, MA: South End, 2006), 50. See also Barbara Katz Rothman, *Weaving a Family: Untangling Race and Adoption* (Boston: Beacon, 2005); and Sandra Patton, *BirthMarks: Transracial Adoption in Contemporary America* (New York: NYU Press, 2000).

CHAPTER 1. REBA, LIVE!

1. See, for instance, Carlos Ball, *The Right to Be Parents: LGBT Families and the Transformation of Parenthood* (New York: NYU Press, 2012); and Marc Stein, *Rethinking the Gay and Lesbian Movement* (New York: Routledge, 2012).

2. See, for instance, Larry Gross, *Up from Invisibility: Lesbians, Gay Men, and the Media in America* (New York: Columbia University Press, 2002); and Suzanna Danuta Walters, *All the Rage: The Story of Gay Visibility in America* (Chicago: University of Chicago Press, 2003).

3. Liza Mundy, *Everything Conceivable: How the Science of Assisted Reproduction Is Changing Our World* (New York: Knopf, 2007), 11.

4. Charis Thompson, *Making Parents: The Ontological Choreography of Reproductive Technologies* (Cambridge: MIT Press, 2005), 7.

5. Mundy, *Everything Conceivable*, 134.

6. Arlie Russell Hochschild, *The Outsourced Self: Intimate Life in Market Times* (New York: Metropolitan Books, 2012), 13, 222.

7. Hochschild, *Outsourced Self*, 74.

8. Hochschild, *Outsourced Self*, 83.

9. Hochschild, *Outsourced Self*, 13, 950, 225. See also Amrita Pande, "Commercial Surrogacy in India: Manufacturing a Perfect Mother-Worker," *Signs* 35 (Summer 2010): 969–992. As Hochschild and others describe, the labor conditions for Indian women working as surrogates are tightly controlled. They typically are housed in dormitory-style "surrogacy hostels" with tight quarters, strict monitoring, rigid schedules, and restrictions on family visitations, a "systemic and near-total domination of surrogates' lives" that also "becomes a space for resistance and networking" (Pande, "Commercial Surrogacy," 970–971).

10. Some scholars question the assertion that breast milk provides early health benefits that formula does not; see, for instance, Joan B. Wolf, *Is Breast Best? Taking on the Breastfeeding Experts and the New High Stakes of Motherhood* (New York: NYU Press, 2010).

11. For a lively recent critique of the normalization of gayness and the sidelining of queer difference, see Suzanna Danuta Walters, *The Tolerance Trap: How God, Genes, and Good Intentions Are Sabotaging Gay Equality* (New York: NYU Press, 2014).

12. Thompson, *Making Parents*, 8.

13. Thompson, *Making Parents*, 146.

14. Richard F. Storrow, "Rescuing Children from the Marriage Movement: The Case against Marital Status Discrimination in Adoption and Assisted Reproduction," *UC Davis Law Review* 39, no. 2 (2006): 310. See also Tiffany L. Palmer, "The Winding Road to the Two-Dad Family: Issues Arising in Interstate Surrogacy for Gay Couples," *Rutgers Journal of Law & Public Policy* 8, no. 5 (2011): 895–917.

15. Richard F. Storrow, "Marital Status and Sexual Orientation Discrimination in Infertility Care," *Law Journal for Social Justice* 3 (Fall 2012): 107.

16. Maureen Sullivan, *The Family of Woman: Lesbian Mothers, Their Children, and the Undoing of Gender* (Berkeley: University of California Press, 2004), 35.

17. Palmer, "Winding Road," 905.

18. Palmer, "Winding Road," 909.

19. For a nuanced critical account of the rise of Caesarean section procedures, see Theresa Morris, *Cut It Out: The C-Section Epidemic in America* (New York: NYU Press, 2013).

20. Hochschild, *Outsourced Self*, 13.

21. Thompson, *Making Parents*, 7.

CHAPTER 2. STRANGER THINGS HAVE HAPPENED

1. Edward Albee, preface to *The American Dream and The Zoo Story: Two Plays* (New York: Signet, 1961), 53–54.

2. Edward Albee, *The American Dream*, in *The American Dream and The Zoo Story: Two Plays* (New York: Signet, 1961), 97.

3. Single Mothers by Choice, "About Jane," n.d., http://www.singlemothersbychoice.org/about/aboutjane/ (accessed August 1, 2014).

4. Ross D. Parke, *Future Families: Diverse Forms, Rich Possibilities* (Malden, MA: Wiley, 2013), 66.

5. Andrew J. Cherlin, *The Marriage-Go-Round: The State of Marriage and the Family Today* (New York: Knopf, 2009).

6. Rosanna Hertz, *Single by Chance, Mothers by Choice: How Women Are Choosing Parenthood without Marriage and Creating the New American Family* (New York: Oxford University Press, 2006), 12–13.

7. Hertz, *Single*, xviii.

8. Parke, *Future Families*, 67.

9. Parke, *Future Families*, 66.

10. Kathryn Edin and Maria Kefalas, *Promises I Can Keep: Why Poor Women Put Motherhood before Marriage* (Berkeley: University of California Press, 2005), 6.

11. Edin and Kefalas, *Promises*, 46.

12. Hertz, *Single*, 4.

13. Hertz, *Single*, 3.

14. Hertz, *Single*, 36.

15. Sara K. Dorow, *Transnational Adoption: A Cultural Economy of Race, Gender, and Kinship* (New York: NYU Press, 2006), 167.

16. Dorow, *Transnational Adoption*, 25.

17. Bonnie Buxton, *Damaged Angels: An Adoptive Mother's Struggle to Understand the Tragic Toll of Alcohol in Pregnancy* (Boston: Da Capo, 2005); Laurie C. Miller, *The Handbook of International Adoption Medicine: A Guide for Physicians, Parents, and Providers* (New York: Oxford University Press, 2004).

18. Deborah D. Gray, *Attaching in Adoption* (Indianapolis: Perspectives, 2002).

19. Orphan Doctor, "Alcohol Related Disorders and Children Adopted from Abroad," last updated November 16, 2006, http://www.orphandoctor.com/medical/commondiseases/fas/alcoholrelated.html#incidence.

20. E. J. Graff, "The Lie We Love," *Foreign Policy*, November–December 2008.

21. David Katz, "China Restricts Adoption Policies," ABC News Online, December 21, 2006, http://abcnews.go.com/Health/story?id=2743016.

22. Sandra Patton, *BirthMarks: Transracial Adoption in Contemporary America* (New York: NYU Press, 2000), 3.

23. Melissa Fay Greene, *There Is No Me without You: One Woman's Odyssey to Rescue Her Country's Children* (New York: Bloomsbury, 2006), 12.

24. Greene, *No Me without You*, 12, 14.

25. Greene, *No Me without You*, 116.

26. Greene, *No Me without You*, 29.

27. Greene, *No Me without You*, 136.

28. National Institutes of Health, "ELISA/Western Blot Tests for HIV," last updated December 2014, http://www.nlm.nih.gov/medlineplus/ency/article/003538.htm.

29. U.S. Department of Health and Human Services, "HIV Test Types," last updated February 9, 2012, http://aids.gov/hiv-aids-basics/prevention/hiv-testing/hiv-test-types/.

30. Greene, *No Me without You*, 19.

31. Greene, *No Me without You*, 12, 14.

32. See Dorow, *Transnational Adoption*.

33. E. J. Graff, "Don't Adopt from Ethiopia," *American Prospect*, May 3, 2012, http://prospect.org/article/dont-adopt-ethiopia; Schuster Institute for Investigative Journalism, "Adoption: Ethiopia," last updated November 25, 2014, http://www.brandeis.edu/investigate/adoption/ethiopia.html.

CHAPTER 3. BIRTH CONTROL

1. Mattilda Bernstein Sycamore, "There's More to Life than Platinum: Challenging the Tyranny of Sweatshop-Produced Rainbow Flags and Participatory Patriarchy," in *That's Revolting! Queer Strategies for Resisting Assimilation*, ed. Sycamore (Berkeley, CA: Soft Skull, 2008), 2–3.

2. Michael Warner, *The Trouble with Normal: Sex, Politics, and the Ethics of Queer Life* (Cambridge: Harvard University Press, 2000), 113.

3. Warner, *Trouble*, 60.

4. Warner, *Trouble*, 60.

5. Warner, *Trouble*, 53.

6. See Kath Weston, *Families We Choose: Lesbians, Gays, Kinship* (New York: Columbia University Press, 1991).

7. Laura Mamo, "Biomedicalizing Kinship: Sperm Banks and the Creation of Affinity-Ties," *Science as Culture* 14, no. 3 (2005): 248.

8. Maureen Sullivan, *The Family of Woman: Lesbian Mothers, Their Children, and the Undoing of Gender* (Berkeley: University of California Press, 2004), 45.

9. Suzanne Pelka, "Third-Party Reproduction: Creating Kinship through an Intent to Parent," *Anthropology News*, February 2009, 8.

10. Mamo, "Biomedicalizing Kinship," 247.

11. Corinne P. Hayden, "Gender, Genetics, and Generation: Reformulating Biology in Lesbian Kinship," *Cultural Anthropology* 10, no. 1 (1995): 56.

12. Rachel Lehmann-Haupt, "Mapping the God of Sperm," *Newsweek*, December 16, 2009.

CHAPTER 4. THE KIDS IN THE PICTURES

1. It's important to note that existing research does not suggest that the children of lesbians are less well adjusted than are their peers raised by heterosexual parents, and they actually fare better on some psychological and behavioral measures. See, for instance, Nanette Gartrell and Henry Bos, "US National Longitudinal Lesbian Family Study: Psychological Adjustment of 17-Year-Old Adolescents," *Pediatrics* 126, no. 1 (2010): 28–36; Timothy J. Biblarz and Judith Stacey, "How Does the Gender of Parents Matter?," *Journal of Marriage and Family* 72 (2010): 3–22.

2. E. J. Graff, "The Lie We Love," *Foreign Policy*, November–December 2008, 62–63.

3. Deborah H. Wald, "The Parentage Puzzle: The Interplay between Genetics, Procreative Intent, and Parental Conduct in Determining Legal Parentage," *American University Journal of Gender, Social Policy & the Law* 15, no. 3 (2007): 381.

4. Barbara Crossette, "Birendra, 55, Ruler of Nepal's Hindu Kingdom," *New York Times*, June 3, 2001, http://www.nytimes.com/2001/06/03/world/birenda-55-ruler-of-nepal-s-hindu-kingdom.html.

5. See John Whelpton, *A History of Nepal* (Cambridge: Cambridge University Press, 2005).

6. Schuster Institute for Investigative Journalism, "Orphaned or Stolen? The U.S. State Department Investigates Adoption in Nepal, 2006–2008," last updated March 3, 2011, http://www.brandeis.edu/investigate/adoption/nepal-behind-the-scenes.html.

7. Schuster Institute for Investigative Journalism, "Adoption: Nepal," last updated February 21, 2011, http://www.brandeis.edu/investigate/adoption/nepal.html.

8. Schuster Institute for Investigative Journalism, "Orphaned or Stolen?"

9. Scott Carney, "Meet the Parents: The Dark Side of Overseas Adoption," *Mother Jones*, March–April 2009, http://www.motherjones.com/politics/2009/03/meet-parents-dark-side-overseas-adoption.

10. Arun Dohle, "Inside Story of an Adoption Scandal," *Cumberland Law Review* 39, no. 1 (2008): 131–186.

11. The limited research on multiparent families like these suggests that tensions among coparents are often quite pronounced. As the Australian researcher Deborah Dempsey put it, "the parties involved may have very incompatible expectations of these relationships," the lived reality of which "may deviate from relationships planned before children"; "issues come up about the complex meaning of 'paternal involvement', the difference between a 'father' and a 'parent' and who is entitled to be included in children's social families"; gendered power in the relationships is complex, with the men sometimes "naïve and insensitive" to the "messy, demanding day-to-day reality of life with young children," while the women "as resident parents have a good deal of power and control." Deborah

Dempsey, "Gay Male Couples' Paternal Involvement in Lesbian-Parented Families," *Journal of Family Studies* 18, nos. 2–3 (2012): 163.

CHAPTER 5. MY NEW KENTUCKY BABY

1. Liza Mundy, *Everything Conceivable: How the Science of Assisted Reproduction Is Changing Our World* (New York: Knopf, 2007), 132.
2. Quoted in Mundy, *Everything Conceivable*, 133.
3. Quoted in Mundy, *Everything Conceivable*, 133.
4. Rainbow Surrogacy is a pseudonym.
5. Mundy, *Everything Conceivable*, 132.

CHAPTER 6. QUEER CONCEPTIONS

1. See, for instance, Jane Jeong Trenka, Julia Chinyere Oparah, and Sun Yung Shin, introduction to *Outsiders Within: Writing on Transracial Adoption*, ed. Trenka, Oparah, and Shin (Boston: South End, 2006), 1–15; and many of the essays in that volume.
2. Paisley Currah, "Gender Pluralisms under the Transgender Umbrella," in *Transgender Rights*, ed. Paisley Currah, Richard M. Juang, and Shannon Price Minter (Minneapolis: University of Minnesota Press, 2006), 5.
3. In some ways, Min's experience is an indicator of the social changes taking place around gender identity. In addition to greater transgender cultural visibility and a slowly growing patchwork of antidiscrimination protections, for instance, the most recent edition of the American Psychiatric Association's *Diagnostic and Statistical Manual of Mental Disorders* (*DSM*) replaced the designation Gender Identity Disorder (GID) with the title Gender Dysphoria, a condition in which the disjuncture between the assigned gender and the felt one causes *distress*. Officially speaking, that is, the incongruence between gender identity and socially assigned gender is no longer considered in and of itself a pathological condition—something transgender activists and their allies have been pushing against for decades. The diagnosis might have been eliminated entirely were it not for the fact that people still need it for access to treatments like hormones and sex reassignment surgery, insurance coverage, and social, legal, and occupational protection. American Psychiatric Association, "Gender Dysphoria," 2013, http://www.dsm5.org/documents/gender%20dysphoria%20fact%20sheet.pdf; Wynne Parry, "Gender *Dysphoria*: DSM-5 Reflects Shift in Perspective on Gender Identity," *Huffington Post*, June 4, 2013, http://www.huffingtonpost.com/2013/06/04/gender-dysphoria-dsm-5_n_3385287.html; see also Judith Butler, "Undiagnosing Gender," in Currah, Juang, and Minter, *Transgender Rights*, 274–298.

For the most part, though, the relative ease of Min's experience is uncommon outside of certain cultural and geographical pockets. The binary gender order, in which you must be either male or female, remains both taken for granted and institutionalized; it regulates gender options for everyone, in part by penalizing gender crossing. As the historian Susan Stryker has described it, because most people have a hard time seeing the humanity of someone whose gender isn't recognizable, "the gender-changing person can evoke in others a primordial fear of monstrosity," which can manifest itself as "hatred, outrage, panic, or disgust," often expressed as "physical or emotional violence." People who don't easily fit binary gender categories are sometimes shunned, sometimes denied basic needs, and face all manner of problems in their encounters with social institutions, including "inability to marry, for example, or to cross national borders, or qualify for jobs, or gain access to needed social services, or secure legal custody of one's children." Susan Stryker, *Transgender History* (Berkeley, CA: Seal, 2008), 6.

4. Kathleen Silber, "Benefits of Open Adoption," n.d., http://www.adoptionhelp.org/open-adoption/benefits (accessed July 28, 2014).

5. Silber, "Benefits of Open Adoption."

6. Oparah, Shin, and Trenka, introduction to *Outsiders Within*, 4.

7. Oparah, Shin, and Trenka, introduction to *Outsiders Within*, 4.

8. Chris Jones, "8 Simple Ways to Make Your Birthmother Letter Stand Out," *Open Adoption Blog*, Independent Adoption Center, July 31, 2013, http://www.adoptionhelp.org/blog/2013/8-simple-ways-to-make-your-profile-stand-out/#ixzz38085QUh2.

9. Adoptive Families, "5 Tips for Writing a Dear Birthmother Letter," 2002, http://www.adoptivefamilies.com/articles.php?aid=326.

10. As an institutional structure in which to make or maintain family, the binary gender order is particularly rough on people who "don't experience a natural connection between genitalia, gender identity, and gender expression." Kristen Schilt, *Just One of the Guys: Transgender Men and the Persistence of Gender Inequality* (Chicago: University of Chicago Press, 2010), 46. Medical institutions, while claiming the right to determine whether or not trans people are sick and in need of treatment, argue about "the ethics of helping transgender men and women have children." Timothy F. Murphy, "The Ethics of Helping Transgender Men and Women Have Children," *Perspectives in Biology and Medicine* 53, no. 1 (2010): 46–60. Legal institutions determine both what constitutes legal sex and what constitutes valid marriage or parenthood. Legal sex and family status, in fact, are interdependent within family law: sex distinctions can affect "whom you can marry, whether you can inherit your spouse's estate, or whether you provide an 'appropriate' role model for your children"; yet different jurisdictions have reached different conclusions about how to make the determination of who is legally male or female. Taylor Flynn, "The Ties That (Don't) Bind: Transgender Family Law and the Unmaking of Families," in Currah, Juang, and Minter,

Transgender Rights, 33. If you're trans and have a family, or want to make one, you face these additional obstacles and often without a lot of support.

CONCLUSION

1. Francesca Poletta, *It Was Like a Fever: Storytelling in Protest and Politics* (Chicago: University of Chicago Press, 2006), 12.
2. Patricia Ewick and Susan S. Silbey, "Subversive Stories and Hegemonic Tales: Toward a Sociology of Narrative," *Law & Society Review* 29, no. 2 (1995): 205, 206, 208.
3. Poletta, *Like a Fever*, 2–3.
4. Poletta, *Like a Fever*, 3.
5. Ewick and Silbey, "Subversive Stories and Hegemonic Tales," 212–213.
6. Cathy J. Cohen, *The Boundaries of Blackness: AIDS and the Breakdown of Black Politics* (Chicago: University of Chicago Press, 1999), 27.
7. Ewick and Silbey, "Subversive Stories and Hegemonic Tales," 200.
8. Ewick and Silbey, "Subversive Stories and Hegemonic Tales," 223.
9. Ewick and Silbey, "Subversive Stories and Hegemonic Tales," 219.
10. Melanie Thernstrom, "My Futuristic Insta-Family," *New York Times Magazine*, January 2, 2011, MM28.
11. Jennifer Readings, Lucy Blake, Polly Casey, Vasanti Jadva, and Susan Golombok, "Secrecy, Disclosure, and Everything In-Between: Decisions of Parents of Children Conceived by Donor Insemination, Egg Donation and Surrogacy," *Reproductive Biomedicine Online* 22 (2011): 485.
12. Thernstrom, "My Futuristic Insta-Family."
13. Sara K. Dorow, *Transnational Adoption: A Cultural Economy of Race, Gender, and Kinship* (New York: NYU Press, 2006), 272.
14. Dorow, *Transnational Adoption*, 273, 278.
15. Dorow, *Transnational Adoption*, 272.
16. Dorow, *Transnational Adoption*, 280.
17. Karen Dubinsky, *Babies without Borders: Adoption and Migration across the Americas* (New York: NYU Press, 2010), 3.
18. Susan Markens, "The Global Reproductive Health Market: U.S. Media Framings and Public Discourses about Transnational Surrogacy," *Social Science & Medicine* 74 (2012): 1745–1753.
19. Dorothy Roberts, *Killing the Black Body: Race, Reproduction, and the Meaning of Liberty* (New York: Pantheon Books, 1997), 6; emphasis in original.

INDEX

Note: Subjects of the book are identified with pseudonyms; readers will find references to the subjects under their given names as identified in the text. The author's family can be found under their actual surnames (e.g., Knight, Richard; Gamson-Knight, Reba Sadie).